Alexander Henry Abercromby Hamilton

Quarter Sessions from Queen Elizabeth to Queen Anne

Illustrations of local government and history

Alexander Henry Abercromby Hamilton

Quarter Sessions from Queen Elizabeth to Queen Anne
Illustrations of local government and history

ISBN/EAN: 9783337204044

Printed in Europe, USA, Canada, Australia, Japan

Cover: Foto ©ninafisch / pixelio.de

More available books at **www.hansebooks.com**

QUARTER SESSIONS FROM QUEEN ELIZABETH TO QUEEN ANNE.

LONDON:
GILBERT AND RIVINGTON, PRINTERS,
ST. JOHN'S SQUARE.

QUARTER SESSIONS FROM QUEEN ELIZABETH TO QUEEN ANNE;

ILLUSTRATIONS

OF

LOCAL GOVERNMENT AND HISTORY

Drawn from Original Records

(CHIEFLY OF THE COUNTY OF DEVON).

A. H. A. HAMILTON,

AUTHOR OF "MEMOIR OF SIR JOHN NORTHCOTE," ETC.

LONDON:
SAMPSON LOW, MARSTON, SEARLE, & RIVINGTON,
CROWN BUILDINGS, 188, FLEET STREET.
1878.

[All rights reserved.]

Dedicated to

THE RIGHT HON. WILLIAM REGINALD, EARL OF DEVON, P.C., D.C.L.,

AMONG WHOSE MANY TITLES

TO THE GRATITUDE OF HIS COUNTY

IS THAT OF HAVING DISCHARGED THE DUTIES

OF A CHAIRMAN OF QUARTER SESSIONS

FOR A PERIOD OF FORTY-TWO YEARS.

Fairfield Lodge, Exeter,
Michaelmas, 1878.

CONTENTS.

	PAGE
INTRODUCTION	ix
QUARTER SESSIONS UNDER QUEEN ELIZABETH	1
QUARTER SESSIONS UNDER JAMES THE FIRST. PART I.	35
QUARTER SESSIONS UNDER JAMES THE FIRST. PART II.	66
QUARTER SESSIONS UNDER CHARLES THE FIRST	100
QUARTER SESSIONS DURING THE CIVIL WAR	127
QUARTER SESSIONS UNDER THE COMMONWEALTH	150
QUARTER SESSIONS UNDER CHARLES THE SECOND. PART I.	172
QUARTER SESSIONS UNDER CHARLES THE SECOND. PART II.	201
QUARTER SESSIONS UNDER JAMES THE SECOND	225
QUARTER SESSIONS UNDER WILLIAM AND MARY	251
QUARTER SESSIONS UNDER QUEEN ANNE.	267
THE TRIAL OF TWO QUAKERS IN THE TIME OF OLIVER CROMWELL	295
THE JUSTICES OF THE PEACE FOR THE COUNTY OF DEVON IN THE YEAR 1592	321
THE JURISDICTION OF THE LORD WARDEN OF THE STANNARIES IN THE TIME OF SIR WALTER RALEIGH	349
THE CASTLE OF EXETER	354
INDEX	361

INTRODUCTION.

THIS volume consists almost entirely of a series of papers contributed to *Fraser's Magazine* during the last two years. I have been encouraged to reprint them in a more permanent form, but the utmost that I can hope for them is that they may be recognized as affording some glimpses of the history of England from a new point of view. It is not easy to find any material for history which has been neglected by the diligent explorers of recent times, but I cannot discover that any use has been hitherto made of the records of "Quarter Sessions." They are not a very inviting study, for the great bulk of them is composed of merely formal and very monotonous documents, from which the more valuable facts can only be extracted by much patient labour. I venture to think, however, that the labour has not been without its reward, as it has recovered some clear and most trustworthy evidence respecting the condition of the provincial districts of England in former times.

Introduction.

These papers are founded in great measure on the records of the County of Devon, which I have had the fullest opportunities of investigating. But I think I am justified in asking my readers to accept that county as a type of the more civilized parts of England during the space of time to which this volume relates. It happens, too, that the records of Devon commence at an earlier period, and are fuller in detail, than those of any other county with which I am acquainted. The earliest records are in this case certainly the most valuable. The affairs transacted by Quarter Sessions were undoubtedly of greater importance in the reigns of Elizabeth and James I. than they have been since. It is perhaps not too much to say that they have been continually dwindling, and it seems to be fated that the reign of Queen Victoria should reduce them to utter insignificance.

The records of Quarter Sessions in Devonshire commence in the year 1592. There are very few counties in which they are older than the time of the Civil War. In Somerset they begin in 1647. In Bucks they commence in 1678. An account of the records of that county down to the death of Queen Anne is comprised in the present volume. In Oxfordshire there are no papers earlier than the Revolution of 1688, and those subsequent to that date are very scanty. There are no regular Sessions Books earlier than the year 1761. I am informed that in Cheshire, Westmoreland, and Wilts, there are records extending from the reign of Elizabeth, with some few *lacunæ*. These, I believe, are the only counties which can be compared in this respect with Devonshire. As Quarter Sessions were established certainly as early as the reign of Edward III. we ought to have records of them for two centuries before the time of Elizabeth. But very little care was bestowed upon such matters in former ages. Until the present century, scarcely any county had provided a Record Room. It was the practice for the Clerk of the Peace to keep the public papers at his private residence, or anywhere he pleased, and at his death they were transferred, or supposed to be transferred, to his successor, who was probably not very anxious to be burdened with several waggon-loads of damp or dusty documents.

In conclusion, I must express my thanks to the Duke of Somerset, *Custos Rotulorum* of Devon, and to Acton Tindal, Esq., Clerk of the Peace for Bucks, for the facilities they have kindly afforded me for examining the documents under their care, as well as to J. R. Pine Coffin, Esq., for the curious letters of the time of James the Second.

QUARTER SESSIONS.

QUARTER SESSIONS UNDER QUEEN ELIZABETH.

HAVING an opportunity of examining the records preserved in the office of the Clerk of the Peace for the county of Devon, it occurred to me to see whether I could find anything bearing upon the heroic age of Devonshire, when that county had to stand in the front of the battle against the Spanish invaders. In the primary object of my search I was disappointed. Nothing relating to the Armada occurs in the books containing the orders of Sessions, except the familiar names of certain actors in that great drama. It happens that those books commence just after the time of the Armada, in the year 1592. Whether any previous books existed, or whether the records had up to that time been kept in detached papers, is not certain. But, from some of the first entries, it would seem that the county business had been done in a somewhat lax way, and that the commencement of these books coincided with a stricter rule, and a more accurate performance of the duties of that ancient body the Justices of the Peace, the form of whose commission had been remodelled by the King's Bench in the year 1590.

One of the first documents entered in the order-book is a letter from the Lords of the Council to the Justices of Devon, dated October 20, 1592. It is signed by the Lord Keeper Puckering, and by Burleigh, Howard, Hunsdon, Buckhurst, Cecil, Wolley, and Fortescue, and is addressed to the Earl of Bath, Lord-Lieutenant of Devon, Sir William Courtenay, Sir John Gilbert, and Sir Francis Drake. It begins by reciting that the Queen's Majesty has been informed that some persons exercise the office of Justice of the Peace without having taken the necessary oaths, and, as it is difficult to distinguish those who have done so from those who have not, her pleasure is that all justices, "without prejudice," should immediately take them. Copies of the oath of a justice, of the oath of supremacy, and of the writ of *Dedimus potestatem* are enclosed. Minute and strict directions follow. The oaths are to be taken in open court, first by the four to whom the commission was addressed, and then to be administered by them to the other justices, " saving that the Lords of Parliament are excepted by the Act from taking the oath of supremacy." Those justices who refuse the oaths, who are resident out of the county, or who are absent from any cause, are to be reported to the Lord Keeper. And then follows what appears to be the real cause of the order, the increased activity of the Government against "recusancy," which marked the latter years of the reign of Elizabeth. Her Majesty has been informed—

" That divers persons doe occupy the offyces of Justice
" of the Peace whoe doe not repayer to there churche or
" chappell accustomed, or upon reasonable lett thereof to

"some other place where common prayer is used and "accustomed for divine servyce, or whose wyves lyvinge "with their husband, or sonnes and heyres lyvinge in there "houses or within that county where there fathers doe "dwell are known to refuse to come to the churche, contrary "to the statutes in that behalffe made. A matter not "agreable with the vocacon of any that ought to enquyer "of such offenders, and to reforme the same."

It was, therefore, her Majesty's pleasure that all recusants, or husbands or fathers of recusants, should be left out of the commission of the peace.

In the reply of the Earl of Bath and the three knights we have what is probably an almost complete roll of the justices of Devon in the year 1592. They were fifty-five in number. Some of them, perhaps, were not much wiser than the gentlemen of the "coram" and "custalorum" immortalized by Shakespeare, though we may suspect that the mind of the poet was somewhat prejudiced by his poaching propensities. But they were certainly not all Shallows or Silences. Besides Drake and Gilbert, there were several who showed themselves fit for greater things than guiding the Court of Quarter Sessions. Such were George Cary, of Cockington, afterwards Lord Deputy of Ireland; John Wolton, Bishop of Exeter; William Peryam, Chief Baron of the Exchequer: Serjeants Harris, Glanvyle, and Edward Drewe, Recorder of Exeter, and afterwards of London; and Hugh Pollard, who raised the county, as Sheriff of Devon, in the year of the Armada. The "three Serjeants" were those thus immortalized by Fuller:—

One { spent / gave / gained } as much as the other two.

Other well-known names occur in subsequent entries, such as that of Sir Ferdinando Gorges, who attained an unenviable notoriety at the trial of Essex ; and Edward Earl of Bedford, appointed Custos Rotulorum (not Lord-Lieutenant) in 1596.

Many of the names are still flourishing in the county, such as Courtenay and Seymour, Fortescue and Bampfield, Acland and Carew, Parker, Wrey, and Walrond. We remark the absence from this list of the greatest name that we might have expected to find in it. Sir Walter Raleigh, though he sat in Parliament as member for Devon, held, as Lord Warden of the Stannaries, an independent jurisdiction over a great part of the county; and we find more than one communication from him to the sessions regarding the rights and privileges of the "Tynners."

We have a letter of Sir Walter's, written from "Durham House," February 15, 1592, complaining that several "tynners" had been summoned to appear before Mr. Serjeant Glanvyle for refusing to contribute to the repair of a bridge, which had been accustomed to be repaired by the borough of Okehampton. The letter civilly urges the charter and customs of the Stannaries, and represents that the rates and taxes are "overburthensome to poor men in regard of their daily travell and disbursements employed about the mynes." But it ends with a threat to have the cause heard before the Privy Council, and then comes the characteristic postscript : " I will myselffe give order that the tynners shall contribute unto the bridge, if, upon examynacon, I find cause to urge them thereunto, but *not by any forren aucthoritie.*"

What answer the county authorities returned to this letter does not appear ; but in the next year we find a letter from the Queen, "Given under our signett at Nonesuch," confirming in the amplest manner the privileges, liberties, and immunities of the "tynners" and tenants of the Duchy of Cornwall; "amongst which the chiefest was that they should not be mustered, taxed, charged, or rated with any ymposicon, chardge, or servyce, but only by there warden or chieffe councell;" also that they should not be compelled to answer for any cause ("pleas of land, lyfe, or *meyhem* only excepted") before any judge, officer, or magistrate, other than the warden and officers of the Duchy, from whom the appeal lay to the Privy Council, and from them to her Majesty's royal person.

The victory evidently remained with Sir Walter, and he seems to have been not unwilling to improve it. In 1595 we have a polite letter from the justices to the Lord Warden, in answer to one in which he seems to have accused them of having "gone about to intermeddle" in his jurisdiction. They assure him that he has been "misinformed by some unadvised and undiscrete persons, who, we think, rather desire to sett some discord between you and us than to uphold your liberties."

Sir Walter had also written that two persons (Voysy and Wright) had "delivered slanderous and skoffing speeches touching his late occasion at sea," to which the justices reply that they had examined into it, and "fynd noe such matter," for if they had, "you should assure yourselff we would have dealt in ytt according to the quality of the offence." With which somewhat ambiguous assurance the justices send their "very harty commendacons."

The privileges and immunities of the Stannaries led to frauds and abuses, as such things usually do, and the last order entered in the reign of Elizabeth recites "that dyvers of the principall inhabitants of sundrye parishes within this countye have of late tyme verie fraudulently interested themselves in some Tynworke, under colour thereof to be protected and discharged against the generall and necessarie charges for the service of her Majestie." And it is ordered that such as are "newly crept in to be Tynners," and had not acquired any "Tynwork" by descent or marriage, shall pay the same as the "foreyners" of the said parishes. But, having the fear of Sir Walter before their eyes, the justices conclude thus : " This order is conceyved to agree with the pleasure of the L. Warden in this behaulfe formerlie signified unto this Court, and not with anie intent to make wilfull breach of the priviledges rightfullie belonging to the Court of Stannery, or to the aucthority of the L. Warden in that behaulfe."

A matter that troubled the squires and yeomen of Devonshire considerably more than the privileges of the Stannaries was the ancient right of purveyance, one of the worst grievances that survived the conclusion of the middle ages. Hallam, speaking of the accession of James I., says that purveyance had been restrained by no less than thirty-six statutes :—

" In spite of which, the impressing of carts and carriages,
"and the exaction of victuals for the King's use, at prices
"far below the true value, and in quantity beyond what
"was necessary, continued to prevail under authority of
"commissions from the Board of Green Cloth, and was
"enforced, in case of demur or resistance, by imprisonment
".under their warrant. The purveyors, indeed, are described
"as living at free quarters upon the country, felling woods
"without the owners' consent, and commanding labour
" with little or no recompense."

We find in these volumes frequent entries respecting

this subject, and the means taken to compound with the Queen for her rights of purveyance. The first entry is the commission of Christopher Walton, to take forty fat oxen and three hundred muttons from the county of Devon, for the use of her Majesty's household. This is dated from Westminster, March 21, 1593, and authorizes the same purveyor to take twenty fat oxen and two hundred fat muttons from the county of "Northfolcke and Marsheland." It also authorizes him to take hay, pasture, and *drivers*, and all other necessaries meet and convenient for that service, "for our reasonable prices and payments to be made in that behalf." And all justices, mayors, sheriffs, bailiffs, constables, head-boroughs, and all other officers, ministers, and subjects, are directed to aid and assist the purveyor, so long as he does nothing contrary to the statutes touching purveyors.

This commission is immediately followed by a letter from the Council, dated March 29, 1593, and signed by Puckering, Buckhurst, Burghley, Fortescue, and Howard. The Lords begin by referring to the complaints of the abuses of the purveyors in taking greater quantity than came to her Majesty's use, and blame the justices for sending up to Court only one of their number, "and the same without aucthoritie" to conclude an agreement. Nevertheless they consent to reduce the provision to twenty oxen and two hundred muttons, "upon mocion made unto us by Mr. Seymour." They complain of most contemptuous and disloyal abuses committed by some, who had taken violently from one Richard Owen the oxen and muttons he had lawfully taken by commission, and especially of one John Treberie, "who with most contempt demeaned himself" in seditious manner and speeches, and who was to be bound over in good security to appear personally before the Privy Council.

The answer to this letter, signed by Edward Seymour, William Courtneye, John Gilbert, and four others, is an ingenious plea on behalf of Devonshire. The justices had appointed Mr. Carye of Cockington, as well as Mr. Seymour, to attend their lordships, but he returned from London sooner than they expected. They omitted to give them authority to compound, because they assuredly trusted that their lordships would have freed "this poore countye of that charge." Her Majesty, "of her princely and gracious favour," had been contented heretofore to have this county spared from the purveyors, "for that this countie is farre remote, and doth not in truth of itselffe feede soe many oxen yerelie as is able to maintayne the inhabitants, but doth yerely buye fyve thousand fatt oxen at the least out of Cornwall and Somersett." "And yet this countie contynually victualleth both her Majestie's navies and all other shippinge when any occasion of servyce is required to the Westward." But, if their lordships do not allow these allegations, the justices humbly submit themselves, only most humbly praying that the composition may be "with as much ease and favour unto our poore countrye as may be, whoe in very truthe, thoughe there welthe is greatly decayed thoroughe the wante of trade by sea (on the wch the estate of this county chiefly consisteth), yet are they willinge even beyond there abilities." They appoint Mr. Seymour and Mr. Carye, not to make a bargain, but to make such composition as they may obtain at their lordships' hands. And, by a final stroke of ingenuity, they find that the chief offenders against the purveyors reside not in Devon, but in Cornwall.

Soon afterwards we come to the composition made with the Lords of the Council by Mr. Seymour and Mr. Cary on behalf of the county. It is evident that the representatives of Devon were not unfavourably received at the Court of Elizabeth. Seymour belonged to a family which had often stood very near the throne, and sometimes overshadowed it. A cadet of Cary's family had married a sister of Anne Boleyn, and became the father of that Henry Cary who was created a Privy Councillor and Baron Hunsdon by his royal cousin. Another of the Council, Fortescue, was a Devonshire man, and another, Lord Howard, had married Hunsdon's daughter. The provisions claimed were reduced to ten fat oxen and 150 "fatt muttons." Every ox was to weigh 6 cwt., and to be delivered at the Court gate on April 20, at 4*l.* a piece; every mutton was to weigh 46 lb., and to be delivered at the Court gate at 6*s.* 8*d.* a piece; sixty to be sent on April 20, and ninety on November 20. Ready money was to be paid. In case of the oxen or sheep being "misliked," there was a provision for arbitration, and, if the objection was maintained, the county was to pay a penalty of 40*s.* for every ox "soe misliked," and for every mutton, 2*s.* 6*d.*; and the deficiency was to be supplied within fourteen days.

As long as the composition lasted there was to be no purveyance within the shire, except it happened that her Majesty came in progress within twenty miles of it. The justices were to rate the county for the expenses of the composition, and any person refusing to pay was to be apprehended and brought before the Council to answer their contempt. The composition might be terminated by half a year's notice being given either by the justices or by the officers of her Majesty's "Grene-clothe."

I have quoted this agreement as bearing upon the question of prices. It appears that beef was delivered at the Court of Elizabeth in 1593 at 13s. 4d. per cwt., or rather under 1½d. per lb., and mutton at about 16s. per cwt., or 1¾d. per lb. The price of beef at the Metropolitan Cattle Market at the end of February, 1876, varied from 63s. per cwt. for inferior to 79s. 4d. for first quality ; and of mutton, from 77s. for inferior to 98s. for first. At the same time the contract price for meat at the Workhouse of St. Thomas, the rural Union adjoining Exeter, was 66s. per cwt.

The copy of the composition is followed by a letter from the Lords of the Council, dated " Nonesutche, 29th May, 1593," addressed to the Sheriff and Justices, acknowledging their " dutiful consideration of the Queen's Majesty's gracious desire," and ordering them to take immediate steps for rating the county. It is remarkable for its admission of the "intolerable abuses " of the purveyors, who had taken far greater quantities and numbers of sundry provisions, " abusing their commission and the subjects, which never came to her Majesty's use."

The next letter is from the Justices to the Earl of Bath, Lord-Lieutenant of Devon, informing him of the arrangements they had made, and asking his assistance in levying 108*l.*, divided equally between the three divisions of the county, for the expenses of the composition. This appears to have been settled rather by guess-work than by valuation, as it is by no means probable that the three divisions were equal in wealth or population. The amount to be repaid by the Queen was 90*l.*, viz., 40*l.* for ten oxen and 50*l.* for 150 sheep. In 1594 it appears that an arrangement was made by which the charge was defrayed by a contractor for the sum of 103*l.*, which shows that the payment made by the Queen was not very unfair, as it left only a margin of 13*l.* for the contractor's profit. Prices, however, continued to advance, and in April 1597 we find a regular contract made between Edward Seymour and George Cary for the county, and Christopher Walton, the former purveyor. The latter was to receive 13*l.* 6*s.* 8*d.* for each of the last two years, probably the balance due to him after he had received 90*l.* direct from the "Grenecloth." For the current year he was to have 113*l.* 6*s.* 8*d.*, and 10*l.* for his expenses "in riding to and from about these busynes." For this purpose 150*l.* was to be levied, and the northern division was to pay 10*l.* more than the other two, "in respect of their backwardnes for the effecting of this service."

It may be suspected that an old purveyor was not the fittest person for a contractor, or that the arrangement was disturbed by the rapid fall in the value of money, with which we are too familiar in the reign of Queen Victoria. Anyhow, we find in the very next year a curious letter from Walton to Sir George Cary, in which he declares that he had lost money by the service of the county for the last four years, and that, while people were complaining that he had so much, he was really losing "not so lyttle as £xx." He further complains that the money was not paid punctually, and that he had to make three journeys a year to receive 120*l.*, which he could not endure any longer. He expresses great regard and esteem for Sir George personally, but, as to the rest of the justices, he will have no more to do with them, and if he cannot get what is due, he will be forced to take "that course as will be more grievous unto them than the taking of their oxen." It seems, however, that Mr. Walton, like many others since his time, continued to contract and complain for some years longer, for in October, 1602, we find a brief entry that Mr. Walton do have half-a-year's warning, and that he be dismissed from "making provision of beefes for Her Majesty's household."

We have seen what evidence these records afford respecting the price of meat in the sixteenth century. More direct, and more important perhaps, is their evidence respecting the price of labour. On April 10, 1594, the justices assembled at the Chapter House agreed upon a new rate for servants' and labourers' wages, according to the statute of the fifth year of Elizabeth. It may be noticed in passing that "William Strode, High Sheriff," appears in the middle of the list of names of those present, not as having any precedence over the others. In modern times the Sheriff, as is well known, takes no part in the business of Sessions. He had no right to act as a justice in the reign of Elizabeth, as the statute disqualifying him was passed in that of Mary. But it may have been the practice for the Sheriff to present the juries, and execute the orders of the Court in person, instead of leaving all such duties to the Under Sheriff.

The maximum rates of wages were as follows:—

No bailiff of husbandry, "chiffe hyne" (chief hind), or miller was to take above 53*s*. 4*d*. by the year and his livery, or 13*s*. 4*d*. for the same.

No common manservant of husbandry, between the ages of 16 and 20, was to take above 30*s*. by the year, and after the age of 20 above 40*s*. These two classes of course received their board and lodging.

No woman-servant under the age of 14 was to take any wages but meat, drink, and clothes; from the age of 14 to 18, not above 12*s*. and livery, or 6*s*. for the same; and

Quarter Sessions under Queen Elizabeth. 13

after the age of 18, not above 16s. 8d. and livery, or 6s. 8d. for the same.

No woman "labouring at hay" was to take above 2d. a day and meat and drink, or 6d. without meat and drink. In corn harvest, 3d. or 7d. respectively, and at all other work, 1d. or 5d.

All labourers at task-work might take as they could agree.

All husbandry labourers were to take from All-hallowtide (Nov. 1) till Candlemas (Feb. 2), but 3d. a day with meat and drink, or 7d. a day without. From Candlemas till All-hallowtide, 4d. or 8d. respectively, except when mowing corn or grass, for which they might take 6d. or 12d.

Master-masons, carpenters, joiners, plumbers, helliers, plasterers, and thatchers, having servants or apprentices according to the statute, and able to take charge of the work, were to take by the day, with meat and drink, not above 6d., or 12d. without.

Other masons, carpenters, &c. were to take not above 5d. or 11d., and apprentices and boys not above 2d. or 6d.

A pair of sawyers were to take not above 12d., or 2s.

The rates of wages were settled yearly at the Easter Sessions, and proclaimed by the sheriff; but they do not seem to have been altered during the rest of the reign of Elizabeth. In October, 1601, we find an order that all constables are to ascertain the names of all masters and servants that give or take more wages than those appointed, and report them to the justices, and five sub-committees are appointed specially to attend to this matter in the different districts.

The most remarkable point in these tables of wages is the slight difference they show between the wages of agricultural labourers and those of men employed in the building trades. A farm-labourer earned 4s. a week for three-quarters of the year, and 3s. 6d. for the remainder. In corn and hay harvest he received a shilling a day, which was equal to the wages of what was called a "master mason." A journeyman mason earned no more than 5s. 6d. a week.

When we consider the frequent interruptions of work in the building trades, and, on the other hand, the "privileges" of the agricultural labourer, especially in the commons which were then so numerous, we are led to the conclusion that there was no great disparity in the condition of the two classes. But while the wages of the former class have rapidly increased, the increase in those of the latter has been very slow. A hundred years after the time of this order, in 1685, a small work was published by Richard Dunning on the condition of the poor in Devonshire. In that work, as quoted by Macaulay, the wages of the Devonshire peasant are stated at 5s. a week. In Warwickshire, the rate of wages in 1685 was rather lower than that in Devonshire in 1594. Within the last ten years, the rate in some parts of Devon has been as low as 7s. or 8s. The average may now be about 12s. or more. But it is not too much to say that the wages of artisans increased fourfold by the time that the wages of husbandmen were doubled. And, if we compare the price of meat with the price of agricultural labour, we may fairly say that the former has increased fivefold since the time of Elizabeth, while the latter has been trebled. But we must not forget that the price of food was formerly liable to fluctuations such as we have never known, and that seasons of plenty were often succeeded by seasons of scarcity, if not of famine. Such a scarcity is mentioned in Jenkins's *History of Exeter* as having occurred in the year 1593.

Another entry bearing on the cost of living is an order that no liquor except wine should be sold for more than one penny a quart. In an affiliation case, we find the father of a child ordered to pay 8*d*. a week for the first three weeks, and afterwards 4*d*. a week. The mother was to keep it up to the age of five years, and from the age of five until twelve the father was to pay 6*d*. and the mother 1*d*. a week to the constables and churchwardens of the parish.

Closely connected with the questions of prices and wages is the great question of pauperism, which weighed so heavily on "Merrie England" in the days of good Queen Bess. Into the causes of that widely spread suffering—the uprooting or the change of established institutions, the discovery of the New World, the universal derangement of the values of labour and property, the struggles that accompany the birth of a new era,—

> With many shocks that come and go,
> With agonies, with energies,
> With overthrowings, and with cries,
> And undulations to and fro—

there is no need that we should inquire. Many of the records of Sessions relate to the details of this subject. The Court had not only to try questions of settlement and the like, but to discharge duties which now belong partly to Boards of Guardians, and partly to the Local Government Board. Of the strenuous measures adopted to repress vagrancy we find numerous traces. The chief duty of a constable, as we know from a higher authority, was to " comprehend all vagrom men."

In April, 1597, we find a letter from the Lord Lieutenant, commending to the especial consideration of the justices the relief of the poor, and the restraint of the multitude of vagrant persons. This is immediately followed by an order of the Court, providing, in the first place, that all "lycences for beggars," which had been formerly granted by the justices, should be suppressed, and that no such licences should be granted in future. Means for setting the poor to work were to be provided by the local justices, imposing some good sums of money on those of best ability in every parish. Constables and sidesmen were to "take a view" of all the poor, and also of all the men of ability, and to report to the justices. To every householder in a parish containing poor, *or in the adjoining parish*, were to be assigned one, two, three or more poor, to be relieved with two meals a day. In default, the justices might make an order for the payment of a sum not exceeding 18*d*. weekly " for every pole." This is somewhat remarkable, not only for the heaviness of the burden, but also as containing the principle of a "rate in aid," if not of " Union chargeability."

The poor being thus "settled and provided for," none were to be suffered to wander or beg, on penalty of being dealt with as common vagabonds, and any " Tithingman " found negligent in enforcing the law was to be bound over to his good behaviour. Vagrants were to be punished, and sent to their places of abode. Search was to be made in every parish once a fortnight for " roagues and vagrant persons," and reports sent to the justices respecting the execution of the orders. The constables and sidesmen were to publish the orders in every church once a fortnight.

In October of the same year we find an order for a special search for vagabonds on Sunday night, the 16th of the same month. The poor were not to be removed from the place where they were born or had been "most conversant" by the space of three years. The removable poor were to be sent to their birthplace, or where they had been most conversant for three years, at the discretion of the justices. Punishment was again threatened on negligent officers, and the justices of each division were to sit on the day following the search to execute the orders, and also to make inquiry for "regraters of corne."

On another occasion (in 1595) the Lords of the Council appear to have suggested that the poor should be relieved with corn at lower prices, to which the justices reply that they do not see cause for such a step, finding the markets well supplied, the price daily falling (except near Plymouth), "noe poore to exclame for want, and harvest near." Yet, at the end of the same letter, they declare that the number of poor and impotent is increasing.

At Easter, 1598, the statute for the punishment of rogues and "sturdie beggers" was ordered to be proclaimed. Four houses of correction were to be erected or hired at Tavistock, Honiton, Chulmleigh, and Newton, and the orders for their government, and the rates for their support, were referred to the local justices. Another general search for rogues was ordered for "Sondaie come sennighte," and every parish was rated at a halfpenny a week for the relief of hospitals and prisons. In 1601, this was raised to a penny a week.

In the same year appears an "exposition" by the judges upon the statute for rogues and relieving the poor, which bears a considerable resemblance to the modern circulars of the Local Government Board. It is chiefly occupied with questions of removal and chargeability; but is remarkable for a declaration that parsons and vicars are bound to

C

the relief of the poor as well as others, and also owners of "tythes impropriate, cole mynes, and saleable woods."

In 1599 three parishes appealed to Sessions against being compelled to contribute to the relief of the poor of Holsworthy, and the question was referred to a committee, who reported that the parish of Holsworthy was well able to provide for its own poor. It seems, however, that the report was not adopted, for at Midsummer, 1600, the Court ordered nine parishes, including the three appellants, to pay certain proportions, varying from $4d.$ to $18d.$ a week, to the parish officers of Holsworthy.

Many matters strange to the modern court came within the cognizance of the Quarter Sessions of Elizabeth. They not only cancelled indentures, but bound apprentices, rather loosely sometimes, as in the case of Ellis Collinge, of the age of twelve years or "thereabout," who was bound to serve Baldwin Hele until the age of twenty-three or twenty-four years. They appointed and dismissed constables. A considerable part of their work consisted in granting pensions or gratuities to "maymed souldiers and maryners." Two treasurers were appointed from among the justices every year for this special purpose, and a separate rate was made. Every applicant was obliged to produce a certificate from the officer under whom he had served, and, as might be expected, we find some who had been wounded at the Groyne or at sea, certified by Drake, and Hawkins, and Fulke Greville ; and some who had served under Sir Francis Vere at Ostend, as well as some who had been hurt by accident in the annual musters. In 1602 there seems to have been a revision of the list, and we have "a true noate" of all the pensioners in the county. They only amount to fifty-two, but they served the justices for an argument when they wanted to show the Council how peculiarly heavy were the burdens of Devonshire. The pensions varied from 26s. 8d. to 10l. a year. A letter dated from the Court at Greenwich, the last day of June, 1595, complains of the insufficient execution of the statute on behalf of maimed soldiers, whereby they are constrained to wander and beg, contrary to the " charitable intent and purpose of her Majesty and the whole Parliament." Their lordships require minute returns of everything that has been done in this matter, and the causes why relief has been refused in certain cases, so that many poor maimed soldiers have come back, complaining that no regard has been had to them. In answer to this the justices defend their administration of relief, and complain that the number of persons chargeable is increasing, " and more likely to follow, having a late impresse of one hundred men made within this countie by order from Sir Fraunces Drake and Sir John Hawkins." This must have been for Drake's last voyage, as he died in 1596. The letter is signed by the Bishop of Exeter (Gervase Babington) and thirteen other justices.

Another matter that came within the cognizance of the Court in those ante-insurance days was the relief of such as had had their houses burnt. Fires were evidently prevalent among the thatched farmhouses and cottages of Devon, as they have continued to be even to our own time. The amounts granted were not large, generally from 5l. to 10l. At one time we hear of twenty-eight houses being burnt at Torrington, but only 30l. was voted for the relief of the place.

In 1596 a great calamity befell the town of Tiverton, and special measures were adopted to relieve the houseless poor. Three hundred of them were quartered on other parishes.

It was ordered that a benevolence should be gathered throughout the county, for which purpose the justices in each division were to call before them the constables and chief of the parish, and "exhorte them by all the means they can to extend their liberalityes in this behalf according to the necessitie of the place." The money collected was to be distributed at the discretion of Mr. Sparry, Mr. Walrond, and Mr. John Acland. It appears from another place that 160*l.* was assessed on the county, and that collections were made in other counties for the same purpose.

In October, 1602, the justices met to take measures for the relief of the inhabitants of Cullompton, whose loss by fire was estimated at 8000*l.* For their immediate necessities the sum of 50*l.* was voted out of the hospital money, and the justices present individually advanced certain small sums *by way of loan*, to be repaid at the next sessions. Only two advanced 5*l.*, the rest only 40*s.* But they all agreed to make collections in their several divisions for the relief of the said town, and to "persuade men to deal the more liberally in regard of their great loss." Nothing is more characteristic of the age than the reliance of men in authority, while saving their own pockets, on their power of extracting money from those under their influence by means of "benevolences," or quasi-voluntary exactions, a mode of action which might be characterized by a phrase used in the educational talk of the present day, "permissive compulsion."

This practice was of course derived from the example of the Government in its system of benevolences, and of "privy seals," or forced loans. Of the last we have a curious example in a letter of June 25, 1598, addressed to

"Our verie loving friend Sir George Carie, knight, Collector of the loane to her Matie in the countie of Devon," and signed by Thomas Egerton and eight other Lords of the Council. As it appears to prove that more direct intimidation than is generally supposed was employed in compelling wealthy persons to lend their money to the Queen, it may be well to quote the letter at length, merely modernizing the spelling:—

"After our hearty commendations. Understanding that
" you have paid to her Majesty the sum of 3000*l.* for the
" loan in the county of Devon, and that there are yet divers
" persons of the better sort that have not paid the sums
" required by their privy seals, amounting to a good sum of
" money, for the which you have no knowledge of any dis-
" charge from hence for the same ; and thereby as we do
" hear you have been and are at great travail and charge
" in sending up and down to their houses for the money, and
" yet cannot procure the payment thereof to her Majesty's
" use ; these shall be, therefore, to require you to prefix a
" day certain to all such as have privy seals, and be not to
" your knowledge here discharged, to make their undelayed
" payment of the sums required by their privy seals, and in
" case any of them shall by contempt obstinately refuse this
" order, or to conform themselves to what you shall in good
" reason appoint them to do for the better service of her
" Majesty herein, then you shall take bond of them to
" answer their contempt before us of her Majesty's Privy
" Council at a day certain by you to be appointed ; and if
" any person shall refuse to be bound according to these
" letters, you shall certify their names to us at the days
" appointed for their appearance, before which day you
" shall likewise signify unto us the manner of their ill-

"behaviour and contempt herein, so as at the time of their appearance such order may be taken with them as their contempt and delays in this so necessary a service to her Majesty and the realm deserveth. And we have thought good to require you to have a special care that all such privy seals as have been delivered by you to any persons within this county and be discharged, that the same be brought unto the Clerk of the Privy Seal, so as no privy seals be left in any person's hands, lest hereafter they may be abused to charge her Majesty. And further, that you do admit no discharge of any of them but by warrant from hence. And so we bid you heartily farewell."

This letter is inserted in the order-book without comment, and is immediately followed by one dated in the previous year, which may, perhaps, be a mistake. It is said that Elizabeth, unlike most of her immediate predecessors and successors, was generally punctual in the repayment of the money she had borrowed, and this letter seems to refer to one of those exceptions which prove the rule. It purports to proceed from the Queen herself, and appears to be somewhat characteristic in the dignified frankness with which she takes her subjects into her confidence, and appeals to the patriotism and good feeling of her creditors. It will be remembered that George Cary's family was connected with the Queen's by marriage :—

"Elizabeth R.   By the Queen."

"Trusty and well-beloved, we greet you well. Where this last year we did commit to your charge sundry privy seals directed from us and in our name to divers persons of good ability, by which there was required to be paid to you by way of a loan some portions of money to be employed by us this last year for the necessary public "service in defence of our realm, of which portions mentioned "in our said privy seals you have with good diligence "received the greatest part, and paid the same into the "receipt of our Exchequer, from whom also we mean to "have the same repaid as soon as we may conveniently, "which upon some occasions unlooked for we cannot readily "perform, both by reason of the present preparations which "by the enemy's mighty attempts against our realm we are "forced presently to make both by sea and land, and also "for that the first payment of such subsidy as by this last "Parliament hath been granted to us is not to be paid to us "before the twelfth day of February the next year. So as "for these respects we find it very necessary to defer the "payment of the said sums so lent some few months, where-"with we hope our loving subjects will be content, con-"sidering they shall be assuredly fully paid by the end of "six months or sooner as we shall find commodity. And "for this purpose we require you to give knowledge of this "our determination to every person of whom you have by "virtue of our said privy seals received any money, whom "you shall require in our name to be content with the for-"bearing of the sums lent for six months from the month "when they ought to have had the sum repaid, whereby "they shall deserve our thanks, and so also shall further our "service for their defence and safety. Given under our "signet at our Palace of Westminster the 23rd day of "March, 1597, in the fortieth year of our reign.

"To our trusty and well-beloved George Cary of Cock-"ington, knight, Collector of the loan in the county of "Devon."

Of the storm that raged against the system of monopolies during the last years of Elizabeth we find some traces in these records. The Crown had assumed the prerogative of regulating all matters of commerce; and patents to deal exclusively in particular articles had been granted lavishly to courtiers and others with little advantage to the revenue, but with the effect of greatly enhancing prices to the unfortunate consumer. Scarcely any article, even of necessity, was excluded from these oppressive patents. The grant which appears to have borne with special severity on the counties of Devon and Cornwall was one held by a certain Henry Marner for salting fish, probably pilchards. It seems to have been resisted at one time by an action at law, for we meet with several instances of money being repaid which had been advanced by individual justices in this cause; and we may perhaps infer that the resistance was successful, at least for a time, from an order for raising a sum of 260*l*. for defraying expenses in *overthrowing* the patent of Henry Marner. But the justices seem to have shrunk from imposing a regular rate for the purpose, until they had tried their favourite course of a "benevolence;" and it was ordered that the members of the court in their several divisions should, "by their wise persuasions and good discretions, move the marchaunts, masters of saynes, and owners of boats, to contribute;" and also should "deale with the inhabitants of all the welthiest townes within the county as a speciall matter tending to the ease and good of the whole country."

The Crown seems to have been willing to retreat, under some decent pretext, from an untenable position. A letter from Lord Treasurer Buckhurst, dated Sackville House, London, September 13, 1599, after reciting that it has been alleged on the patentee's part that to continue the execution of the said patent in restraint is prejudicial to her Majesty, both in her prerogative and in the omission of the rent payable by the patentee, declares that he is desirous, with due regard to her Majesty's right and prerogative, to moderate, so far as he may, the use of the said patent, as may stand with the convenience of the country. And he therefore requests the justices to furnish him with their opinions, allegations, and objections.

This letter is followed by certain notes drawn up by a Mr. Hancock, who may, perhaps, have been Mr. Edward Handcock, clerk of assize, setting forth good reasons against the patent. He begins by a legal argument, that no grant of the kind could be found since the eighth year of Henry III., and that the practice had been suppressed for more than 300 years until revived by her Majesty; that the new grant was far more extensive than the old; and that a tax had been laid upon the fishermen in lieu of the rent formerly reserved. He then shows that it was most unreasonable to revive the patent "when the country was never so greatly burdened and decayed, as impoverished with long great dearth of corn, hinderance of trade, spoil of their shipping, goods, and some of their towns by the enemy, greatly charged for their defence and maintenance of wars, also with continual subsidies and great loans." Then he tries a *reductio ad absurdum.* Such a precedent might bring it to pass that none but patentees shall license any "to bake their own corn into bread, or to convert the same into malt or drink, or to salt their flesh, or to clothe themselves with their own wool." Fishermen, he argues, are commonly "the poorest of any other company," and, if they have greater burdens laid on them, they will be forced to give over "their most painful, hazardous, and yet most necessary trade," from which will follow the decay of shipping, want of sailors for the navy, of food for the country and the navy, decline of foreign trade and the Customs, and depopulation of the sea-coast towns. This grant would also ruin the fishing off Newfoundland, Ireland, &c., and would more generally discontent and dismay the people than any hitherto granted.

We have also a copy of the "Reasons for which the Justices and Gents of Cornwalle humblie praye that the patent for the saltinge, drying, and saving of ffishe maye be revoked and cancelled." This paper expatiates at greater length on the topics contained in Mr. Hancock's "Notes." I quote one paragraph :—

"The rent increased by this patent is only 20s., whereas "the profit of this lease, by estimation, will amount unto "1000l., by the year, or, rather, to so much as the lessee "shall be disposed to value the same ; and yet we as- "sure ourselves her Majesty doth more tender the good "and loyal hearts of her subjects than so much gain to "herself."

We hear no more of this patent, and it was probably swept away, like most of the other monopolies, by the torrent of opposition that broke out in the Parliament of 1601.

Almost all trades that were not the subject of monopolies appear to have required a licence from the Court of Quarter Sessions. We find frequent licences to buy and sell corn, generally for so small a quantity as three or four bushels a week. The licencees were called *badgers*, a word which has dropped out of the language, or has been converted into *cadger*, but which is to be found in Johnson's first folio, with the derivation from *bajulus*, a carrier. They were required to give security that they would not "forestall, regrate, or ingross," practices which appear to have been the special terror of ancient legislators. Persons were licensed to buy and sell butter and cheese, peas and beans, serges, &c., and probably to exercise all kinds of trades, as we find that the "Clarke of the Markett" was authorized to take certain fees for recording the names of victuallers, innholders, butchers, grocers, chandlers, mercers, clothiers, and "other artificers." Some were licensed to beg, but these licences were revoked, as we have seen. Some were licensed to shoot fowls with "hand gunnes" and "hailshotte." We find one man licensed to exercise the trade and "scyence of Tynkyng." An immense number of people had to give security for one reason or another, so that one feels a sort of impression that half the inhabitants of the county gave bail for the good behaviour of the other half.

One of the matters for which the Sessions frequently granted a licence was to build a cottage. A most curious Act had been passed in the thirty-first year of Elizabeth "for the avoiding of the great inconvenicnces which are found by experience to grow by the erecting and building of great numbers and multitude of cottages, which are daily more and more increased in many parts of this realm." It was provided that no person might build a cottage unless he assigned to it at least four acres of land, to be continually occupied with it. From this statute the Courts of Assize and Quarter Sessions had a dispensing power, and they were frequently moved to exercise it, though not so frequently as might have been expected.

Towards the close of the reign we have more evidence of the activity of the Government against "recusants." A list of persons who were to be bound over for this offence to appear at the next gaol delivery was sent to the justices by the Judges of Assize. Two of these recusants, living at Ottery St. Mary, bore the suspicious name of Babington. The justices, having some doubts as to the manner of procedure, sent certain questions up to the Judges, which were answered thus :—

"1. A recusant refusing to appear may be apprehended "by the Constable, and forced to appear, or else "committed.

"2 and 3. Converts (before the assizes), and such as are "excommunicated and forbear the church for debt, and not "Popish recusants, may be spared.

"4. Let not conference be denied a recusant, and if he "come to the church, his binding may be spared.

"5. If the woman refuseth to appear, and her husband "refusing to be bound, bind the husband to his good "behaviour, and if he refuse commit him."

The growth of Puritanism may be considered to be evidenced by an order made in July, 1595, at a Sessions held in the Chapter House, the bishop being apparently in the chair. It is declared that all

"Church or parish ales, revels, May-games, plays, and such "other unlawful assemblies of the people of sundry parishes "unto one parish on the *Sabbath day* and other times, is a "special cause that many disorders, contempts of law, and "other enormities, are there perpetrated and committed, "to the great profanation of the Lord's 'Saboth,' the "dishonour of Almighty God, increase of bastardy and "of dissolute life, and of very many other mischiefs and "inconveniences, to the great hurt of the common- "wealth."

It is therefore ordered that these assemblies shall be

abolished on the Sabbath; that there shall be no drink "used, kept, or uttered" upon the Sabbath at any time of the day, nor upon any holiday or festival in the time of divine service or preaching of the Word; nor at any time in the night season; nor yet that there shall be ": any Mynstralsy of any sort, Dauncying, or suche wanton Dallyances," used at the said May-games, &c.

In January, 1599, the justices took a long step further, and having discovered that many inconveniences, "which with modestie cannot be expressed," had happened in consequence of these gatherings, they ordered that parish ales, church ales, and revels should thenceforth be utterly suppressed. A market which had been held on the "Saboth" at East Budleigh was also abolished.

Of the ordinary business of Sessions we need not say much. They were held generally in the Castle of Exeter, as at present, but sometimes in the Chapter House, and sometimes adjourned elsewhere, as to Ottery St. Mary or Totnes. It does not appear that a Chairman was regularly elected. The name highest in rank appears first on the list, and probably its bearer took the chair, as is the practice of the grand jury at Assizes. The bishop appears to have acted frequently as a justice, contrary to the custom of the city of Exeter, in which his pretensions to exercise the office were successfully resisted by the mayor in 1558. The justices repaired bridges, as they do now. They maintained the gaol, not as they do now. The condition of the prisons in that age, and long afterwards, was disgraceful to humanity. At the "Black Assize" at Exeter, in 1586, the wretched prisoners brought the gaol fever from their foul dungeon into the Court. Most of those present were infected by it, and it proved fatal to the judge, eight magistrates, eleven jurymen, and many constables and others who were in attendance. The difference of jurisdiction between Sessions and Assizes seems to have been at this time very small. The justices not only decided cases of settlement and affiliation (which were very numerous), but sometimes even tried questions of title. In criminal cases, their jurisdiction ranged from the business of Petty Sessions to the power of life and death. They committed many persons to be tried at the next Sessions or Assizes. They sent many to execution. The offences are seldom mentioned, but we have the calendars of both Sessions and Assizes, the names of prisoners being arranged in batches according to their punishment. The numbers vary very much, which is, probably, owing not so much to the fluctuations in the amount of crime as to the spasmodic efforts which were occasionally made to repress it. Of the ferocity with which the law, and something more than law, was sometimes enforced, there remain abundant records. In the year 1595 martial law was declared in London and the suburbs against vagrants and suspected persons, and the " most notorious and incorrigible " were to be executed on the gallows. In 1597-8 there seems to have been a crusade against offenders in Devonshire.

At the Lent Assizes of 1598 there were 134 prisoners, of whom 17 were dismissed with the fatal *s.p.*, it being apparently too much trouble to write *sus. per coll.*; 20 were flogged ; 1 was liberated by special pardon, and 15 by general pardon ; 11 claimed " benefit of clergy," and were consequently branded and set free,—" *legunt, uruntur, et deliberantur.*" At the Epiphany Sessions preceding there were 65 prisoners, of whom 18 were hanged. At Easter there were 41 prisoners, and 12 of them were executed.

At Midsummer there were 35 prisoners, and 8 hanged. At the Autumn Assizes there were 87 in the calendar, and 18 hanged. At the October Sessions there were 25, of whom only one was hanged. Altogether there were 74 persons sentenced to be hanged in one county in a single year, and of these more than one-half were condemned at Quarter Sessions. As it may be supposed that most of them were young, if a similar ratio prevailed in other counties, the numbers executed must have seriously affected the increase of the population. A paper preserved by Strype, which was written by a Somersetshire justice in the year 1596, says that 40 persons had been executed in that county in one year, and yet "the fifth part of the felonies committed in the county were not brought to trial; the greater number escaped censure, either from the superior cunning of the felons, the remissness of the magistrates, or the foolish lenity of the people." Some felons, we find, were "reprieved for the service of her Majesty's galleys," and a claim of 3*l.* a year for each was made for their maintenance by the Lords of the Council. This was resisted on the usual ground of poverty, "because the county is chargeable with many other taxes coming thick one in the neck of another." It would seem that Macaulay made an unusual mistake when, writing of the year 1690, he tells us that galleys had never been seen in the English Channel until the time of Louis XIV., and that their discipline was a thing strange and shocking to Englishmen.

A favourite punishment for small offences, such as resisting a constable, was the stocks. The offender had to come into the church at morning prayer, and say publicly that he was sorry, and was then set in the stocks until the end of evening prayer. The punishment was generally repeated on the next market-day. But the most common of all punishments was whipping. At every Sessions and Assizes there appears a long list of names to which the Clerk of the Peace appended the word *flagell*, with a flourish at the end strongly suggestive of the lash. This infliction was considered peculiarly appropriate, not only to rogues and vagabonds, but also to women, as we learn from certain passages in Shakespeare, as well as from the present records. At Easter, 1598, it was ordered that every such woman as shall have a bastard child be whipped. Also the reputed father of such child was to be whipped, if, as is added with a grim facetiousness, " the proves be so pregnant and apparent in the conscience of the justice before whom the cause shall be examyned, as maye deserve that punishment, unless it shall otherwise seeme meete in the discretion of the same justyce." In one case we find an order that a woman be whipped until she confess the father of her child. In this case we may believe that the gaoler was more merciful than the Court, for we find a note that she escaped out of custody.

The setting of "that bright Occidental Star, Queen Elizabeth of most happy memory," and the appearance of James I., "as of the Sun in his strength," found little reflection in the Sessions books of the county of Devon. The Clerk of the Peace did not even begin a fresh volume. He turned over a new leaf, took a new pen, or mended the old one, and, instead of the familiar title that had headed all official papers for forty-five years, wrote,—

" Anno regni Domini nostri Jacobi Dei gratiâ Angliæ,
" ffranciæ et Hyberniæ Regis fidei defensoris, &c., primo *et*
" *Scotiæ Tricesimo Sexto.*"

Quarter Sessions under Queen Elizabeth. 33

NOTE.

As a contribution to the history of crimes and punishments, I append a specimen of a Calendar of this period. I have discovered the offences by examining a large mass of depositions.

LIST OF PRISONERS TRIED AT THE CASTLE OF EXETER AT MIDSUMMER SESSIONS IN THE FORTIETH YEAR OF QUEEN ELIZABETH, 11TH JULY, 1598.

To be hanged. *Offence.*

Richard Rundell . . . . . Horse-stealing.
Margery Pedell . . . . . Cutting a purse.
William Rowe . . . . . . Picking pockets; two charges.
William Weekes . . . . . (Depositions wanting.)
John Delbridge . . . . . House-breaking, &c.; four charges.
Englishe Sanders (a woman). Receiving stolen goods from Delbridge.
Trystram Crosse . . . . . { Picking a pocket, and stealing in a house; two charges.
John Capron . . . . . . Sheep-stealing.

To be branded and set free, being able to read.

Richard Payne . . . . . Stealing clothes; three charges.
Stephen Juell . . . . . } Sheep-stealing; two charges.
Andrew Penrose . . . . . }
John Reed . . . . } Stealing clothes.
John Collacott . . . . . }
Anthony Shilston . . . . Sheep-stealing.
Andrew Jordon . . . . . Stealing clothes; four charges.

Acquitted.

Nicholl Hooper . . . . . Stealing or receiving a shirt.
Andrew Bragge . . . . . House-breaking.
Joan Cooke . . . . Stealing or receiving clothes.
Nicholas Shilston . . . . Sheep-stealing; four charges.
Alice Wylkyns . . . . . Stealing a bed.
Alice Bowden . . . . . . Receiving ditto.
Richard Greenslade . . . Stealing corn, &c.

To be flogged.

Henry Sellock	(Depositions wanting.)
Temperance Drake	Stealing clothes.
Joan Bowne	(Depositions wanting.)
Phineas Horsham	Sheep-stealing.
John Dodridge	(Depositions wanting.)
Thomasina Baron Elizabeth Baron	} Stealing or receiving clothes.
Alice Bagwell	Stealing a smock.
William Ackland	Stealing cheeses, &c.; two charges.
Blanche Symons Thomas Jellard	} Stealing gloves, stockings, &c.
Gregory Talman	Sheep-stealing.
John Chalmer	Ditto.

It seems probable that flogging was generally thought a sufficient punishment for a first offence, while repeated offences, though not of a very heinous nature, were considered to deserve capital punishment.

QUARTER SESSIONS UNDER JAMES I.

PART I.

ON a former occasion I brought forward some evidence respecting the state of the country during the last ten years of the reign of Elizabeth, which I had gleaned from the records of Quarter Sessions in the county of Devon. I now propose to pursue the same subject through the reign of James I., a period unmarked by events as startling as those which distinguished the reigns of his predecessor and successor, but during which those forces were silently growing which were destined in the next generation to overturn the Monarchy and Church of England. Before relating those facts which bear upon the condition of the people in their daily life, it may be convenient to advert to certain occasions on which the little round of Devonshire business crossed or coincided with the larger orbit of the government of these islands, then for the first time united under "the twofold balls and treble sceptres."

The first communication from the Court to the justices, during the reign of James, which is recorded in these volumes, is on the old subject of purveyance. How deeply that grievance was still felt is shown by a very vigorous speech of Bacon's delivered in presenting a petition to the King, during the first Parliament of the new reign. The

Devonshire justices, with a somewhat flattering appreciation of the Scottish character, seemed to have imagined that the Stuart King might be expected to relinquish his prescriptive rights in this matter. They had agreed during the late reign, as we have seen, to supply the Royal Household with ten oxen, for which they were to receive 4*l.* a-piece, and 150 sheep, at the price of 6*s.* 8*d.* each. They had had constant quarrels and misunderstandings with the contractor who undertook to perform the service, and they had at last summarily dismissed him. They appear to have taken advantage of a new reign to omit the appointment of a successor, indulging, no doubt, a fond hope that the system of purveyance might be altogether abolished, or at least that the county of Devon might be suffered to escape the burden, as, in fact, it had escaped during the greater part of the reign of Elizabeth. From this dream they were suddenly awakened by the following letter from the Treasurer and officers of the household :—

"Whereas the neglect of the service of your composition, "at the time prefixed, hath already enforced us to provide "four score and ten muttons at 18*s.* the piece, whereof the "country's money amounteth to 51*l.*, and by reason the "next day of service is so near, being the 20th day of "April, we must of necessity buy Oxen, being ten at 8*l.* "the piece, and the charge thereof to the country will "amount to 40*l.* ; three score muttons at 20*s.* the piece, the "charge whereof to the country will amount to 40*l.* And "further upon complaint made by Christopher Walton, "your undertaker, for default of his money at due times, a "Marshal hath been sent down two several times, and had "no satisfaction from the country, but the said Walton hath "paid him 13*l.* 10*s.*, and likewise hath paid for oxen, taken

"upon the breach of your composition in Anno xxxix⁰, 6*l*.
" all which sums we expect that you see present satisfaction
" of, yet we have stayed sending down of his Majesty's
" Commission, and certified you hereof, at the intreaty of
" Mr. Edward Seymoure and Sir Thomas Ridgwaye, who
" were before us. And therefore we require you forthwith
" to take order that the foresaid provisions and arrerages
" past, together with those that rest now to be made, be forth-
" with paid and satisfied by the country. And so expect-
" ing your due care in better performance of your composi-
" tion hereafter, we bid you heartily farewell.

" From his Ma⁽ⁱ⁾ˢ Compting House at Whitehall, this 9th
" day of April, 1604."
The letter is signed by Wm. Knollys—a name not unknown at Court since that time—and six others.

It is evident that the officers of the household wished to make the justices feel the weight of their displeasure, and "surcharged" them most heartily. It is clear, too, that they had been stirred up by Christopher Walton, who must have had some influence at Court, and who had long before threatened, in a letter to Sir George Cary, that he would take some course that would be more burdensome to the county than the taking of their oxen. The prices charged in the letter are, no doubt, excessive, even supposing, as is probable, that it was a year of remarkable dearth. Prices were rising rapidly ; and they were rising, as usual, like the tide, in waves that advanced and recoiled alternately. But we may safely suppose that the household took the opportunity of laying on something beyond the extreme limit of prices. The total cost of the required provisions, according to their statement was 81*l.* for 90 sheep already purchased, 80*l.* for 10 oxen, and 60*l.* for 60 sheep about to be purchased, making in all 221*l*. The King was entitled to have sheep supplied at 6*s*. 8*d*. a-piece, and oxen at 4*l*.; so that he was only liable for 90*l*., leaving a balance against the county of 131*l*., besides the arrears and expenses claimed by Walton. It is probable that the average price of sheep at that time was nearer that given by Justice Silence, " A score of good ewes may be worth ten pounds." The poet is more likely to have given the price of his own day than to have investigated that current in the reign of Henry IV.[1]

In reply to the requisition the justices (or their clerk) composed a humble and elaborate letter, addressed " To the right honourable our verie good lords, the L. Knollys, Treasurer, the L. Wotton, Comptroller of his Majesty's household, and to the rest of the principall officers of the said household."

They explain that they had given Walton notice to terminate his contract, because they had had an offer from some of their own countrymen " to serve that provision, and to discharge us, better cheap than Walton dyd," and that they " lystened thereunto much the rather because this Walton had made many complaints against us without cause, as now again we are informed he doth." When they were about to send up the provisions the year before, " Yt pleased God to call her late Majestie to Him, whereupon we held yt meete to staye them, untill we had receyved directions from your Lordships, what would be expected

[1] It is certain that the household of James was far more extravagant than that of Elizabeth. In the letters written by Bacon, when Lord Keeper, there are many suggestions for the retrenchment of these expenses, though he was willing to admit some large allowance for waste, " because the King shall not lose his prerogative to be deceived more than other men" !

from us, which till nowe we never did." Finding it is their Lordships' express pleasure that the composition should hold, they are taking steps to collect the money " undelayedlie," and promise to have it ready by the end of Midsummer Term. They pray their Lordships to have patience for a reason which commands universal sympathy, " for that we perceive by our countrymen, and knowe yt ourselves to be true, that money is exceeding skant in theis partes; and much the more, for that att this tyme they paie their last subsidye." The rest of the letter is chiefly occupied by a recital of their dealings with Mr. Walton, and by their defence against his "imputacons." And "if this man have cause so to declaime against us, we leave it upon due consideracon of the premisses to your Lordships to judge of." And, " because many things maye causelesslie be further objected in our absences," they appoint Sir Thomas Ridgwaye and Mr. Edward Seymour, the knights for the shire, to give their Lordships all explanation and satisfaction.

In October of the same year we find an agreement made with John Stookie of Abbotskerswell, by which he undertakes, in consideration of a yearly payment of 110*l*., "to make purveyance of beeves and muttons for the King's Majesty's house according to a composition made in the late Queen's time," and gives security in 200*l*. for the performance of the contract. But this contract was a complete failure. In July of the following year the "undertaker" gave notice to terminate it. He had received from the constables, who then collected the county rates, more money than he had accounted for, and a committee was appointed to examine his accounts. Both he and his son were threatened with committal to prison. And the justices who purposed to be in London during the ensuing term were requested to take measures for supplying his Majesty with fourscore muttons on the 20th November, or for compounding with the officers of the household.

To our great surprise, we find that they could think of no better course than to recur to their old enemy, Christopher Walton. He seems to have been the only man who understood the business of contracting, and of keeping his Majesty's household in good temper. He now consented to resume his contract for the sum of 125*l*. a year. Soon afterwards we find that the Court allowed Stookie 20*l*. for his losses during his contract.

The contract with Walton appears to have held good for several years. We find occasional applications for an increase in the terms, which were referred to a committee, and probably granted. Not until 1621 does another crisis seem to have arisen. In that year the contract was offered to one William Burride, of Chard, for the sum of 145*l*. and was apparently declined. At the beginning of the next year we find 160*l*. ordered to be paid to Mr. Serjeant Lancaster, who had undertaken to manage the business at that price. He also seems to have got into difficulties. In one letter he says that he expects to buy 90 sheep at 9*s*. each. In the next he declares that they cost 18*s*. 8*d*., and, as the King only paid 6*s*. 8*d*., he expects the county to pay 12*s*. for each, or 54*l*.

At last we find the system terminated in the only satisfactory way, by an agreement between commissioners appointed on behalf of the King and certain knights and esquires on behalf of the county, whereby the King agreed to accept a money payment of 140*l*. a year in lieu of the provisions formerly supplied in kind. The agreement recites the great trouble caused by the frequent breaches of contract by the "undertakers," many of whom had "become *non solvent* or Bankrupte," whereby the household had been much inconvenienced, and the counties had to pay twice over. The justices and "many gentlemen of worth and quality" of many counties humbly desired his Highness to accept of some composition in money, to which his Highness "out of his grace and favour to his subjects" inclined to agree. The payment was to be taken "in lieu of all compositions and purveyance now served or taken in kind, and of all carriages for the use and provision of his Majesty's household and stable, as well in progress as otherwise." All persons refusing to contribute their share of the charge according to the assessment of the justices were to be liable to "all manner of purveyance and *cart-taking*" (written cartaking), and were also to be brought by warrant before the officers of the Green Cloth to answer their contempt. His Majesty was in future to buy all his provision, and hire all his carriages, and pay for the same to the contentment of the parties who served him. But if this composition should be found inconvenient to his Majesty or his "imperiall crowne" through the obstinate and wilful denial of his provisions and carriages at the same price as other men paid for the same, it was then to be lawful for his Majesty, upon six months' warning, to break the composition, and to "use his commission as in former tyme." And the justices might determine the composition upon similar notice.

This agreement, dated Sept. 7, 1622, appears to have held good during the remainder of the reign. We find a committee appointed to apply for certain alterations respecting "cart-taking" and other points, but the Clerk of the

Peace did not enter the reasons or the results of their mission.

The important events of the year 1614 are clearly reflected in these records. In that year took place the first great breach between the King and the Parliament, the origin of the myriad woes that befell both Crown and people in the next generation. James had lost the guidance of Lord Salisbury, the last representative of that wise race of statesmen who had met around the Council Board of Elizabeth. The Stuart King was fond of being compared to Solomon, but he rather resembled Rehoboam in his attachment to flattering and violent counsels. The discontent which had been gradually gathering head broke out openly in the Parliament of 1614. The Commons refused to consider the question of supply until their grievances were redressed. The King sent for them to Whitehall, tore up their Bills before their faces, and dissolved the Parliament without having passed a single Act. Some of the members were flung into prison; and the King appealed from his Parliament to his people, not by ordering fresh elections, but by asking for a "benevolence" instead of a subsidy.

The manner of raising that benevolence, so far as concerned the county of Devon, is recorded in some detail in the volumes before us. The first document should, perhaps be quoted at length. It is a letter from "ye Lordes of ye Councell" to "our verie lovinge friends" the Sheriff and Justices of Peace in the County of Devon. I have not preserved the manner of spelling.

"After our hearty commendations. You cannot be "ignorant that upon the dissolving of the late begun Parlia- "ment, there hath not been yielded to his Majesty such "supply of wants as in Congruity of State he might have

"expected from his loving subjects. Whereupon as well
" the Lords Spiritual with many of the Clergy, as the Lords
" and others of his Majesty's Privy Council, with many other
" Lords and gentlemen of worth and quality, taking the same
" into serious consideration, out of their dutiful love and great
" affection to his Majesty, in contemplation of the many
" blessings and happiness which we enjoy by his most gra-
" cious government, have of their own free motion, every one
" for himself, with great alacrity presented and given to his
" Majesty Plate or money, or both. Which example we are
" informed the reverend judges for their parts, as also the
" gentlemen and others of ability in these adjacent Shires and
" some Cities and Boroughs, have lovingly and readily re-
" solved to follow. And therefore we, very well understand-
" ing the forwardness of your affections upon all occasions,
" and in all things tending to his Majesty's service, have
" thought good to make the same known unto you, wishing
" you to impart the same to other gentlemen, and all such
" within that county that you shall discern to be persons of
" good ability or otherwise fit to further the service. Whereby
" the return and success thereof (which will rest much in your
" industry and discreet handling) may carry with it a worthy
" demonstration, as well of your own zeal and forwardness as
" of the general love and good affection of that county towards
" his Majesty. Whatsoever shall be given, be it money or
" Plate, they whom in your discretion you shall depute to
" have the collection and custody thereof, are to cause it to
" be sent to his Majesty's Jewel House in Whitehall, with a
" register in writing of the value of every particular gift, and
" the names of the several givers, that they being presented
" to his Majesty's view, he may be pleased to take notice of
" their good affections, which he will ever retain in his

"grateful remembrance. And it is resolved that it shall
"only be employed for the payment of his debts, as namely
"for Ireland, the Navy, and the Cautionary Towns in the
"Low Countries ; and so, leaving the carriage of this busi-
"ness to your discretions and wisdoms, we bid you heartily
"farewell.

"From Whitehall, the 4th day of July, 1614. Your loving
"friends,

" G. CANT.	" T. ELLESMERE, *Canc.*
" LENOX.	" T. SUFFOLKE.
" GILB. SHREWSBURIE.	" E. WORCESTER.
" PEMBROKE.	" R. SOMERSETT.
" E. ZOUCHE.[2]	" W. KNOLLYS.
" E. WOTTON.	" RALPHE WINWOODE.
" JUL. CÆSAR.	" THO. PARRY.
" EDW. COKE.	" THO. LAKE.
	" *Ext.* GEO. CALVERT."

It may be observed that this letter is signed by Sir Edward
Coke, who is said at one time to have given an opinion
adverse to the legality of benevolences, and who afterwards
fell into disgrace for his opposition to the Court. Like most
other letters from the Council, it bears a large number of
signatures, probably those of all the Councillors present. It
is evident that the "solidarity" of what we call the Cabinet or
the Ministry was considered far more important in that age
than it was in the eighteenth century, and perhaps more important than it is at present. Under the Georges there were
instances of Ministers opposing each other, even in Parliamentary debate. At the present time it is generally under-

[2] Sir Simonds D'Ewes mentions Zouche as Lord Warden of the
Cinque Ports at this time, Worcester as Privy Seal, and Somerset as
Lord Chamberlain.

stood that a Cabinet must be agreed on all great questions of public policy, but considerable latitude is left to individual Ministers in directing the business of their several departments. We have seen that a paper which attracted so much public attention as the Fugitive Slave Circular was issued by a department without the previous concurrence of the Prime Minister. Under Elizabeth and James it seems to have been the practice for the whole Council to sign almost every public document. We find this done not only in the case of a benevolence, which was no doubt a matter of first-rate constitutional importance, but in communications relating to the ordinary administration of justice and the relief of the poor, which in our day would bear no signature except that of the Home Secretary or the President of the Local Government Board.

We may well believe that the demand for a benevolence caused no small consternation among the justices of Devon. They met in considerable force, and, after long and repeated consultations, they managed to agree upon the following answer :—

"Right Honourable. Our humble duties remembered.

"By virtue of your Lordships' letters dated the 4th of July
" last, we assembled ourselves to consider by what means
" we might best be able to give your honours satisfaction.
" And entering into a serious consideration of the matter by
" your Lordships propounded, according to the weight and
" importance of it, there were presented unto us so many
" doubts and dangers as did not a little distract our resolu-
" tions, and therefore, having spent much time and many
" meetings in the free discovery of our own opinions, and also
" private trial of others of best sufficiency, we fell at length
" into this resolution (with as much speed as a matter of so

"extraordinary consequence would suffer), to make known
" to your Lordships our general scruple, which under your
" Lordships' favour is briefly this : The exceeding prejudice
" that may come to posterity by such a precedent. His
" Majesty's great necessity to be supplied (which we perceive
" by your Lordships) wrought much upon the affections of
" every particular of us, so as *nothing but the fear of the*
" *just blame of after ages* could have abated our forward
" dispositions from performing a service in itself so requisite,
" propounded by your Lordships, and advanced by so many
" reverend examples. Many other great and important
" reasons, in our opinions, were presented to our considera-
" tions, with which in respect of the sufficiency, as we think,
" of this one which we have alleged, we thought best not to
" trouble your Lordships. And therefore, to conclude, we
" trust that this our plain answer shall stand just in your
" favourable constructions, and shall not lessen the opinion
" which your Lordships have ever had of our good and duti-
" ful affections towards his Majesty in regard of the many
" blessings which we daily receive by his most peaceable
" and gracious government; for we humbly entreat your
" Lordships to rest assured that none of his Majesty's sub-
" jects whatsoever shall be more ready and forward than
" ourselves, in all the ancient lawful and laudable courses
" of this kingdom, to lay down our goods at his Majesty's
" feet for the supply of his wants, of which we are at this
" time so sensible as we are very sorry that we are deprived
" of the present means to show our faithful zeal and loyal
" affections in that behalf. Thus leaving the farther consi-
" deration hereof unto your Lordships' approved wisdoms,
" we most humbly take our leaves and rest Your Lord-
" ships to be commanded.

"From Exon, the 26th of August, 1614."

This letter is signed by no less than thirty justices, no doubt with the hope that a demonstration by so large a body might induce the Government to reconsider its determination, and might, at any rate, prevent its anger being visited upon individuals. The justices express so much regard for the opinion of "after ages," that it would be an act of ingratitude to abstain from publishing their letter. But it can hardly be expected to excite much admiration. Nobody could blame them for their unwillingness to contribute for a purpose which was in fact the abolition or weakening of Parliamentary government ; but their excuse was a very lame one, and was accompanied by expressions of servility remarkable even among the servile compliments peculiar to the period. The only particle of spirit shown is in the insinuation that benevolences were not among "the ancient lawful and laudable courses of this kingdom." But no doubt they had good reason to be timid in their opposition. In another of the western counties, Wiltshire, Oliver St. John wrote on this occasion a letter to the Mayor of Marlborough, in which he remarked in good constitutional terms on the illegality of the King's conduct. He was instantly arrested for a seditious libel, carried before the Star Chamber, prosecuted by Bacon, who was then Attorney-General, and sentenced to pay the enormous fine of 5000*l*. and to be imprisoned during pleasure. It was not to be expected that every county would produce a St. John or a Hampden. But the justices of Devon might as well have consented to pay at once as have rested their objection on their fear of creating a new and dangerous precedent. Of the legality of benevolences there had always been considerable doubt. They had been actually condemned by a statute of Richard III., which had never been repealed, though the Crown lawyers had argued that it was void, as having been passed by a usurper. But there had been many benevolences levied since his time, and the attempt to deny that there were precedents for such a course was as useless as it would have been to deny that the Tudors had ever reigned in England.

It did not require a Government that could command the services of Francis Bacon to dispose of such a pretext. The council followed the old course, which had been so often successful under the previous dynasty. They sent for some of the leading men of the county to appear before them; frightened them thoroughly, and sent them back to their companions with a letter in which contempt was thinly covered with a veil of decent politeness, and adorned by an appropriate quotation from the recently published Preface to the Bible.

"After our very hearty commendations. We did of
" late address our letters unto you, signifying upon what
" occasion the Lords Spiritual, with many of the clergy,
" together with the Lords and others of his Majesty's Privy
" Council, and many other Lords and gentlemen of quality,
" were moved to make a free and voluntary contribution
" for the supply of his Majesty's occasions, wishing you
" to impart it to other gentlemen, and such within that
" County of Devon as you should discern to be persons of
" good ability, or otherwise fit to further the service. In
" answer whereof we received yours of the 26th of August
" last, subscribed by most of you the Justices of that
" county, imparting a general scruple of exceeding prejudice
" that may come to posterity by such a precedent, so as
" nothing but the fear of the just blame of after ages could
" have abated your forward dispositions from the perform-
" ing of a service in itself so requisite. Whereupon we
" thought it very expedient both to certify this mistaking, and
" to justify our proceedings herein to be safe and free from

" any such doubts or exceptions. And having informed
" ourselves more particularly thereof, as also of such other
" reasons as are mentioned for important, nor expressed in
" your letter, nor found to be such upon enquiry ; it was at
" this board in the presence of some of yourselves evidently
" proved and manifested by constant and continual prece-
" dents and records, that the like voluntary and free gifts
" (without coercion or constraint) have from age to age
" been made to his Majesty's most noble progenitors for
" the supply of their necessities, as by the same precedents
" and records particularly appeareth. Whereof, as of the rest
" then delivered, the gentlemen then present can give you
" farther and more particular satisfaction ; and therefore,
" forasmuch as the said general scruple is thus cleared, and
" that it is not meant to exact upon the country, but only to
" move such as are of ability and sufficiency (to) cheer-
" fully and willingly contribute as at the first, so now again
" we wish you to resume this service, tending so much to
" the public good as by our former letter appeareth, which
" we refer to your better considerations, and that now at
" length you so effectually dispose yourselves as that of
" Devon be not noted to be the only county that is not
" moved to concur with the whole kingdom in this free and
" voluntary supply, but rather that you endeavour to re-
" deem that which is passed with such alacrity and demon-
" stration of thankfulness and good affection as *the great*
" *and manifold blessings* you enjoy under His Majesty's
" most gracious and just government may move or induce,
" and as we are persuaded upon better advice ye will readily
" perform. And so we bid you very heartily farewell.

" From Whitehall, the last of November, 1614.

" To our very loving friends the Sheriff and Justices of
" Peace within the County of Devon."

It is not uninstructive to compare these proceedings with Bacon's speech upon the trial of Oliver St. John, in which he argues that this was "a true and pure benevolence," not an exaction called a benevolence, which the Duke of Buckingham had defined to be not what the subject of his goodwill would give, but what the King of his goodwill would take. In this case—
"the whole carriage of the business had no circumstance "compulsory. There was no proportion or rate set down, "not so much as by way of a wish; there was no menace "of any that should deny; no reproof of any that did "deny; no certifying the names of any that had denied ". . . . . This was a benevolence wherein every man had a "prince's prerogative, a negative voice; and this word "*excusez moy* was a plea peremptory."

We may doubt, perhaps, whether the justices of Devon thought that "the carriage of the business had no circumstance compulsory," and that their minds were convinced by pure argument. But, at any rate, they saw the inutility of remonstrating, and set to work to do the bidding of the Council. They met together on the 12th of January in large numbers at Bedford House in Exeter, the residence of the Earl of Bedford, *Custos Rotulorum*. At the head of the list appears the name of Sir John Dodridge, one of the many eminent lawyers that Devonshire has produced, who had been recently appointed to the Bench, and was probably sent down by the Council to indicate to his fellow-countymen the way in which they were desired to proceed. They divided the whole county into districts, to each of which a small committee of justices was appointed, and they sent out orders to the constables throughout the county, "as they would answer their Lordships to the con-

Quarter Sessions under James I. 51

trary," to give notice to all "subsidy men," and to all others able to contribute to "his Majesty's free guift," to be present at their several meetings on the next Monday. The appointment of committees gives us a list of fifty-four justices, probably the whole number in the county. As the number is exactly the same as in the year 1592, it seems possible that it may have been limited. The justices were to bring all the moneys they collected, with the names of the givers, to Bedford House in Exeter on the Wednesday in the next sessions week, at eight o'clock in the forenoon, and to pay the sums over to Sir George Smyth, "Highe Shrieve of the Countie." And at the Michaelmas Sessions we find an order that the justices in every division are to "take a strict course" with the constables of hundreds of parishes to send in accurate lists of such persons as had paid, and of such as had not paid, which lists were to be sent to Sir Francis Fulford and William Cary, Esq., for examination.

This is the last entry relating to the benevolence of 1614-15. Master Charles Vaughan, who held the office of Clerk of the Peace (*clericus pacis*) at that period, was not so accurate a man as might be desired in that position. Many facts recorded by him have to be dug out of masses of irregular minutes, entered in exceedingly bad writing. He often records the beginning, middle, or end of an affair, omitting the corresponding portions. So, in this case, we are enabled to trace every step taken in the matter of the benevolence, except the last. We find no record of the total sum collected in the county, or of the portions subscribed by individuals.[3] But this *hiatus* is partially supplied

---

[3] By the records of the Exchequer it appears that 23,500*l.* was

on another occasion. After the other great quarrel between the King and his Parliament, in 1621, James had recourse to another benevolence. As this event does not seem to have attracted the attention of historians so much as the other, it may be advisable to quote the letter of the Council on this occasion also. It appears to me to show a distinct advance in boldness on the part of the Court since 1614. At that time the benevolence was represented as a strictly voluntary subscription, initiated by the Lords Spiritual and Temporal. In 1622 it appears as an appeal made by the King in person to his people, or rather to his magistrates, and the intimidation of individuals is enjoined with very little circumlocution.

"After our very hearty commendations. What en-
"deavours his Majesty hath used by treaty and by all fair
"and amiable ways to recover the patrimony of his chil-
"dren in Germany, now for the most part withholden from
"them by force, is not unknown to all his loving subjects,
"since his Majesty was pleased to communicate unto them
"in Parliament his whole proceedings in this business. Of
"which treaty his hopes being at last frustrate, he was en-
"forced to take other resolutions, namely, to recover that
"by the sword which by other means he saw no likelihood
"to complish. And his Majesty was confident that in a
"course so nearly concerning him and his children's interest
"his people in Parliament would have yielded him a liberal
"and speedy supply. But the same unexpected not suc-
"ceeding, his Majesty is constrained, in a cause of so great
"necessity, to try the dutiful and forward affections of his
"loving subjects in another way, as his predecessors upon

received from the City, bishops, and courtiers, and only 42,600*l.* from all the rest of England.

Quarter Sessions under James I. 53

"like occasions have done in former times, by propounding
"a voluntary contribution. And therefore as we doubt not
"but yourselves will herein readily follow the good and
"liberal example of such as have been before us, which we
"may assure you his Majesty will take in very gracious part,
"so his pleasure is, and we do hereby authorize and require
"you with all convenient expedition to call before you all
"the knights, gentlemen, subsidy men, and all others of
"known ability within that county, and to move them to
"join cheerfully in this contribution in some good measure
"answerable to that yourselves shall and divers others well
"affected have already done, wherein his Majesty is as-
"sured that, besides the interest of his children and his own
"Crown, the Religion professed by his Majesty and happily
"flourishing under him in his kingdom (having a great
"part in the success of this business) will be a special
"motive to persuade and incite them thereunto. For the
"better advancement of which service you are upon your
"first general meeting to divide yourselves in such sort as
"may best advantage the same, and not to call too many
"to one place at one time, but to take their answers and
"offers severally, calling in the persons unto you one by
"one. For the collectors we doubt not but you will con-
"ceive how requisite it will be to make choice of meet and
"sufficient persons, who are to call for the moneys that
"shall be given so as the same may be all paid in by the
"30th of June next. And so, recommending the service
"to your best care and endeavours, praying you to return
"unto us by the 10th of June next a schedule of the names
"of such as shall contribute, and the sums given by them,
"that his Majesty may take notice of the good inclination
"of his subjects in a cause of such importance, as likewise

"of such others (if any be) that out of obstinacy or dis-
"affection shall refuse to contribute herein, we bid you
"heartily farewell.
  "From Whitehall, 31st March, 1622.
  "Your very loving friends,

  "G. Cant.   "G. Carew.
  "Jo. Lincoln, C.S.   "J. Mandeville.
  "Hamilton.   "Pembroke.
  "H. Falkland.   "T. Edmonds.
  "T. Arundel.   "Ju. Cæsar.
  "La. Winton.   "Rich. Weston.
  "L. Cranfield.   "Jo. Suckling.
  "J. Lenox.

  "To our very loving friends the High Sheriff and Jus-
"tices of Peace of the County of Devon."

On this occasion the justices could not profess their former scruple as to creating a bad precedent for after ages. Their "forwardness" was no doubt quickened by a rumour recorded in the Diary of Walter Yonge, a Devonshire gentleman of the period, that all persons refusing the benevolence would be sent to serve as soldiers in Ireland or the Palatinate. They at once issued an order in exact conformity with the letter of the Council, repeating the special direction about "calling persons severally unto them one by one." All moneys collected were to be paid to Simon Leach, Esq., "at Mr. Walter Boroughe's house, now Mayor of Exon." Simon Leach was sheriff in 1625, and was knighted on the accession of Charles I.

At the same sessions we find a sum of money appended to each name in the usual list of those who attended. Although no explanation is given, I think we may farly suppose that this represents the amount which each subscribed to the benevolence; and it therefore shows what the burden really was, or, perhaps we ought to say, how little a country gentleman might venture to give without attracting the unfavourable notice of the Government. Edmund Parker, sheriff of the county, gave 40*l*. "Barronett Vincent" and Sir William Courtenay each gave 30*l*. Sir Henry Rolle gave 20*l*., Sir John Whiddon 15*l*. Sir W. Pole and J. Drake, Esq., gave 10*l*., and all the rest of the knights and esquires, twenty in number, gave 4*l*. each, except one gentleman who limited his offer to 50*s*. Sir W. Strode, it is mentioned, had "given to the Lords."

From this it appears that the contributions of twenty-seven of the principal gentlemen of the county, being half of the whole body of justices, amounted to 233*l*. 10*s*. What was the amount collected from the whole county does not appear, but it can hardly have been very large. The people, though not bold enough to refuse, were becoming bold enough to reduce their subscriptions. At the time of the benevolence raised by Henry VIII. in 1545, the county of Devon produced 4527*l*. His Council had plainly intimated that the least which his Majesty could reasonably accept would be twenty pence in the pound on the yearly value of land, and half that sum on movable goods. There can be no doubt that the value of land had increased enormously during the three quarters of a century that had elapsed since that time. The fair mansions and abundant plate of the period are material proofs of the comparative wealth of the country gentlemen of the reign of James I. There was no "Domesday Book" or "Return of Landowners" in that age; but it is certain that the contributions on this occasion did not amount to anything like twenty pence in the pound. Sir Henry Rolle, who was very probably the largest landowner in the county at that time, as his representative is at the present day, subscribed 20*l*., which, at twenty pence in the pound, would have represented a rental of only 240*l*.! According to Walter Yonge, the Bishops granted the King on this occasion a benevolence of 3*s*. 10*d*. in the pound on all "spiritual men's lands;" which caused much discontent among the clergy, "yet most paid the same not without a kind of muttering." The estimated amount to be raised from all England was 200,000*l*., but only 88,000*l*. was obtained.

Among James's expedients for raising money was, as is well known, the creation of the order of baronets. The first created in Devonshire were Seymour (whose title has been inherited by the present Duke of Somerset) Vincent, and Prideaux, whose baronetcy became extinct in 1875. The new title seems to have puzzled the Clerk of the Peace, and its recipients are entered in his books for several years as "Barronett Seymour, Barronett Vincent, and Barronett Prideaux."

There is nothing new under the sun, except things that are so old as to have been forgotten. We have heard much in our own time of "foreign loans," but we should hardly have expected to find one recorded in the sessions books of an English county in the reign of James I. So, however, it is. An appeal for a foreign loan was made to the British public, not by a republic of Central America, but by a King of Central Europe. We have seen in the last letter of the Council the anxiety of the King respecting "the patrimony of his children in Germany, now for the most part withholden from them by force." His only daughter,

Elizabeth, had in the year 1612 married Frederick, Elector Palatine, who had been in 1619 elected King of Bohemia. The new monarch was instantly attacked by the whole power of the Empire, supported by an army of Spaniards. He assumed the character of the champion of the Protestant cause, and appealed for help to the Protestant nations. Even the pacific James was half inclined to go to war; and, though he could never fully make up his mind to so dangerous a step, he allowed an English contingent to serve under his son-in-law. He also permitted the agents of Frederick to apply to the English people for pecuniary support.

It is on this occasion that we find a letter addressed by the Bohemian ambassador, "the Baron of Dona,"[4] to the Earl of Bath, Lord Lieutenant of Devon, and by him communicated to the Court of Quarter Sessions through the High Sheriff, Christopher Savory. In transmitting the letter, the Lord Lieutenant mentions that he is about to join with others of his rank in this contribution, but that he is also ready to do anything the justices wish to forward the business.

The letter of the ambassador, which was brought down to Devonshire "by a messenger of his Majesty's Chamber," runs thus:—

"Right honourable and my very worthy friends,—
"I need not here remonstrate unto you the state of the "affairs of the King of Bohemia my master, for the fame

---

[4] Baron Achatius of Dohna, or Dhona, as his name is spelt by Bacon, was for some time resident in England. He was disliked by Buckingham, and consequently by James, and was compelled to leave the country in January, 1621.

"thereof is so public, and your affection is so good to the "welfare of your Sovereign's children, that you cannot be "ignorant thereof, insomuch as I doubt not but you are "partakers of the general joy and gladness for those mani- "fold blessings and prosperities which God hath been "pleased every day more and more to confer upon them, "and will not exempt yourselves out of the number of "those who in their zeal to the service of the blood royal "do jointly contribute to the assistance and preservation "thereof. The reasons are apparent, and the means offer "themselves to our wishes, if it please you to lay hold on "them, whereunto I know you are all well addicted. I "have, amongst other things, received charge from the "King my master, to desire the Lord Mayor, and his "brethren the Aldermen of the City of London, that in con- "sideration of the present necessity of the affairs of my said "master it will please them to furnish him with the loan of a "good sum of money. I find that they are very well disposed "that way, yet so as they desired to leave a place open for "you and others, the well-affected of this kingdom, to "come in and concur with them in so good a work. And "for example divers, together with those of the city, have "already begun to enter the lists, namely the clergy and "many of the nobility and others ; yea some of the princi- "pal lords make no difficulty to embark themselves therein, "and therefore I hope you will not be the last. That "which I so earnestly entreat is in behalf of the King, my "master, and of his Queen, the only daughter of the King "your sovereign, *the most glorious mother and fruitful* "*nursery of the royal plants*. The only consideration where- "of, and of those heavenly blessings which do so clearly "appear in her, will incite you to this holy enterprise ; and

"on the contrary, I assure myself the adverse practices,
"apprehensions, or suggestions of others will no way hinder
"you, especially when the examples of so remarkable per-
"sons of the kingdom as aforesaid, and the examples
"of some of the shires already, do lead and encourage
"you, as also in the entire affection of his Majesty him-
"self, whereof there can be no doubt made, it being
"unlikely that his Majesty will not heartily desire and
"consent to that which is for the good of his blood and
"issue. I cannot therefore but hope well of the real
"effects of this overture unto you, being for the assistance
"and consolation of those whom I assure myself you
"would not willingly frustrate of the hope and expecta-
"tion, nor of the good opinion which they have of
"your affections, but that you will rather oblige them
"by your present and worthy resolutions therein, where-
"of I promise you a grateful acknowledgement here-
"after under the hands of the King and Queen of Bohe-
"mia ; which shall also assure you of the right employ-
"ment of your favours in their occasions. I will entreat
"you to communicate this to all parties of the county, as
"you shall judge it most proper for the advancement of so
"good and acceptable work ; and so, committing you to
"the protection of the Almighty, and praying Him, so to
"direct you and to bless your counsels as they may tend to
"His glory and the good of His chosen, I take my leave,
"and remain ever
            " Your very assured to do you service.
"Westminster, this 26th of May, 1620."

One can hardly help admiring the honest and straightforward letter of the Bohemian nobleman. He has a most lordly disdain for the base details of business. He speaks of a loan, but he scorns to allude to the total amount of it, or to the rate of interest, or the time of repayment. A modern State under similar circumstances would have promised twelve per cent., and paid nothing. The Baron of Dona soars far above such considerations. The King, his master, wants "a good sum of money." England has money, so the accommodation will be mutual. "The reasons are apparent, and the means offer themselves." It is fortunate for Devonshire people that there is "a place open for them," and that they have an opportunity of not being the last.

It seems probable that this spirited appeal had considerable success. The English people were becoming tired of the piping times of peace, and anxious once more to "drink delight of battle," as in the glorious days of Elizabeth. They did not know much about Bohemia, except that it was "on the seacoast." The old buccaneering sailors who hung about the harbours of the southern counties told their tales of Drake and Raleigh, and how they had hunted down the gold-laden galleons. The imaginations of earnest Protestants were fired by the idea of the daughter of their king being hard pressed by Popish enemies. Indeed they were far more ready to go to war for her sake than her own father was. Walter Yonge says that Dr. Sutclif, Dean of Exeter, was "sent for" (by the Council) for speaking against the Spanish match, and saying the King showed no natural affection to leave his daughter in distress. James was not only constitutionally averse from war, but his notions of the Divine right of kings could hardly have permitted him to approve of the way in which Frederick had obtained the crown of Bohemia. Afterwards, when his unfortunate son-in-law had lost not only his new kingdom, but his old hereditary dominions, James was, as we have seen by his letter of 1622, extremely indignant at his family being deprived of their patrimony, and talked big about recovering by the sword what he had failed to obtain by all amiable ways. But, even so, his indignation did not proceed to extremities. The King of England, according to a farce of the period, swore he would send a hundred thousand—ambassadors! Indeed, his conduct can hardly be better described than in a clever fable of our own day :—

> In a wordy despatch full of menace and moral,
> Then the Trout call'd the Perch a bad lot,
> And declared that he enter'd the lists of that quarrel
> With the sternest resolve to fight—not.

The fact was, that James was aiming at two different objects, both of which he hoped to attain. He flattered himself that his alliance with Spain might be the means of recovering the Palatinate from the Emperor. But, on the whole, he cared more for a possible Spanish daughter-in-law, than for an actual German son-in-law.

Such, however, was not the feeling of his people. The King of Bohemia was for the time a very popular personage. In Devonshire his projected loan was recommended by the Lord Lieutenant and High Sheriff, and adopted by the Court of Quarter Sessions. It was resolved that copies of the ambassador's letter should be sent to the justices in every subdivision, with a suggestion that they should appoint collectors and receivers, and bring all they could collect to the next general sessions.

In this case, too, we unfortunately do not find any record of the amount subscribed. The business passed out of the hands of the justices. At the October sessions a financier of the period appears upon the scene—Mr. Abraham Jennings, merchant, of Plymouth. He had obtained a commission from the Baron de Dona and Abraham Williams, Esq., the King of Bohemia's agent, to receive all the money collected in Devon and Cornwall. All constables living near Exeter were therefore ordered to pay in their collections to him or his deputy at Mr. Garland's house in Exon, and the rest were to make their payments at his house at Plymouth. Mr. Abraham Jennings writes to Sir William Strode to say that "his business at home by reason of the fleet" is such that he may not well be absent, and he deputes his man, Peter Goodman, to receive the loan for him. The fleet at Plymouth at this time was, no doubt, that of Sir Richard Hawkins, prepared for the purpose of attacking Algiers.

One would like to know whether the unfortunate king ever got any of the money.[5] It certainly did not reach him in time to have any influence on his affairs. Within a few days of this time, on November 8, 1620, was fought the decisive battle of Prague, which ruined his cause for ever. From that time the fate of Frederick was even as the fate of Banquo—the ancestor of a long line of kings, though he himself was none.

Other foreign powers had different ways of raising money in England. Turkish bonds were by no means unknown in those days, though not exactly of the same description as those of the nineteenth century. We frequently find in

---

[5] I find this suspicion confirmed by a passage in the Autobiography of Sir S. D'Ewes : " There were indeed divers moneys now collecting here in England for the aid of the Palatinate, but much of it, as was feared, came short of so good a use."

these volumes entries authorizing the collection of charitable contributions for redeeming Christian captives from the Turkish galleys. Sometimes they are for the benefit of a single individual. As a specimen I may perhaps quote an order of October, 1607 :—

"It is ordered that friendly letters be written by the
" Clerk of the Peace to the constables of every particular
" Hundred, that they, by their letters to the petty constables
" of every particular parish within their several divisions, do
" entreat the said constables thereby to appoint two of the
" fittest men of every parish, on some Sunday after Divine
" service, to stand at the church-door and to persuade all
" men to extend their charitable devotions for the enlarge-
" ment of a poor Christian, an Englishman, and born in
" Plymouth, who hath been long time a captive in the
" Turks' galleys. And that the same money so collected
" be by the said constables of parishes brought at the next
" sessions, with the particular names of the givers, and the
" sums what they gave, and to pay the same to such as shall
" be appointed by the Justices to receive the same at the
" next sessions."

It would appear that 30*l.* was considered sufficient at this time to redeem a captive ; and that sum was paid to a Mr. Carkeet, of Plymouth, who undertook to manage the business. From time to time we find mention of the progress of this case and others. Sometimes the unfortunate captive was reported to be dead, and sometimes to have been released. The practice of kidnapping, of course, went on increasing, and the price of redemption went on rising. In July, 1623, we find a curious general order, showing how common such crimes were at this period :—

"The Justices in their several subdivisions are ordered
"and entreated to command the head-constables to bring
"them a note from the petty constables of all the names
"who, in their several parishes, are in Turkish captivity,
"and what their friends will give to bring them home, and
"to bring that on Tuesday to Bedford House, at the next
"assizes."

And in October we find that—
"the Justices do undertake with Mr. Neale, that so much
"as is fit shall be paid for those persons who shall be
"brought out of *Turkish Captivity* to the English shore.
"And what is not raised by their friends, the same to be
"laid out of the remainder of the hospitals till it be levied."

The name Turks of course meant especially the pirates of Algiers and the adjoining coast. In 1619 the city of Exeter paid 500*l.* "towards suppressing pirates." At the beginning of the reign of Charles I. we meet with a pitiful story :—

"Whereas this bench is by a very large certificate unto
"them exhibited under the hands of the Lord Bishop of
"Exon, the Mayor and divers Aldermen of the city of Exon,
"and also divers Justices of this county, given to under-
"stand that Julyan Vynton, of Topsham, widow, hath of
"late suffered a very great loss, to the value of 700*l.*, by
"means of a ship which she had taken by certain *pirates*
"*of Sallye*, and in the same one son of her's and two sons-
"in-law, together with divers other mariners in the said
"ship, who by the said pirates were carried into Barbary,
"where they remain in most miserable captivity and torture,
"until they shall either deny the faith of Christ professed,
"or pay 200*l.* or 300*l.* for every of their ransoms, which the
"said Julyan Vynton or any other friends for her said sons

"are no way able to satisfy; it is therefore ordered that "the said Julyan Vynton shall receive from the treasurer "of the Hospitals of the South Division the sum of 10*l*., "towards the payment of the ransoms for her said sons, "who have many poor children depending upon the welfare "of their said parents."

The premisses would seem sufficient to have supported a larger conclusion, supposing it was right to deal with pirates at all in such a manner. It was evidently time that a Blake should arise, and show the corsairs that the arm of England was long enough to reach them.

NOTE.

Names of the Justices of Devon who subscribed to the benevolence levied by James I. at the Quarter Sessions held in May, 1622 :—

	£	s.		£	s.
E. Parker (Sheriff)	40	0	J. Northcott	4	0
Baronett Vincent	30	0	E. Chudley	4	0
Sir W. Courtenay	30	0	W. Bastard	4	0
Sir T. Prideaux	4	0	N. Gilberte	4	0
Sir J. Whiddon	15	0	R. Reynell (Creedy)	4	0
Sir T. Drewe	4	0	J. Davie	4	0
Sir R. Chichester	4	0	H. Clifford	4	0
Sir H. Rolle	20	0	M. Frye	4	0
Sir W. Pole	10	0	T. Ford	2	10
Dr. Clifford	4	0	J. Welshe	4	0
J. Drake	10	0	H. Burye	4	0
W. Walrond	4	0	B. Berie	4	0
R. Reynell (Ogwell)	4	0			
J. Woode	4	0		£233	10
R. Haydon	4	0			

QUARTER SESSIONS UNDER JAMES I.

PART II.

THE reign of James I. was an age of great lawyers. A long list of such names is known to students, and some of them, as Coke, Bacon, and Selden, are familiar to everybody. We find in the records of Quarter Sessions evidence of considerable efforts made at this time to improve and organize the administration of law, if not of justice. There seems to have been a conception of the duties of judges far more extensive than that to which we are accustomed. Besides their usual work in the trial of prisoners and of causes, they appear to have been employed as what we should call inspectors of the county justices. They were directed to inquire during their circuits into the manner in which the justices exercised their functions. They were to require the justices to furnish them with reports on various subjects, especially on " recusants," alehouses, rogues, paupers, and so forth. Matters of county business, such as those relating to rates and assessments, were referred to them, and orders upon these affairs were frequently issued by them. They adverted in their charges to questions concerning the trade and manufactures of the district, and they gave interpretations of law for the guidance of the justices, without requiring individual cases to be argued before them. James himself, who was not without considerable capacity for public business, took much interest in the details of this work. We find in a speech of Bacon's that the King is specially praised for this,—that he constantly consulted the judges,—that he conferred with them regularly on their returns from their visitations and circuits, that he gave them liberty both to inform him and to debate matters with him, and in the conclusion commonly relied upon their opinions. This system, though adopted no doubt with the view of extending the power of the Central Government, can scarcely have failed to be beneficial in some respects, especially at a time when the greater number of the justices were by no means too well educated, and not altogether above suspicion of corruption.

It had been the practice frequently to adjourn the Quarter Sessions, and sometimes to adjourn to another town for some special reason. It had also been usual to refer particular cases to two or more justices resident in the district where the matters in question had occurred. But the establishment of regular Petty Sessional Divisions, and the administration of justice in them, were clearly provided for in the following orders, which were sent down, with a letter from the Council, in June, 1605:—

"Orders conceived fit to be put in execution in these "several counties of this realm for the better preservation "of his Majesty's subjects in peace, order, and obedience "within the same. At the Court, Greenwich, 23rd of June, "1605.

"(1) First, that the Justices of the Peace resident within

"any county of the realm (except they have just cause of
"impediment) be at every quarter sessions for that county
"or part of the county in which they are resident from the
"beginning of the same sessions to the end thereof.

"(2) That the Clerk of the Peace give a true certificate
"upon his oath at every assizes to the justices of the assizes,
"what Justices of the Peace resident as aforesaid were absent
"from any such quarter sessions of the same county holden
"mean between that and the assizes next before, or who,
"being at the same sessions, were not there at the beginning
"thereof, or held not out till the end, according to the tenor
"of the former article.

"(3) Item, that the Justices of Assize do examine the truth
"of the cause of such justices' absence or not-attendance at
"any of the said sessions, and for such as shall be found to
"have offended therein without just cause or excuse, the
"Justices of Assize to advertise the same to the Lord Chan-
"cellor or Lord Keeper of the Great Seal for the time being,
"whereby his Lordship may deliver it to his Majesty and
"Council, that such course may be taken therein as shall
"stand with justice.

"(4) Item, that upon Conference between the Justices
"of Assizes and the Justices of the Peace of every several
"county at the next assizes to be holden in the same, con-
"venient and apt divisions be made through every county
"and riding, and that fit Justices of the Peace be assigned
"to have the special charge and care of every such division,
"and these to be answerable for such defects as through
"their defaults shall happen therein. And every such divi-
"sion to be so made as none be driven to travel above seven
"or eight miles, that then the same part be assigned to the
"division of the county next adjoining.

"(5) Item, that the Justices of the Peace of every such
" division be assigned to assemble themselves together
" once between every general Sessions of the Peace near
" about the midtime between each such sessions, at some
" convenient place within their several divisions, to en-
" quire of, and see the due execution of these things fol-
" lowing, viz.

" (6) The Statutes of Labourers, the Statutes concerning
" Alehouses and Tipplers, the Statutes of the Assize of
" Bread and Drink, the Statutes concerning Rogues and
" Vagabonds, the Statutes for setting of the Poor on Work
" and to bind their Children Prentices, but especially to
" bind them to husbandry and housewifery, and to be in-
" formed of all manner of Recusants as well Popish as
" Sectaries, Murderers, Felonies, and Outrages within that
" limit. And to execute the Statutes concerning Artificers,
" matters of the Peace, and all other things within their
" several divisions as aforesaid, appertaining to their office
" to deal as Justices of the Peace, and thereupon to take
" such course that the same be dealt in and reformed
" according to the law. But especially such as keep ale-
" houses without licence may there be examined and pre-
" sently punished according to the law. And that such
" as having licence do abuse the same, or not observe these
" articles, be put down and proceeded with upon their
" recognizance and such like.

" (7) Item, that the Constable of the Hundred and
" Wapentake and Petty Constables and other inferior offi-
" cers, touching matters of justice, inhabiting within any
" the limits aforesaid, be at the said assemblies, to deliver
" their knowledges touching the premises. And by warrant
" from the justices of that division to bring to the assemblies

"such as offend in remissness or otherwise touching rogues
"and idlers, or in keeping of tippling houses without lawful
"licence, or which do not observe the articles and orders
"prescribed unto them.

"(8) Item, that they appoint a clerk to keep notes of
"their proceedings at these assemblies.

"(9) Item, that the same clerk and constables of the
"Hundreds inhabiting within every such limit certify the
"Justices of Assize at every assizes upon their oaths what
"Justices of the Peace were absent from any such assem-
"blies, that the cause may be examined and if need be
"certified as aforesaid.

"(10) Item, that at those assemblies they punish by the
"good behaviour such as be common drunkards, and all
"common haunters of alehouses, and that they also take
"order that all idlers be dealt with and punished according
"to the laws, and that also at those assemblies they examine
"the negligences, disorders, and misbehaviours of constables,
"petty constables, and other inferior ministers, and there-
"upon to take order for proceeding against them for the
"same according to the laws.

"(11) Item, that the Justices of Assizes do at every
"assizes inform themselves as well by the Clerks of the
"Peace, Constables of the Hundred, as otherwise, what ser-
"vice have been performed by every Justice of the Peace
"since the assizes last before in apprehending of murderers,
"robbers, and thieves, in punishment of rogues and vaga-
"bonds, in suppressing and putting down of alehouses and
"tippling houses, and in punishing such other offences and
"disorders wherewith the country is most infected, and who
"hath been negligent in doing their duties therein, and to
"make relation thereof to the Lord Chancellor, and his

"Lordship thereupon to make it known to his Majesty "and his Council aforesaid.

"T. ELLESMERE, *Canc.*   "SALISBURY.
"NORTHUMBERLAND.   "E. BRUCE.
"H. NORTHAMPTON.   "LENOX.
"E. WOTTON.   "DEVONSHIRE.
"ASHLEY.   "W. KNOLLYS.
"T. DORSET.   "J. HARBERT."
"E. WORCESTER."

This letter gives additional evidence of the well-known desire of James that country gentlemen should live at home and attend to county business. We are reminded of the "good thing" he is reported to have said, to the effect that a country gentleman in London was like a ship at sea, which looked very small, but in his own county he was like a ship in a river, which looked exceedingly big.

These orders lay down pretty plainly the "whole duty" of a justice, and point to the establishment of a sharp system of discipline in enforcing its performance. That system could hardly have been maintained, but it may perhaps be doubted whether the practice of succeeding generations has not erred in the opposite direction. Among the points prescribed, the discovery of "recusants" soon after assumed the first place. The Gunpowder Plot took place in the following November. But, for the present, the regulation of alehouses and "typlers" appeared the most pressing question, as it still does after the lapse of two hundred and seventy years. The orders were accompanied by a list of articles which all persons licensed to keep "typling-houses" were to be bound to observe. No children or servants were to be allowed to tipple at all. No one was to be allowed to tipple above one hour in any one day. No tippling was allowed during the time of "sermons or service," nor at any time after nine o'clock at night. No "carding," dicing, or drunkenness was to be permitted. Brewers were to sell "the best" at 6s. the barrel, and "the small" at 4s. Alehouse-keepers were to sell the best at 3d. per gallon, and the worst at 2d. the gallon. The number of such houses was to be "as few as may be," and certificates of the number in each division were to be produced to the Judges of Assize. No brewer or alehouse-keeper was to be a "retayner" to any justice.

Even before this, at Easter 1604, the justices of Devon had adopted stringent measures for "abridging" alehouses, which they declared were the "nursery of lawless persons." All unlicensed or ill-ordered houses were to be forthwith suppressed, and no more to be licensed "than are of necessity;" for the use of unlawful games there, "and the abuse of God's good creatures by quaffing, drinking, and gluttony, is found by lamentable experience to be the cause of manifold dangerous effects." We find many instances of such houses being "suppressed," and sometimes the reasons are given at length, as in the case of one Liswell, who kept an alehouse in the parish of St. Budeaux, in the high-road leading from Plymouth to Tavistock. His house is declared to have been "the receptacle of many lewd and wicked persons;" some convieted for murders, others for robberies, and many rogues, vagabonds, and other lewd people suspected of sundry misdemeanours, had been harboured and had relief there. Readers of *Westward Ho* may remember the "Rogues' Harbour" Inn, on the road between Plymouth and Lidford, where Salvation Yeo slew the King of the Gubbings.

Towards the end of the reign we find mention made of a name that has passed into history in connexion with the subject of monopolies. Three persons were complained of for selling ale at Newton Abbott, under pretence of a licence from Sir Giles Mompesson.

Cakes and ale were evidently obnoxious to the virtue of the authorities. An order of Easter 1607 declares that church ales, parish ales, young men's ales, clerks' ales, sextons' ales, and all revels, are to be utterly suppressed. Yet we find as late as 1622 that the war against them was still being carried on.

In June, 1608, we have a letter from the Lords of the Council, enclosing new and stricter orders for the regulation and licensing of alehouses. The letter is chiefly remarkable for the explanation of a misunderstanding arising from a passage in a former letter. His Majesty had said that the disorders of such houses arose from the negligence of "inferior and subordinate ministers," which had been interpreted as intended to convey a general imputation upon justices of the peace. The Lords declare that this is not so, and that they are ever ready to represent to his Majesty "the effects and fruits of the service of many worthy gentlemen that bear that office." But they take the opportunity of exhorting them to use great care and diligence in the execution of his Majesty's directions, "as is answerable to the trust reposed in you."

Appended to the new orders is a list of parishes, hamlets, and places in Middlesex in which the alehouse-keepers are to pay the same sums as are paid in cities, towns corporate, and market towns. This gives us an idea of the "Metropolitan district" of that age. It is interesting to observe that it included such rural localities as Chancery

Lane, High Holborn, and Gray's Inn Lane, "Shordich, Hockston, Finneburie, and Islington."

In July, 1608, there were special orders made for alehouse-keepers in Devon. In addition to the provisions in the general order, we notice that they were prohibited from dressing or *uttering* any flesh to be eaten in Lent or upon any day forbidden by the laws, except for persons lawfully licensed to eat the same. Also that they were not to receive into their houses any persons suffering from any horrible or infectious disease, and that they were to inform the constables of any strange or suspicious person that came to lodge with them. But they were bound to "lodge, harbour, entertain, and utter their victual and drink for reasonable money to all wayfaring people that shall require the same."

It is more interesting to trace the administration of the law in matters of religion. In the summer circuit of 1606, the judges were directed to cause complete lists to be made of all freeholders, to obtain from the gaolers a return of all fees that they received, to take an account of the justices of what they had done, and finally to cause all constables to be bound over to inform and give evidence against the "recusants" in their districts. This was the commencement of a period of renewed diligence in inquiring after these unfortunate objects of suspicion, a business in which the local authorities may sometimes have been more keen than the imperial Government. Already, at the Easter Sessions of 1605, a warrant had been issued to search the houses of George Eveleigh and Thomas Babington, of Ottery St. Mary, "upon credible information of great resort made to them in the night season and other unlawful times of Recusants, Papists, and other persons ill-affected to his Majesty." Some also of those that repaired thither were suspected of being either "Semynaries, Jesuites, or massing Priests, and to bringe with them Popishe bookes, vestments, and other unlawful reliques." One would like to know something more of this Babington, and whether he had anything to do with the conspirator of 1586. Walter Yonge mentions in the same year that the judges were to try *Abbington* and two seminaries taken in his house, and there can be little doubt that this was the same individual, though it is curious that in Worcestershire Thomas *Habington* was suspected of complicity in the Gunpowder Plot, and his daughter was believed to be the writer of the famous anonymous letter that revealed it.

In the next calendar we find the names of Thomas and Agnes Babington as recusants—the latter admitted to bail. Thomas seems to have been remanded from time to time,—the usual way of breaking down the spirits in such cases. In another calendar we find him convicted of recusancy, and sentenced "to confer with Mr. Doctor Hutchinson, and if he do not conform himself to be committed," probably for an indefinite period. At the same time thirteen other persons were sentenced to remain in gaol for recusancy, and twelve of them were "to confer with Mr. Doctor Hutchinson," which the judges evidently thought added a new terror to the sufferings of imprisonment.

Gaol chaplains were not invented at this period. Dr. Hutchinson was a magistrate, and a canon of Exeter. One would like to know whether he did his spiriting after the manner of the gentleman who held the post of chaplain to the prison at Exeter towards the close of the last century. There is a story that one of his flock once asked to be allowed the consolation of a visit from a Roman Catholic priest. The chaplain sent for the culprit, and thus addressed him: "Miserable wretch, do you think Father Whatshisname can save you? Why, it's as much as I can do myself!"

On another occasion we find a person convicted of recusancy ordered to be imprisoned by himself, and not to have access to any others of the recusants, and we shall probably not be doing him an injustice if we suppose him to have been one of the "seminary priests." In 1610 we find that Robert Venner, being committed to prison, confessed that he was one. At Michaelmas, 1606, we have a list of persons who had not attended their parish church for two months presented by the constables, who were entitled to a reward of 40s. for every person they convicted of recusancy, according to the violent Act of 3rd James, cap. 4, passed in vengeance for the Gunpowder Plot. And at the end of the same volume is a list of thirty-four recusants compiled by the Clerk of the Peace. It is noticeable how many of these are women. There are four of the name of Fursdon alone. There can be no doubt that the female sex were more prone to cling to the ancient religion, and many husbands had to pay heavily for their wives' recusancy. A letter to Lord Burleigh from Richard Topclyff, "a discoverer and taker up of Popish seminaries," in 1590, declared that the women were worse than the men in harbouring and relieving priests and traitors, and in readiness to assist foreign invasion. "Of these patronesses of priests it is incredible how great a number there lurketh in and about London." Walter Yonge has a story of a priest being arrested by a pursuivant at the house of a Mr. Flear, near Lyme Regis. Mrs. Flear gave the pursuivant a hun-

Quarter Sessions under James I. 77

dred "angeletts" to let him escape. The officer took the money, but carried off the priest as well.

In the calendars after this time there are many instances of persons imprisoned for *præmunire*. This, of course, generally meant refusing the oath of allegiance prescribed by the statute I have already quoted, and prohibited by an order of the Pope. It became the test of loyalty as well as of religion, and seems to have been tendered with much impartiality to any who had given cause for suspicion by absence from church or otherwise. We find many certificates of magistrates and members of "county families" having taken the oath either in open court or before two justices. At Michaelmas, 1610, there is a list of such, with their signatures, and soon after a certificate that Sir William and Lady Courtenay had taken the oath, and another respecting Sir Ferdinando Gorges. A warrant was issued for Sir William Kirkham, John Gifford of Halsberry, Amias Chichester, and John Coffyn, and all such others as the Clerk of the Peace could call to mind "that do not usually use the Church and receive the Sacrament according to his Majesty's laws," requiring them to appear at the Castle of Exeter at the next sessions, and take the oath of allegiance. At Epiphany similar orders are given respecting Lady Kirkham, wife of Sir William, Mrs. Carew of Haccombe, and "Mrs. Joan Cruse of Cruse Morchard" (Cruwys of Cruwys Morchard), a family which is said to have held their land from Saxon, if not from British, times. The proceedings seem to have been deferred from time to time, for in 1613 we find "Mrs. Joan Cruse" actually committed to prison, not having taken the oath when ordered by the Lord Chief Baron. Sir W. and Lady Kirkham were indicted in 1612 for recusancy, and Sir

William and Giles Kirkham (probably his brother) then took the necessary oath, but were bound over for contempt of court. On another occasion they were bound again, perhaps on Lady Kirkham's account. She does not seem ever to have taken the oath, and was evidently very much the reverse of a Protestant. I had the curiosity to discover who this lady was. She belonged to an old Roman Catholic family in Hampshire, who have had fame thrust upon them in our time. Her maiden name was Tichborne. It seems not improbable that her father was that Chidiock Titchbourne who was executed for his participation in Babington's conspiracy. He left an only child, a daughter.

Among the State Papers of the reign of James are several relating to these Devonshire recusants. There are grants made to individuals of " the benefits of the recusancy" of Amias and Gertrude Chichester of Arlington, of John Coffin, and of " John Jefford of Halsbury." In October, 1614, the Earl of Bath writes to the Council that, on arrival of orders for disarming recusants, Sir William Courtenay, a deputy-lieutenant and colonel of a regiment, tendered his resignation, confessing that his lady was a recusant, and that he never received the Communion, though he had taken the oath of allegiance.

In December, 1609, the sheriff and justices received a letter from the Council admonishing them as to the discharge of their duties. Though containing some expressions of regard and confidence, it can hardly be considered as anything less than what is vulgarly called a "wigging," interspersed with moral reflections, after the usual style of the period. The lords begin by reminding the justices how large a portion of power and government is left to their care, not only in the execution of the laws established, but also "concerning the observance of other extraordinary directions derived from the prerogative power of his Majesty by proclamation, letters, and commissions, or from us of his Council by orders and letters in his name." They think it necessary to inform their correspondents, that "our long experience in deliberation and despatch of the greatest and most important causes that concern the State and Commonwealth, hath made us better able to discern and judge in many things what course may be most likely to give expedition in such things as do depend upon the diligence and discretion of subordinate ministers, than those that live more remote from the higher seats of government under his Majesty, from whom all authority is derived." Having thus reminded the justices of their relative places, they proceed to intimate that in divers orders and ordinances there is "a want of good correspondence between direction and execution." Though they are willing to admit that there are many excellent people in the Commission of the Peace, they find that "the rule seldom faileth which common experience hath made so certain, that those duties which concern all men are neglected of every man." They complain that matters relating to the public service are often carried so confusedly or executed so remissly as the vulgar sort of people will in time get a custom of disobedience. They complain that many directions are passed over from one to another without that respect which belongs to matters resolved upon by his Majesty. They therefore recommend them to elect three or four or more of their number to execute the directions received from the Government, and to give an account of what has been done in all such matters. They declare that their intention in taking this course "cannot be ill interpreted of any but those that can interpret nothing well." They reflect that people who undertake public services must often meet with hard and dubious constructions of such as are not moved with the same zeal and conscience that other men are. And they speak of those "who make it a conscience to possess public places, and attend only private things." They commend specially to the justices the choice of "fit and serviceable persons" to be constables. And, reverting to their moralizing mood, they speak of the care they have that the ship of this Commonwealth, which hath so judicial and royal a master to steer it, may be carefully sailed by those that have the charge under him of all sorts. They then admonish the sheriff with some severity for not returning "honest and sufficient juries," and for the partiality and corruption shown in the execution of his Majesty's process. The only excuse they can imagine for the sheriffs is the ill choice of the under-sheriffs, whereof there are so many that are "bred in nothing but in craft, extortion, and corruption." They speak of great negligence on the part of the sheriff in not distributing his Majesty's proclamations and ordinances, "which pass not lightly from the King or State, but upon mature and advised deliberation."

It seems clear that the chief object of this letter was to increase the power of the King, and enhance the authority of proclamations issued by virtue of his prerogative. The Justices replied by appointing six of their number "for the execution and despatch of such directions as shall be received concerning his Majesty's service." It may be that this was the commencement of the practice of electing regular Chairmen of Quarter Sessions. I do not find at this time any mention of a chairman, but soon afterwards there was an order made that the Justices at every Sessions should appoint one of their number to give the charge at the next sessions.

At the Lent Assizes of 1612 it was expressly ordered by the Judges that the justices in each division should meet at least once between every sessions, and once before every assizes, not only for ordinary business, "but most principally to take course that the statute made in the first year of Queen Elizabeth, for forfeiting 1*s.* for not repairing every Sunday or holyday to some church or chapel to hear Divine service, be duly and with great care put in execution." In 1613 still stricter orders were made. The Clerk of Assize and the Clerk of the Peace were to compare their records with the presentment of the Ordinary, and to draw up " a perfect note " of the surnames, Christian names, dwellings, and conditions of every party who had been convicted of recusancy. They were to inquire and inform the Court whether the wives and children of such recusants, their guests, servants, and tenants, duly resorted to church. Also whether any recusants had conformed themselves, and when, and how ; and if so, whether they received the Sacrament. Also whether recusants were confined to a limit of five miles from their houses, and so certified by the minister, and registered by the Clerk of the Peace. Also whether any had refused to abjure, "or abjured and not gone, or gone and returned." Also whether the constables and churchwardens had omitted to present any recusants. Also " whether any be carrier from recusant to recusant, or be holden dangerous in corrupting others." Also whether persons refusing the oath of allegiance had been committed. And lastly, " what Jesuits or priests doe harbour, lurke, or runne to and fro in the country, and who receive them."

In accordance with these instructions an order was made

that the Clerk of the Peace was to inform the justices of the name of every recusant in their neighbourhood. And the justices were thereupon to call before them the "parson, vicar, or curate," and examine him as to whether the recusants ever came to church, or received the Sacrament, and, in case of default, to bind such recusants over to appear at the assizes.

A similar series of minute questions, to be answered to the satisfaction of the Judges of Assize, was issued respecting the laws and orders for the poor, for alehouses, and for rogues. But enough evidence has been adduced to prove the prying and inquisitorial character of the system which it was intended to establish. On some occasions the justices remonstrated. In 1622 they resolved to acquaint the judges with the grievance felt by reason of the constables' presentments being made to the assizes, and to desire that the presentments might be transferred to them (the justices) as formerly. We find repeated orders made by the judges in local matters, signed generally by Sir H. Montague, who succeeded Sir E. Coke as Chief Justice, and by Sir Lawrence Tanfield, Chief Baron of the Exchequer. The name of the latter, a great man in his day, was merged in that of Cary. His daughter and heiress married Lord Falkland, and became the mother of the Falkland of the Civil War. His name is now kept alive only by Tanfield Court in the Temple.

In the letter of the Council quoted in a previous page there is mention made of the corruption and extortion of the under sheriffs. These practices were certainly not limited to personages of their rank. It is beyond a doubt that the offence which reflects eternal disgrace on the greatest man who ever held the post of Lord Chancellor was very common in the reign of James I. These volumes contain plenty of evidence of the extent to which corruption had permeated through all ranks and degrees of officials. We find charges of extortion preferred, and proved, against constables, rate collectors, bailiffs, "clerks of the market" and other similar persons. We are reminded of Bardolph taking money from Mouldy and Bullcalf, to free them from the obligation of serving the King under Sir John Falstaff. That valiant knight, to use his own words, "misused the King's press damnably." He had got three hundred and odd pounds in exchange of a hundred and fifty soldiers. The clerks and deputy treasurers cheated the "maimed souldiers" of the whole or part of their pensions, "dishonouring the country, and injuring a great number of poor men, whose wants were meet to be relieved." In October, 1604, the justices sent a letter to the Chief Justice respecting an "apparator," who had been found guilty of four cases of extortion, and complained of for many others. "Of this kinde of offenders manie complaints are made, but of none so much as of this Collacott, and we doe finde yt verie meete to make some example therein, which we humbly recommend to your lordship's favour and good helpe."

It may be that these offences had been restrained in the previous reign by the strong hands of Elizabeth and Cecil. It may be that the growing spirit of liberty made men bolder in unmasking the misdeeds of official personages. The history of more than one nation makes it certain that the existence, or the exposure, of such scandals, is the surest symptom of coming revolution.

Many curious offences and sentences may be picked out of these volumes. Sometimes we find persons sentenced "premi ad mortem," the old penalty for refusing to plead.

Four men were committed to prison for a year for baptizing a mare. In another place we have a similar offence described at length. Michael Jeffrye was bound over, one surety in 200*l*., and one in 100*l*., for naming a "dogge" John and sprinkling of water upon him, and signing him with the sign of the cross, saying that it was in the name of the Father, Son, and Holy Ghost. A "parson" was charged with being privy to making a child drunk in the church. Another was accused of exchanging a good *bande* (bond?) and delivering a counterfeit bande. Some of the clergy were brought into collision with the magistrates by claiming the old privileges and exemptions of the pre-Reformation era. One Nicholas Gill seems to have been a reverend gentleman of almost profane audacity. He was committed to gaol "for that he, being taxed according to the law for the relief of the poor of the parish of Brent, where he is parson, refuseth to pay, and being distrained for the same, he arrested such as took the distress, and used divers very great and contemptuous speeches of this whole bench, *tearmynge yt an ale-benche*, refusinge to com to the benche beinge sent for, with divers contumelious words of contempt and reproach, besides maney other mysdemeanors." Roger Richards, parson of Cotley, seems to have been a similar character. He was proved to be guilty of "lewd, turbulent, and unquiet courses," but sentence was deferred upon the motion of the "right reverend father Lord Bishopp."

We only find one instance of that admirable punishment *cucking*, afterwards corrupted into "ducking." From the elaborate way in which the sentence is set forth, and the *locus pœnitentiæ* that is left for the offender, it would seem to have been rare at this time, although it is said to have survived even into the present century. Archbishop Trench in one of his books laments the disuse of the old female termination *ster*, of which "spinster" is the only remaining example. He does not mention *scolster*, which has been superseded by the word scold being exclusively appropriated to females. Our ancestors were wise enough, or gallant enough, to admit that a scold, like an old woman, might sometimes be of the male sex. By the entry in the Sessions Book, it appears that Agnes Pringe was indicted for a *Skolster*. The hearing of the case was referred to three justices, who reported that, having heard her, her accusers, and sundry witnesses concerning the unruliness of her tongue, they had directed the constable to *cucke* her, except she should demean herself more modestly among her neighbours than heretofore. The Court " well approved." of the order, and resolved that if the said Agnes Pringe was ever again found to offend in a similar manner, she should be punished by being set upon the " cucking-stool."

The ceremony in question is described with great gusto by Hudibras:—

> There is a lesser profanation,
> Like that the Romans called ovation ;
> For, as ovation was allow'd
> For conquest purchased without blood,
> So men decree these lesser shows
> For victory gotten without blows,
> By dint of sharp hard words, which some
> Give battle with, and overcome ;
> These, mounted in a chair curule,
> Which moderns call a cucking-stool,
> March proudly to the river's side,
> And o'er the waves in triumph ride,
> Like dukes of Venice, who are said
> The Adriatic sea to wed,
> And have a gentler wife than those
> For whom the state decrees these shows.

We notice a somewhat involved sentence passed at the assizes in 1603. Two men were to remain in gaol for a year "unless they pay 10*l.* to their wives whom they have murdered." A relic of the system of penance appears in the frequent orders that offenders are to come into the church and confess their faults publicly at the time of morning prayer, and ask pardon of those whom they have offended, and then are to be set in the stocks until the end of evening prayer. The penalty for drunkenness was fixed even then at the familiar sum of 5*s.*, at which it remained until our own time, but to be "a common haunter of alehouses" appears to have been an indictable offence. Some persons were fined 3*s.* 4*d.* for being more than one hour in an ale-house.

Monthly, and sometimes weekly, searches were made for rogues and vagabonds, and incorrigible rogues were "dealt with by marking them in the left shoulder with a Romaine R." "Marshals" were appointed for the special purpose of apprehending such characters, and paid at the rate of 4*d.* for every rogue that they caught. Any amateur rogue-taker was paid 3*d.* a head, like a modern mole-catcher. The unfortunate rogues were treated like poor Tom, "whipped from tithing to tithing, and stocked, punished, and imprisoned."

John Knight was ordered to be discharged by Mr. Richard Reynell "when he hath confessed to him who gave him the love-charm he used to *cossen* wenches with." A warrant was granted against "Jayne Rugge" of Woodbury, for the practice of witchcraft, enchantment, or sorcery, "to the great dishonour of God and offence of well-disposed Christians. The penalty in such cases for the first offence was one year's imprisonment, and to be set in the pillory once every quarter for six hours in a fair or market. For the second offence the punishment was death.

Arthur Davie was sentenced to be hanged in chains near the place where he committed the felony, *but not in view of his father's dwelling.* Philemon Pearce was to be whipped once every day,—for how many years does not appear. Three men were to be "spared of their whipping" because they promised to serve the King as soldiers. Richard Mutter was committed to prison until two justices certified that William Smith was well of his wound.

A "claimant" appears in those days also, and is somewhat summarily dealt with. We find that William Machim had falsely usurped and taken upon him the name of Devereux, and untruly affirmed himself to be the son and heir of Walter Devereux, Esq., deceased without issue, being brother to the Right Honourable Robert, late Earl of Essex, and by colour of this false naming of himself had cozened and abused divers of his Majesty's subjects, and, being a man altogether ignorant and unlearned, had also taken upon him the profession of physic, to the great hurt and danger of the health and lives of divers and sundry of his Majesty's subjects, "and also had tempted and allured one of the daughters of Mr. Steaninges, of Broad Clyst, promising to make her a countess, by means of which doubtful promises she, as is supposed, is grown to be a lunatic." Further, being called in question for his lewd life and ill behaviour, he "carried himself in a most contemptuous manner." It was therefore ordered that the said William Machim should be manacled and safely conveyed to the house of correction at Honiton, there to be kept at work and punished until further orders. Also he was not to be permitted to have any people resort unto him for any cause of physic, but was to be "utterly restrained from any further practice therein." The claimant, however, was evidently not destitute of friends. He managed to escape, and the gaoler was consequently fined 20*l.* for his neglect, and the constables were bound over to appear at the next sessions. It is satisfactory to find, by a subsequent entry, that the claimant was recaptured. However, this was not the end of him, for in the year 1628 William Machim *alias* Devereux was again sentenced to be imprisoned for one year, and to be pilloried once in every quarter, for deceiving Mistress Margaret Copleston, no doubt by a promise of making her a countess.

We regret to observe that piracy was practised at this time by Englishmen as well as by Turks. A letter was sent to the Council representing that the inhabitants of the haven town of Salcombe, in the county of Devon, were sorely oppressed and endangered "through the insolence of sundry dissolute sea-faring men, who often came into the town in great numbers, 200 armed men at one time, and threaten, when they are denied such things as they would have, that they will burn the town." It was represented also that they often foraged and stripped the country adjoining of sheep and other commodities, and took from poor fishermen and others their boats and barks. Moreover, as it is somewhat inaccurately expressed, they "murdered each other, and buried them in the sands by night," and committed daily sundry other outrages. The authorities of the county felt quite unable to suppress them, as they could always take refuge in their ships lying off the harbour. The justices therefore called upon the Council to send down his Majesty's forces to subdue them. They give the names of some captains or chieftains among the pirates. It may be supposed that their advice was taken, for we afterwards find a charge of 6l. for conducting "pyratts" to gaol from Salcombe. It may also be inferred that the pirates showed fight, for there was a payment made to the surgeon for curing them. But the fair harbour of Salcombe still continued to be a favourite haunt of such characters. In the reign of Charles I., as we learn from Walter Yonge, Sir William Courtenay's castellated mansion of Ilton, near Salcombe, was robbed, and much of his plate and household stuff was carried away. "It was done by certain pirates which came up in boats from Salcombe, and fled the same way they came, without apprehension."

The laws against poaching were, as we might expect, pretty strictly enforced. Salmon were protected as well as game, and nets and engines were frequently ordered to be destroyed. Weirs were pulled down on the Teign and the Dart. The use of nets for taking game was also prohibited, and persons were sent to prison for using cross-bows and "birding pieces," or for "shooting to house-doves, with hail-schotte in hand-gunne," which dangerous implements were becoming common. Many licences for the use of these weapons are entered at length in the books, and perhaps it may be allowable to quote a specimen :—

"A licence is granted in open court to Thomas Algar, "of Plympton, in the county aforesaid, yeoman, servant and "falconer to Sir William Strode, knight, to shoot in hand- "gun and birding-piece with hail-shot at any Crow, Chough, "Pie, Rook, Ringdove, Jay, or smaller birds, for hawk's "meat only, according to the Statute in that case pro- "vided."

And the licensee had to enter into recognizances of 20l. that he would not shoot at any fowl or game at which shooting is prohibited by the laws, nor within six hundred paces of any "hernerie," nor within a hundred paces of any pigeon-house, nor within any park, forest, or chase of which he or his master was not owner, keeper, or governor. Constables were compelled to make frequent searches for guns, crossbows, and "other engines," and were themselves sometimes bound over to answer for their neglect in these matters.

If the country was tolerably free from the scourge of war during the reign of James I., it was by no means exempt from fire, pestilence, and famine. Many applications were made to Quarter Sessions on behalf of towns and villages that had been partially burnt. Tiverton, for example, was again almost destroyed by fire in 1612. A collection was ordered to be made throughout the county, and a hundred houseless poor were quartered on each of the three divisions. A charter of incorporation was granted to it in 1615, "the town having been twice consumed by fire, to the loss of 350,000*l.* (?), through the negligence of some of its inhabitants, *for want of government.*" Other places required relief on account of the plague. At the beginning of the reign there was an outbreak in Exeter, and in various parts of the county. In London more than 30,000 persons are said to have died of it, and the justices of Devon actually put the metropolis into quarantine, and prohibited carriers from going there during the sickness. On other occasions we hear of the prevalence of plague at Otterton, Tormoham, Kingswear, Axminster, and other places, and of special rates made for their relief. "Pest-houses" and "Lazar-houses" were provided at certain spots. In 1624-5 there was a terrible outbreak in Exeter, and the city is said to have been left almost destitute of

Quarter Sessions under James I. 91

inhabitants. The newly-elected mayor refused the office, and retired into the country, but was compelled to serve by a special order from the King. The county justices held their sessions at Crediton, and ordered that any persons who went into Exeter, or any other infected place, or into the company of any person coming from such places, should be shut up in their houses for the space of one month.

The rise in prices, to which I have before alluded, produced much distress, which in unfavourable seasons amounted to actual famine. Such a season occurred in 1608. Orders were issued that "such as be corn-sellers do bring the same to the markets upon the market-days, there to be sold." The justices were to take special care that there might be no *ingrossing*, and that the poor should b first served. The allowance for the prisoners in the gaol was increased. It is stated that their number was very great in consequence of the dearth of all things, and the money allowed for them was so little "that divers of them of late have perished through want." It would appear that no allowance was made to a prisoner until it was proved that his relatives were unable to maintain him, and even then the sum granted was as small as possible. At Michaelmas, in the same year, the making of malt was positively prohibited, in order that all the barley might be used for making bread. The justices in each division were to assemble themselves together "for the reformation of excessive prices of corn." A letter was sent to the Lords of the Council, expressing much alarm at the continued dearth.

"Right Honourable,—Whereas it pleased your Lordships "to send directions unto us this last summer for the abating

"of the great price of corn at that time, and for preventing
"of further dearth. We, in discharge of our duties in that
"behalf, have used our best endeavours in the effectual
"execution thereof in this county of Devon. And yet,
"notwithstanding the price of grain of all sorts at this
"present continueth very high, wheat at 8$s.$ the bushel, rye
"at 6$s.$ 8$d.$, barley at 5$s.$ 4$d.$, and oats at 2$s.$ 8$d.$, and the
"bushel eight gallons : which, although before harvest was
"generally hoped would be much abated, yet sithence, by
"reason of the great store of rain here fallen, whereby we
"have had a very unseasonable harvest, the price is like to
"grow far higher than now it is, unless there be some
"provision had from other countries, of which we thought
"it our duties to advertise your Lordships, to the end such
"farther course for prevention of this dearth may be taken
"as to your good Lordships may seem convenient. And
"for our own parts we do intend henceforth in like manner
"as we have done heretofore to persevere in the due
"accomplishment of your Lordships' former directions.
"And so, with remembrance of our duties to your Lord-
"ships, humbly rest your Lordships to be commanded."

The prices mentioned in this letter agree with those entered in Walter Yonge's Diary in the year 1622. In estimating the sufferings of the poor it must be remembered that the maximum rate of wages for labourers was 4$s.$ a week in summer and 3$s.$ 6$d.$ in winter.

The woollen trade of the West of England was rising rapidly during this reign ; but its prosperity, like that of other manufactures, was varied by periods of extreme depression. We find constant complaints of the "decay of clothing." Special Acts of Parliament were passed for the regulation of this trade in the county of Devon, and many orders in council were issued concerning it. Here is a curious letter from the Bench to the Lords of the Council :—

"Our right humble duty to your honourable good
" Lordships remembered. When at any time the grievances
" of our country are either brought unto or felt by us, we
" have always presumed to offer them to your Lordships'
" grave wisdoms and considerations, who have ministered
" unto us relief, which we, with our humble thanks to God
" for you, and also to your Lordships for it, do retain in
" thankful memory, and do rest now assured to taste of your
" like honourable favours, towards the people of this county,
" his Majesty's most loyal and dutiful subjects. It may
" please your good honours to be advertised that at this our
" present assembly at the session of peace for his Highness'
" service, not only the clothiers, dyers, spynsters, weavers,
" tookers,[6] and others living by their work of clothmaking, but
" divers others whose livelihoods depend thereupon (being
" the greatest part of the people of this county), made known
" unto us their general grief conceived by reason of the late
" demand of a greater custom upon this country kerseys and
" dozens than formerly was paid, wherewith we perceive
" your Lordships have been made acquainted by some that
" solicit your Honours on the behalf of the merchants of
" these parts. And forasmuch as we conceive the same to
" concern the state of the whole country, we made bold to
" break silence and humbly to beseech your Lordships'
" favourable consideration, thereby seasonably to avoid the
" manifold inconveniences which we evidently see are
" like to ensue. For when we look into the condition of

[6] Tuckers, here spelt *tookers*, is the old Devonshire word for persons employed in the trade of weaving. *Tuch* (German), cloth.

"this shire, depending, as it were, wholly upon clothiers
"and traffic by sea, if the same should any way decay, it
"is certain that those who now live by work and maintain
"good families, will, when they want work, become beggars,
"the number whereof will be such as there will not be left
"men sufficient to relieve them, neither shall we be able to
"rule them as were fit, their misery will be so great. And
"that we be not tedious to your Honours, vouchsafe we
"beseech you to accept one instance from us, whereof we
"received even now credible information. That there are
"in the town of Crediton, whereout his Majesty received
"yearly two hundred and forty-six pounds certain rent into
"his treasury, above five hundred poor people who expect
"the success of this business, and are ready to go a begging
"if they be not relieved. And if so many there, in so
"small a circuit, then may your Honours easily make
"estimate what the number will be in the whole shire.
"We need not to amplify reasons in this case to you, whose
"wisdoms can and do discern more than we are able to
"utter. This goodness we doubt not to be made partakers
"of at your Lordships' hands, that you will equal our con-
"dition with others of his Majesty's subjects, making our
"burden no heavier than theirs, and that in custom paying
"our merchants may receive like weight in their kerseys as
"others do in their cloths, or at leastwise in such measure
"and proportion near thereunto as they have both in
"Queen Mary's time, and her late Majesty's, done. This, in
"all humility, we crave and desire of your good Lordships,
"whereby you shall add to our bonds of duty to pray unto
"God for the increase of your Honours in all prosperity.
"From the Castle of Exon. This 12th April, 1605."

At this time, according to the estimate of Hume, nine-tenths of the commerce of the country consisted of woollen goods. The difficulties in this business formed one of the principal reasons for the establishment of the Board of Trade. We find that in Exeter and other parts of Devonshire hundreds of weavers sometimes paraded the streets, demanding food or work. At one time James had an idea of providing a new employment for the people by introducing the culture of silk. At the Epiphany Sessions of 1608 many thousand mulberry-trees were sent down to Devonshire "for the relief of silke-wormes in this countie," to be divided among such of the landowners as chose to pay three farthings a piece for them. The Lord Lieutenant had a thousand, and many knights and esquires took five hundred each. I cannot discover that any remains of mulberry plantations now exist in the county. The white mulberry was found to be too delicate for this climate; but many gardens in South Devon contain one or two large trees of the black species, which may well be as old as the reign of James. It was at this time, no doubt, that Shakespeare planted his mulberry-tree.

A similar experiment has been tried in our own days by an enterprising Frenchman, who planted a tract of ground near Dartmoor with ailanthus trees, with the view of introducing the ailanthus silkworm. But this scheme has, unfortunately, had no better success than that of James I.

Under the date of February, 1621, we have a letter upon the subject of the woollen trade. It is signed by ten councillors, and is called a letter from the Council, but, as they speak of themselves as "this Board," it may be one of the earliest productions of the Board of Trade. They say that they have taken notice of the great " decay of clothing " and the distress fallen upon the weavers, spinners, and fullers, for want of work. And though they think that these complaints are sometimes exaggerated "by the clamorous disposition of some idle persons," and that it cannot be expected that "so great a business as the mystery of clothing, having relation to so many persons, trades, and circumstances," should always proceed in the same manner, and bring equal benefit to all parties interested in it, yet, as it was a matter whereon the livelihood of many poor workmen depended, they have taken certain steps, which they thought it right to communicate to the Justices. They had called the merchants before them, and desired them, as far as possible, to buy the cloth which was in the hands of the clothiers. And they intended to take further means for "vent" of cloth in foreign parts and at home. They were also taking steps to moderate the price of wool. On the other hand, the Justices were to require the clothiers to give employment to the weavers, spinners, and other persons out of work. The clothiers were not to be allowed to dismiss their workpeople without informing the Board, as in such cases they were likely to disturb the quiet and government of those parts. And if there were greater numbers of poor people than the clothiers could employ, the Justices were to put in execution the statute for raising public stocks for their employment. The names of clothiers refusing to obey were to be reported to the Board in London. The wool-growers also were not to be allowed to "engross" their wools, and keep them back in order to enhance the price, but were to be compelled to moderate their demands, so that other persons might thrive and not "want work and consequently meat." It was the opinion of the Board that this was the

"Rule by which both the wool-grower, the clothier, and merchant must be governed, that whosoever had a part of the gain in profitable times since his Majesty's happy reign must now in the decay of trade, till that may be remedied, bear a part of the public loss, as may best conduce to the good of the public, and the maintenance of the general trade."

Such was the political economy of the Jacobean era. The merchants were to buy cloth which they did not want. The manufacturers were to employ the poor, though it might be at a loss. The weavers were to work on such terms as the Justices might prescribe. The wool-growers were to sell their wools at such prices as might be convenient to other persons. And the Government was to interfere all round, and teach every man how to manage his own business.

This system did not succeed in ruining trade altogether, but it no doubt retarded its recovery. We find repeated complaints about the unemployed poor, and the disturbances caused by them. In a letter of May, 1622, the Council say they have been informed of "divers tumultuous assemblies and riots in some of those Western parts," occasioned partly by the "decay of clothing" and likewise "by the practices of lewd and vagrant persons that omit no opportunity of raising tumults and disorders for their own private ends." They state that his Majesty, "in his princely consideration of his people's want, has directed a course for restoring the trade of clothing to as good and flourishing a state as these times will any way admit." They require the Justices to see that the laws for the poor are strictly carried out, especially as to limiting them to their several parishes. A provost martial was to be appointed at the general charge of the county, and the punishment of rogues, which had been much neglected, was to be strictly enforced.

There is an entry in the early part of the reign of James which appears worth recording for its literary interest, though it is unconnected with the other subjects to which I have adverted. We find under the date of March, 1605, " It is by some thought that four score or 100*l.* should rest in the hands of *Mr. Lee of Northam* as a remain of a greater sum collected for the charges of a ship employed at seas in the late Queen's days." And it was agreed that a committee appointed to inquire into the "coat and conduct money," and other matters, should "take the account of Mr. Lee for the money pretended to rest in his hands." None who have ever read *Westward Ho!* are likely to forget how Sir Amyas Leigh of Burrough, in the parish of Northam, bore his part in the battle with the Armada. The spelling of names was of no consequence in those days. Mr. Kingsley himself observes that Sir Richard Grenvile was known as Granvile, Greenvil, Greenfield, with two or three other variations, and the name Cruwys is said to have been spelt nineteen different ways. There was a family of the name of Lee or Leigh, living at Burrough Court at that period. This fact was known to Mr. Kingsley, and upon this foundation he built the brilliant romance that has added a new charm to North Devon. It seems to me a curious coincidence that the only entry in the county records that probably relates to the Armada tends to verify the fancy of the poet, and to prove that a Lee of Northam did really command a ship, or perhaps a squadron, of Bideford, in the days of Queen Elizabeth of famous memory.

NOTE.

Church-ales are thus described by Richard Carew of Antony, who wrote his "Survey of Cornwall" at the end of the reign of Elizabeth :—

"For the church-ale two young men of the parish are yearly chosen by their last fore-goers to be wardens, who, dividing the task, make collection among the parishioners of whatsoever provision it pleaseth them voluntarily to bestow. This they employ in brewing, baking, and other *acates*, against Whitsuntide, upon which holidays the neighbours meet at the church-house, and there merrily feed on their own victuals, contributing some petty portion to the stock, which by many smalls groweth to a meetly greatness : for there is entertained a kind of emulation between these wardens, who, by his graciousness in gathering, and good husbandry in expending, can best advance the church's profit. Besides, the neighbour parishes at those times lovingly visit one another, and this way frankly spend their money together. The afternoons are consumed in such exercises as old and young folk (having leisure) do accustomably wear out the time withal."

QUARTER SESSIONS UNDER CHARLES I.

M. MICHEL CHEVALIER, in his excellent book on the "Probable Fall in the Value of Gold," traces the English Civil War of the seventeenth century to the depreciation of the precious metals caused by the discoveries of the previous hundred years, and to the general inconvenience, suffering, and discontent, following on the "derangement of the value of labour and property."

This opinion is certainly exaggerated, and must be taken as the view of a political economist too much wrapped up in his own "speciality." An irreverent reader might be reminded of Mr. Dick in one of Dickens's books, who could not keep Charles I. out of his memorial. But, on the other hand, it may well be doubted whether historians have not attributed too much influence to the imprudent acts of the Government, and too little to those sources of uneasiness which kings and laws can do little to cause or cure. The records of the county of Devon suffice to show much suffering from the enhanced price of food, caused not only by the change in the value of money, but also by the increase of population, the difficulties of internal carriage and of external trade, and by unfavourable seasons which seem to have frequently occurred at this time, alternating, no doubt, with seasons of comparative plenty.

The favourite remedy for dearth was the prohibition of

making malt and of transporting grain out of the county. Such orders recur very frequently in the Sessions Books of the reign of Charles I. At Michaelmas, 1630, there was a proclamation on this subject received from the Government in London. It speaks of the great excess and abuse of bread corn by reason of the extraordinary conversion of barley into malt, occasioning the dearth of corn and grain within the county. The justices consequently proceeded to " inhibit all common malsters from converting of barley into malt " until further orders. They also resolved themselves "to resort unto markets to endeavour reasonable prices on corn and grain," and to take like care for the prevention of the dearth of salt. All persons who had bought or should buy any corn at the markets, or elsewhere by land or sea, " with intent to sell the same again converted into malt or otherwise," were to be " taken notice of " by the constables. Letters were to be written to the justices of neighbouring counties, and to the mayors and chief officers of corporate towns, inviting them to join in the same course. The chief officers of maritime towns were also to be requested to prevent all transportation of corn, meal, and biscuit, except " for a competent provision of the ships of our own nation for their particular voyage." Inquiry was to be made respecting all " corn-masters and sellers of corn," and " what kind of grain and how much they shall be able to spare from this time until the next harvest." And all " forestallers and regraters of salt" were to be forthwith suppressed.

The distress on this occasion was further proved at the winter assizes by a very long calendar of prisoners, of whom seventeen were hanged. The allowance to the prisoners in gaol, which was very sparingly dealt out, was increased by a halfpenny a day. The price of wheat according to Sir S. D'Ewes, was 8s. a bushel, and of barley, 4s. 6d. We find that one Henry Pincklie was "suppressed from making malt," and obliged to sell all the barley he had at 3s. 8d.

Sometimes, as we have seen, the making of malt was entirely prohibited. Sometimes a reservation was made in favour of persons specially licensed to supply the shipping. Sometimes the manufacture was limited as a precautionary measure, because it was conceived that " by reason of extraordinary *drieth* of the spring there may grow in some parts of this county a scarcity of barley, which grain is commonly used for bread corn among the poor sort."

If Cromwell was really a brewer or maltster, and if similar proceedings were common in the county of Huntingdon, we may imagine that he was not unnaturally irritated by these frequent interferences with his business.

Among other expedients the justices were directed to be severe in punishing tipplers and drunkards, and in suppressing unlicensed alehouses, and all such licensed houses as " do break the Assize of Beare and Ale." A "sufficient person" was to be appointed in every parish to go with the constables "to view and taste weekly the beer and ale brewed or uttered." And if they found any so strong "as in their judgment cannot be with profit uttered for a pennie a quart," they were to complain to the next justice of the peace, who might " cause the said ale or beare to be drawen out and uttered to the poore after the rate of a pennie a quart." We may observe that the prisoners in gaol were allowed in those days to buy beer, but not of a dangerous strength. Their keeper was to permit no other beer to be sold in his house "than ten-shilling beer for the hogshead."

The constables were also required to attend every market in time of dearth, and to take care that the poor were served first. This was done by causing the market bell to be rung "two severall times," the second time an hour at least after the first time, and by preventing any " badger or carier of corne," or any baker, from buying any corn, or being in the market, until after the second ringing. No forestaller, ingrosser, regrater, miller, or maltster was to be suffered to buy any corn at all. If any person promised a price for corn of any kind " to be reserved for him or her till after the second ringing of the bell or after all markett," such person was to be forthwith bound over to the next sessions. No corn brought to market and left unsold might be carried out of the town by the owner or any other, but was to be reserved till the next market day, and then again offered for sale. And the justices in each division were to take care that those who had corn to sell should bring to the weekly markets as much as was needful for the supply of the poor. The price of fish, too, was not beneath the notice of the justices, and they determined to make examples of such as committed the enormity of buying pilchards at two shillings and sixpence the thousand and selling them for five shillings "in our owne countreye." They also resolved to take speedy course for the reformation of the abuse of " ingrossing Newfoundland fish," by binding over the " delinquents " at the next sessions.

Other bad symptoms appear in the frequent orders respecting the poor, the establishment of workhouses and bridewells, and the frequent complaints regarding vagrants or "roagues." Perhaps it may be allowable to quote a specimen of these orders :—

"Whereas the bench is credibly informed that sundry "suspect persons, Roagues both sturdy and begging vagrant, "some whereof pretend to be petty chapmen, others "peddlers, others glassmen, tynckers, others palmesters, "fortune readers, Egiptians and the like, and that some-"time they meet by thirty in a company both upon the "highwaie and in the night tymes in ale houses and other "cottages and obscure places and howsses of evill reporte, "soe as his Ma$^{tie's}$ better subjects are not only much pre-"judiced but terrified. For remedy of the present and "prevention of future damage, these are in his Ma^{ts} name "to will and strictly require you that one daie and one "night weekly till the next sessions you sett a watch and "make a diligent search for the findeing out and takeing "and apprehendeing of the evill members aforesaid, and "the suspect persons and sturdye beggers to carry before "some justice of peace for his direction, and the rest to "punish as the lawe biddeth, and send to their place of "birth or dwelling as the lawe directeth, whereof ffaile you "not as you and every of you will answeare the contrary at "your perills."

A curious feature of the times may be observed in the frequent complaints concerning "wandering Irish," which we do not meet with in the previous reigns. At present Devonshire lies completely out of the line of communication with Ireland, and an Irish vagrant, or even an Irish labourer, is seldom met with. A return of the number of Irish paupers in England, presented to the House of Commons in the last session, shows only 263 in Devonshire, and of these 231 were in Plymouth and the adjoining unions of Stonehouse and Stoke, 26 in Exeter, and only 6 in all the rural unions of the county. In the reign of Charles I.

there seems to have been a regular immigration of Irishmen, imported, perhaps, by some enterprising Devonian. An order of Easter, 1629, speaks of "the Irish rogues with which the countrey swarmes." They were to be "with speciall care taken up and punished and sent awaie." The subject seems to have inspired the justices with an attempt at a bull.

"And for so manie whose birth and landing *cannot be* "*knowen*, to be ponished as rogues and sent from tithing to "tithing to the port where they were landed, and from "thence to the place of their birth or dwelling in Ireland "according to the statute."

A sum of 20*l.* was voted "towards the transporting of the Irish people." One Walter Gibbs, of Beer, was fined 20*s.* for bringing over three Irish people "out of the Realm of Ireland." And on another occasion we find mention made of "Sir George Chudleigh and other commissioners for the relief of poor Irish people."

There were other causes of suffering and uneasiness besides the dearth of food. The plague appears to have pressed heavily upon the county at frequent intervals throughout the reign. At its commencement the sickness was raging in Exeter, and the sessions were removed to Crediton. A strict quarantine was established between the two towns, but the disease followed, and Crediton suffered much from it. The regular course seems to have been to shut up in their own houses persons who were either infected, or had been in the company of infected people, and thus to try to isolate the disease. As such persons could not follow their usual avocations, some small weekly pittance was allowed for their support; and a rate for this purpose was levied upon the adjoining hundred. The burden thus imposed must have been exceedingly heavy. Plymouth and Stonehouse were allowed 40*l.* a week, Cullompton 20*l.*, Dartmouth 15*l.*; Tiverton had 100*l.* a week, and Totnes, Ashburton, Buckland, and North Bovey had 150*l.* a week between them. That these grants represent a vast number of individual cases may be inferred from the instance of Northam. In that parish it is mentioned that 633 persons were "shut up." Yet only 32*l.* 18*s.* 8*d.* a week was granted.

We hear also of the plague at Chulmleigh, Moreton Hampstead, St. Thomas, Dawlish, Withycombe, Chudleigh, Lidford, Barnstaple, Honiton, and in fact all over the county. At Plymouth, 80 persons died in one week. Watches were set at the entrance to towns, and especially on bridges, to turn back any that were suspected of infection. After the Civil War broke out sharper measures were adopted than in the days when the administration of the law was in the hands of Dogberry and Verges. In 1646 it was ordered—

"That all parishes and parts adjoining near unto any
" places infected do appoint and keep very strong watches
" and guards for the repressing the excursions of all persons
" from any such infected places, and if any person infected
" shall presume to press upon such guards or intrude them-
" selves into any company (they having the sickness upon
" them) that then such watches and guards and others *maie*
" *shoote them* if they will not otherwise forbear, and all con-
" stables and other officers and watchmen are required to
" be very careful and vigilant in the performance of their
" duties herein."

Special orders were issued as to the watch and ward to be kept in all market towns. The inhabitants were required to fulfil the duty "in their own persons." And if any inhabitant of the several towns should entertain in their house or houses any infected person, or any person coming from any infected place, such houses were to be forthwith shut up, and the said persons turned out of the town.

As it was found that the weekly tax for the poor infected people of Bideford was much in arrear, through the obstinacy of some people and the neglect of the constables and churchwardens, Lieutenant-Colonel Harris was desired to send a party of horse and foot soldiers to take and apprehend the parish officers, and to levy the rates himself wherever "the officers were negligent or the payers obstinate."

Much discontent was caused in Devonshire at the beginning of the reign by the number of soldiers billeted on the county, especially in the neighbourhood of Plymouth, in consequence of the war with Spain. We find that Sir George Chudleigh was allowed 100*l.* for his expenses "in soliciting the removal of the soldiers." It appears that the army intended for Cadiz was kept for more than two years at the charge of the county, " without pay or clothes, and living disorderly." Three hundred men were pressed for soldiers in Devon in each of the years 1624 and 1625, and four hundred in 1625 for the navy. In one of the calendars we notice ten prisoners "sent for soldiers." We are reminded of Sir John Falstaff's soldiers :—" The villains march wide betwixt the legs, as if they had gyves on ; for indeed I had the most of them out of prison." In 1628 Sir George Chudleigh was requested to answer a letter from Sir James Bagg, and to inform him that all the justices were ready to assist " for the furthering of the pressing of mariners for his Majesty's service," and a privy search was to be made once every week "till his Majesty's fleete be gone." Sir G. Chudleigh was a leading man in the county at this time. He sat in the Long Parliament, and was very active in opposition to the king, though he took the royal side before the conclusion of the war. The orders respecting the "mariners" receive some light from an entry in Walter Yonge's Diary, in which he speaks of a mutiny at Plymouth in consequence of the men being ill fed, and unpaid for nine months. And after the tumult was somewhat appeased, "there was such hiding and flying away of mariners for want of pay and for bad victuals, that the report is that they were fain to man their ships, being but sixteen sail, with lame and untrained soldiers, being very unfit for such a service."

Sir James Bagg was appointed by Buckingham Vice-Admiral of Devon, superseding Sir John Eliot. Two of the captains were named Cook and Love, and a wit of the period remarked that the fleet had a bag without money, a cook without meat, and love without charity.

In 1627, it was ordered that all accounts respecting the charges of billeting and pressing soldiers, and their "coat and conduct money," were to be brought to the commissioners at Plymouth, and the Lords were to be solicited for the said several charges "presently after the departure of the souldiers." The cost of maintaining the troops was met by a special rate upon all persons within the county, "as well tynners as others," and those who refused were to have soldiers billeted on them. In the following year Sir John Chichester was "intreated" to write to the Lord Lieutenant, begging him to take means "to free the sending of the horse to Shaugsbery, because of the great charge and trouble to the county, and the great want of hay and other provision, especially this year," also thanking him for what he had already done, and "for the preventing of two hundred soldiers." If we may identify "Shaugsbery" with Shaugh Prior, the spot must have been near one of the places where a camp was established during the late autumn manœuvres on Dartmoor.

The complaints respecting the suffering inflicted at this time on the county of Devon by the expedition to Cadiz are more than confirmed by the papers of Sir John Eliot, and by the letters preserved in the State Paper Office. We meet with constant representations of the soldiers and sailors being left unclothed and starving, billeted without money, and spreading through the country "the fearful trouble of the infection."

A letter of Sir James Bagg's to Buckingham gives a return of 5000 soldiers billeted round Plymouth. In answer to remonstrances, the Deputy-Lieutenants were desired to levy the pay of the soldiers on the county at 4s. 8d. per week per man. The amount was supposed to be repaid by the Government, but their way of repaying it was by raising forced loans in the county for that purpose. A sum of 9300*l*. was so raised in 1627, being only part of a larger sum. It is impossible to exaggerate the gross mismanagement of the whole business. Captain Love said the fleet had been supplied with "men sick, victuals bad, drink scarce, and ships leaky." Eliot spoke in Parliament of "the miseries, the calamities, which our western parts have both seen, and still feel." "Our honour is ruined, our ships are sunk, our men perished; not by the sword, not by the enemy, not by chance, but by those we trust!"

A letter of 1627 describes the feeling of the county:—
"What, say the people, will his Majesty make war with-

"out provision of treasure, or must our county bear the "charge for all England? Is it not enough that we undergo "the trouble of the insolent soldiers in our houses, their "robberies, and other misdemeanours, but that we must "maintain them, too, at our own cost?"

It seems strange that there was so much loyalty left in Devonshire after such sufferings.

The chief culprit, if we may believe the evidence adduced by Mr. Forster, was Eliot's enemy, Sir James Bagg, M.P. for Looe, who lived in luxury at his seat of Saltram, now Lord Morley's, and embezzled large sums of money which were destined for the fleet and the army. Even Laud, who was not inclined to be severe on a supporter of the Government, could not refrain from characterizing him as "Bottomless Bagg."

The burden of purveyance was increased during the reign of Charles I. The composition made in the former reign, by which the king agreed to accept 140*l.* a year in lieu of his ancient rights, was terminated, and the county had again to supply his table in kind. An arrangement was made with a contractor, who undertook to perform the service at first for 165*l.*, but this sum rapidly rose to 185*l.*, 192*l.* 10*s.*, 200*l.*, and 240*l.*, "besides the king's allowance," which probably remained at 90*l.*, as in the reign of Elizabeth. At one time the contractor was allowed 24*l.* more "for serving the purveyance at York." During a great part of the reign the contractor was one Mr. *Antiochesten* Phillips, a name which I do not remember having met with elsewhere. If one might hazard a guess, I should say it might be derived from Antioch-christian, as the disciples were called Christians first at Antioch.

The ordinary business of sessions went on as usual, and

we need say nothing of the many orders on the staple subjects of the poor and their settlement, alehouses, cottages, forestalling, rogues, affiliation, fires, Turkish captives, maimed soldiers, and the like. An order that "souldiers dead" should have no more allowance reminds one again of Falstaff, who had "a number of shadows to fill up the muster-book." We may note some curious offences and sentences. John Walker was to be committed to gaol, "and to be freed if he marry the woman." Michael Edy was to be whipped three times about the city, and to stand upon a stool with a paper in his hat signifying "This is the fellow that beat his master!" which must have been pleasant for the master as well as the man. Sometimes the justices vouched for a lady's character, as when they sentenced Joane Hill for greatly abusing Mrs. Jane West, "a virtuous gentlewoman, and of known good worth and reputation." A still worse offence was that of William Shapton, who was committed for saying that there were not two honest women in Thorverton. The indictment in these cases probably resembled the accusation in *Much Ado about Nothing*: "Marry, sir, they have committed false report; moreover, they have spoken untruths; secondarily, they are slanders; sixth and lastly, they have belied a lady; thirdly, they have verified unjust things; and, to conclude, they are lying knaves."

Some were sent to prison for being "partridge-shooters and common hunters;" others for "refusing to go with a hue and cry." The Bishop's services were utilized by the matters in dispute between Mr. William Holwaie and his wife being referred to him, and he was "desired by the Court once again to take some pains for settling of a peace between them." The same prelate was expected to take pains "for the satisfaction of the conscience" of Thomazina, wife of Robert Wakeham, Doctor of Divinity, who would not take the oath of allegiance.

The sentences are for the most part entered in dog-latin, with many contractions, and sometimes with a mixture of English or a *soupçon* of Norman French. For example, "Vincentius Morell, *com. gaol p. ball. bon. et comp. in px.* for beating and hurting Ann Berie." The prisoner is sometimes a husbandman, sometimes *agricola*, sometimes a "marryner," sometimes *nauta*. Sometimes he is a "typler," sometimes *tipulator*. Sometimes he sells beer, sometimes "*vendit cerevisiam*." When a rogue is branded, "*ur. ut rogus incorrigibilis.*"

One of these sentences is valuable as proving the duration of the Devonshire dialect. Robert Randle, of Ipplepen, was brought up for shooting a woodcock. Probably he was one of the first persons who ever succeeded in hitting one; and when we consider the "hand-gun and hail shot" of the period, the feat may appear worthy of admiration rather than punishment. The witness no doubt spoke not of his shooting, but of his *shutting* the woodcock, exactly as a Devonshire witness would speak at the present day. The Clerk of the Peace was evidently not much of a Latinist, but he was still less of a sportsman, and he saw no harm in translating *shutting* into *claudendo*. So he entered in his book that the prisoner was fined "xx^s *pro claudendo cum hayle shott* and killing a woodcocke," and bound over in 20*l*. "sub conditione quod non *claudebit iterum!*" This nearly parallels the case where an offender was indicted for stealing "duos suspensores et unum adolescentiorem"—two hangers and one ladder!

We find in Walter Yonge's Diary another proof of the permanence of the local dialect, or at least of the pronunciation of *oo*. He wrote that "the fleet advanced in the form of a half-*mune*."

In another case the prisoner was charged with stealing *wotts*, which is the way that the word *oats* is still pronounced in Devonshire.

At the beginning of one of the volumes the Clerk of the Peace exercised his Latin by entering two mottoes. The first is: "Honestè vivere, neminem lædere, suum cuique tribuere, are the effects of justice, and that the harmony of all virtues." The other is: "Lenitas in impiis est impius in piis"—which, if it meant anything, would somewhat resemble the celebrated "Judex damnatur cùm nocens absolvitur."

It was a frequent sentence that the prisoner should stand in the pillory with a paper in his hat stating his offence, e.g. "cosening the people by telling fortunes." Four prisoners were, "by their own consent," to go to Dartmouth, and from thence to be shipped for the Barbadoes. Similar sentences occur afterwards, and it seems clear that transportation was at first a voluntary commutation of another punishment. Baldwin Whitfield was committed to prison for a year, and once a quarter to stand six hours in the pillory, "for provoking the unlawful love of Mary Herder by witchcraft, charme, and sorcery." Richard Saunders was convicted of literally teaching the young idea how to shoot, for that he "did of late bringe a gunne and chardged him, and delivered him to his said apprentice, willinge him to shoote to pidgeons, who dyd soe and killed fyve, and brought them to his master."

Sometimes the prisoner was branded with a T, which may perhaps have signified traitor, or thief. Sometimes he had one of his ears cut off. Humphrey Moore was sent to the house of correction for an indefinite period for being a "very lewd and dangerous fellow," and especially for having falsely accused his master of slandering some of the justices by alleging that they took bribes of the "trayne souldiers" which were to have been sent into the North. He had also maliciously and falsely accused his master of shooting pigeons, and had advised an apprentice to accuse his master's son of shooting partridges and "feazants."

There were many complaints of outrages committed by soldiers quartered in the county, and the unfortunate constables were strictly charged to apprehend the offenders, an order which was probably more easily given than obeyed. It is likely that they preferred to be guided in such a case by the directions of Dogberry, to "take no note of him, but let him go; and presently call the rest of the watch together, and thank God you are rid of a knave."

A permanent County Treasurer seems to have been first appointed in this reign. The four chief heads of expenditure were the gaol, the hospitals, purveyance, and maimed soldiers. The contributions in aid of the redemption of "Turkish captives," and of those who had suffered losses by fire or at sea, were generally taken out of the "hospital money." Many rates ordered by sessions to be collected by the constables for special purposes, as for the relief of places stricken by the plague, and for building houses of correction, were levied and spent without being brought into the hands of the treasurer. Besides these, voluntary contributions were often ordered to be collected in the same way, sometimes for building churches, and especially for the "reparation" of St. Paul's Cathedral in 1634.

The treasurer's accounts were not generally entered in the books, but in 1639, on the death of Mr. Treasurer Jones, a summary of his account is given, by which it appears that in eight years he had received 3283*l.* and disbursed 3334*l.* It is recorded that Mr. Jones had been a very "good husband for the county." He was succeeded by Mr. Nicholas Vaughan, probably the same who was muster-master for the county, and who was killed in the civil war. The justices seem to have had an excellent plan, when they increased the salary of one of their officers for good service, of diminishing that of another for idleness.

There are many orders against ales, revels, maypoles, and the like. In 1627 the judges of assize, Chief Baron Walter and Sir John Denham, issued a special order against such festivities, and for "the speedy apprehending and punishment of idle and lewd people drawn together to such places." Every minister was to publish the order in his parish church, and every constable was to bring to the judges a certificate from the ministers of their having received a copy of it. And such persons "as usually carry up and downe bulls and beares to baite, being roagues by the statute," were to be punished as such, "for the further prevention of such inconveniences as usually happen upon such meetings." So that Sir Hudibras, when he interfered with the bear-baiting, was acting according to the old law of the land, and not in obedience to Puritanical innovations.

The judges issued a similar order for suppressing the multitude of unnecessary alehouses, declaring them to be

" The seminary of the greatest mischiefs within this coun-
" trye, and the occasion of many manslaughters, bloud-
" shedds, and affraies, and of much dronkenness, and are the
" harbors of idle and dissolute people, and a means to drawe
" men's servaunts and younge tradesmen and beginners from
" their lawfull trades and labors to an idle and disordered

"course of life. And therefore the suppressinge of these "howsses will be a very beneficiall and profitable accon."

In 1631 the Court was credibly informed that much disorder and great misdemeanours had been committed by the setting up of a maypole at Cullompton, which was consequently ordered to be taken down, as the cause of great outrages, disorderly assemblies, and riotous meetings.

In May, 1633, we note an order for the appointment of "foot-posts" in every parish in the county, "to be sent onlie for anie occasion for his Majestie's speedie services or from the sessions, and they to have a peny for every mile forth and back, to be paid by the petty constables of everie parish."

Letters from the Lords of the Council were either not so frequent, or not so frequently entered, as in the previous reign. In 1632 there was a letter received "for quickening the justices to the continuance of their monthly meetings and establishing of bridewells." There was also a communication respecting the "great disorder used in the venting and selling of tobacco," declaring that it was necessary to restrain "the excesse and ungoverned venting of it." The justices were required to report in what towns and places in their county it might be sold by retail, and to obtain written certificates from the chief officers and governors of each place as to how many persons in each should be permitted to sell, and the names and trades of persons who were considered fit to be "admitted to use that trade." This letter was signed by T. Coventry, C.S., B. Ebor, R. Weston, Lindsey, Bridgwater Dorset, Kellie, Wentworth, Danby, G. London, Fra. Cottingdon, J. Coke.

In 1639 a letter was addressed by the Court to the Lords of the Council, declaring that they were "daylie prest by the complaints and peticons of a multitude of necessarie poore people the worsted-combers of this countie." The occasion was "a pattent lately obtayned by the cittizens of Exon and others of that trade which proves in the execucion very molestacious," "farr differing from his Mat's gratious intention or the pretences of the procurers." It is stated that "injuryes of unsufferable nature" had been done to the wool-combers, namely "the suppression of some of the ablest in the trade, if they satisfie not the unreasonable demands of ffines by the pattentees, which their estates will not beare, and admission of others for mony, not much experienced, contrary to their first pretensions, which were the grounds of their incorporation." The justices send by the bearer various petitions and examinations for the information of their lordships, and conclude by a humble but solemn warning of impending danger:—

"We most humbly tender the same to your Lordships'
" serious considerations, to whom the prevention of mischiefs
" wholly appertains, to us only the provision and information
" at this distance, which we humbly desire your Lordships
" to take in good part from those that presume not to pro-
" pose the remedy, but cannot conceal our poor judgment to
" be that the quiet of this country cannot stand long with
" this Pattent, at least extending itself without the limits of
" the city, with whose government it is not proper for us to
" intermeddle, neither, as we conceive, should their incorpo-
" ration of this trade stretch without their bounds, more than
" do their weavers, tuckers, shoemakers, and the rest. But
"submission to your Lordships' approved wisdoms is the duty
" of your Lordships' most humble servants."

Matters relating to the constitutional questions which produced the Civil War are not so fully entered in these records as might be desired. The Clerk of the Peace was too discreet, or too idle, or perhaps too busy, to write more about them than was necessary. We find by an entry at the end of the reign, to which we may refer hereafter, that he was active on the side of the king, and was deprived of his office "for levying war against the Parliament." It seems certain that the majority of those who attended Sessions were always Royalists, so that the entries in the books are generally of a loyal description until the end of the war, when authority passed into other hands, and the tone of the records is completely changed.

Although the requisitions relating to ship-money and loans are not entered at length, we meet with incidental allusions which throw some light on what we know from other sources. It is probable that Devonshire, as an important maritime county, had often borne the burden of ship-money in previous reigns, and did not feel the imposition as a novelty. The demands of Charles seem to have been made upon the west some years before the case of Hampden. On April 5, 1627, it was ordered :—

" That the justices in their several divisions (who are by " letters from the Lords of his Majesty's Council to contri- " bute or join with the ports for the setting out of ships) do " treat with the said towns therein according to the direction " of the said letters, and after to take further order therein " as they shall think fit, &c."

At the Michaelmas sessions of the same year, the Commissioners in every division " are intreated to call such persons before them who have refused or not paid their loans to his Majesty, whose names shall be presented unto them by Mr. Ralph Robynson, his Majesty's messenger, or his assigns, and if the said persons shall refuse to come or make present

Quarter Sessions under Charles I. 119

payment of the said loans, then to leave them to his Majesty's messenger, according to direction of the Lords of his Majesty's most honourable privy council."

These orders receive some explanation from another quarter. Walter Yonge, in his Diary for 1626, records that "Exon, with his members, was required to set forth two ships." Each ship was to be of 200 tons, with twelve pieces of ordnance, and 132 men. "Letters were also directed to the justices of peace adjoining to Exon, to furnish them with a third part of men, if they wanted men, and to supply them with victuals." There was also "a demand made for those four subsidies and three fifteenths which were propounded in Parliament, but not agreed on, but upon conditions." And at the beginning of the next year he records that a commission was sent down to Devonshire, consisting of Lord Russell, Lord Lieutenant, and all justices of peace of the county, to require a loan to the king by all subsidy-men, "after the rate of five subsidies, to be paid within 24 days of such as are able, and all others to pay the one half within 14 days, and the rest within three months." A letter from certain deputy-lieutenants to Lord Russell declares that "the business will be irksome to the country, as it has been unpleasing to the writers." And they hope "that their diligence may not be a means to invite his Majesty to an often recourse to that kind of supply, but rather to those which for their antiquity and indifferency are more pleasing to his subjects."

From Walter Yonge we also learn that in April 1627 there came other letters to the justices of Devon and mayors of port towns, "for the setting forth of eight ships; viz., two for Exon, two for Dartmouth and Totnes, two for Plymouth, and two for Barnstaple." "The towns are to provide the ships, and the country men and victuals, and are to be ready against the 20th May next." And in the next year there were sent letters into Devon, both by King Charles and his Council, "for the raising of 17,400*l.* out of this county, to set a fleet at sea, which was appointed to be at sea the first of March, we having but six or seven days to raise the money and return it to London; but our county refused to meddle therein."

John Northcote, father of the first baronet, was at this time Sheriff of Devon. He was summoned before the Star Chamber, probably in connexion with this business.

It many be interesting, as showing the estimate of the relative wealth of different parts of the country at this time, to compare the demands made on other counties. The sum required from Yorkshire was 10,602*l.*, from Kent, 6711*l.*, from London, 12,135*l.*, and from Middlesex, 4620*l.*

In 1634, when the question of ship-money was beginning to stir the country from its foundations, we only find that the treasurer was ordered to pay Mr. Humfrey Bond "xxx*l.* towards his expences to travel to London and solicit the Lords of his Majesty's Council about the business concerning the shipping." And if he had occasion to disburse any more money "thereabouts," it was to be allowed to him at his return. In the correspondence of Lord Strafford it is mentioned that five Devonshire baronets were summoned before the Council for having asked that some inland towns might be exempted from the payment of ship-money. They appeared, received some reprimand, "and so, I believe, will be dismissed back again, it being punishment enough to them to have travelled 400 miles to so small purpose."

Quarter Sessions under Charles I. 121

In 1639 a constable of Cheriton Fitzpaine was dismissed from his office, and compelled to repay all the money he had exacted from his parishioners "beyond their proportion for the shipping money." On another occasion, in 1641, an inquiry was ordered into the conduct of certain constables who were believed to have received divers sums of ship-money and to have never paid them in. In the next year we hear of rates for martial services "foreign and domestique," of opposition to church-rates, and of commissioners for "the present levy of 400,000*l.*"

The first direct symptom of the impending appeal to arms appears in the measures taken for disarming recusants. "Popish recusants," indeed, can hardly at this time have been objects of terror, except from the traditions of forty or fifty years before. But the sharp laws passed against them were perhaps found to serve equally well against the Puritans. In 1640 we find that the Court had been informed that there was "great resort of recusants unto their several houses in this county," and that "there remained arms in divers of their houses." An order was therefore made for searching the habitations of the said recusants.

At the next sessions we have an order from the House of Commons requiring the prosecution of recusants, and in this case we may suppose that Roman Catholics were really intended. At the same time an order was sent down requiring information to be furnished to a committee of the House appointed to inquire and consider "how there may be *preaching ministers* set up where there is none, and how those preaching ministers may be maintained where there is no maintenance, and when they are in how they may be kept and continued." Also the committee was to inquire and consider "of the true grounds and causes of the great scarcity of preaching ministers through the whole kingdom, and *of some way for removing of scandalous ministers, and putting others in their places.*" This committee was appointed in consequence of a petition from the "inhabitants of Hughenden, in the county of Bucks," a parish which has certainly retained its influence over public affairs, and has frequently had something to do with a change of ministers.

At Michaelmas, 1641, we meet with an order for disarming recusants in Devon and seizing all arms, gunpowder, or other munition of war.

Meanwhile the appeal to arms was becoming inevitable. The county of Devon, like certain States in the American civil war, seems to have thought it possible to mediate between the mighty opposites. Petitions were sent up to the King and Parliament in 1641, and Sir John Pole, Sir George Chudleigh, John Bampfield, and Arthur Basset were allowed 25*l.* apiece for their charges in presenting them. In 1642 Sir Edmond Fortescue and Sir Popham Southcott were paid 50*l.* each for journeying to London and York on the same errand. On this occasion we have the full text of the petitions. Read by the light of subsequent events, they sound like a woeful cry of peace when there was no peace.

" To the Honourable Houses of ye Lords and Commons assembled in Parliament.

" The humble Petition of (the county of Devon)

" Showeth—That your petitioners having made their "humble address unto his most excellent Majesty on the

"behalf of these honourable Houses and themselves, now
"in this time of dangerous distraction, conceive it a duty
"owing to your wisdom, fidelity, and pains, to be made
"acquainted with the contents, whereof a copy is humbly
"presented. Thereby your Honours may perceive what
"sense your petitioners have of your perplexed condition,
"and what esteem of Parliament privileges, the pillars of
"their religion, liberty, and propriety. That we do now
"also apply ourselves to your Honours for a compliance
"with his Majesty, it seems most necessary that we appear
"unpartial in our respects, unchangeable in our loyalty.
"We beseech you, take it in good part, though we be
"suitors for that which we are assured you intend, that for
"the speedy stopping of these miseries of Ireland, and pre-
"vention of our own, you will be pleased above all things
"to continue the study and endeavour of the pacification
"of our royal Sovereign, whom we find to our infinite
"sorrow to be highly incensed. Great hearts are best
"wrought upon by submissive intercessions. It shall be
"your honour to make them in the humblest way your
"wisdoms can devise, saving to posterity the fundamental
"rights of Parliament. Two acts we chiefly pray for, one
"of forgiveness, another of forgetfulness. A few examples
"made upon delinquents are as prevalent warning as a
"multitude. Forbearance doth sometimes win when
"severity exasperates. Distractions are among us through
"various commands, hardly to be reconciled but by the
"unity of King and Parliament. Unity in religion, unity
"in loyal affections to his Majesty, will, according to our
"protestation, by God's mercy keep us still in peace and
"charity. The Lord grant it by your Honours' most

"approved industry to the preservation of his Majesty and
"his dominions in the true Protestant religion to all pos-
"terity. So your petitioners do always pray."

The other petition ran thus :—

"To the King's most Excellent Majesty.

"The most humble Petition of the countie of Devon
from the late General Sessions.

"Most gracious and dread Sovereign,

"Your poor dejected suppliants cannot so far neglect
"our own duties and affections as to be silent in either
"our incessant prayers to God for the augmentation of
"your Majesty's honour, your own and your kingdom's
"preservation, which are inseparably bound up together,
"or, in these times of public calamity, in our petitions to
"your Majesty. The lamentable distractions and convul-
"sions whereby each member is drawn from other, and
"each loyal heart rent within itself, makes us fly to your
"Majesty as a physician to cure us, and fall at your feet
"as a compassionate father to relieve us, being confident
"that your Majesty owns as well a will as an ability to
"help us. The debt we owe, our joy and gratitude through
"your Majesty's bounty and goodness commands to ac-
"knowledge, in the highest pitch of thankfulness which
"either love or duty can present, our obligation to your
"Majesty for passing so many good laws for your and your
"kingdom's benefit. And yet the unhappy differences be-
"tween your Majesty and both Houses of Parliament have,
"to our unexpressible grief, bereaved us of the fruit which
"we were ready to reap, and left us nothing but complaints,
"tears, and prayers to feed on. Your Majesty commands
"our obedience to the commission of array, whilst both

"Houses of Parliament adjudgeth us betrayers of our liberty
"and property if we do so. They persuade submission to
"the militia, whilst your Majesty proclaims it unlawful and
"derogatory to your prerogative. How unhappily are we
"here made judges in apparent contraries, in how hard a
"condition are we *whilst a twofold obedience, like twins in
"the womb, strives to be born to both*. We cannot choose
"but look upon the privileges of Parliament with a natural
"affection. From our father's loins we derive a touch that
"leads us thither as the needle to the loadstone. We de-
"sire to preserve them, because the death of liberty without
"that support is unevitable. Our hearty humble petition
"now is that your Majesty would be pleased, as you have
"graciously offered, to grant your general pardon of all
"things mistaken or misdone, and that you would be
"pleased to reinstate your great Council in the same affec-
"tions you and your royal ancestors have borne towards
"them, to enliven justice by your presence and union with
"it in such way and manner as to your excellent wisdom
"shall be thought meet for closing up the present breaches
"of this distracted and the other bleeding kingdom of
"Ireland. The which we have also humbly supplicated to
"the honourable Houses of Parliament. We are not pre-
"sumptuous to petition for the way, but beg the end.
"Pardon, we humbly beseech your Majesty, this boldness
"of your petitioners, whose lives, fortunes, and utmost
"powers, according to our several oaths and protestations,
"are totally and loyally at your Majesty's command. The
"Lord direct and protect your Majesty and your Parlia-
"ment to his glory. So prayeth, &c."

It may be that Butler was thinking of some attempt of this kind when he put into the mouth of his Presbyterian justice those sage reflections about civil war and bear-fighting, and the declaration that we—

> *Quantum in nobis*, have thought good
> To save th' expence of Christian blood,
> And try if we, by mediation
> Of treaty and accommodation,
> Can end the quarrel, and compose
> The bloody duel without blows.

The petitions were agreed upon on July 12, 1642. On September 23 Prince Rupert drew the first blood in the skirmish near Worcester.

QUARTER SESSIONS DURING THE CIVIL WAR.

IN one of Macaulay's letters we find the reflection : "It is sad work to live in times about which it is amusing to read."

This remark, applicable to any period of civil war, is peculiarly applicable to the English Civil War of the seventeenth century. That war, instead of being confined to one locality, and to the manœuvres of great regular armies, raged over many counties, in a series of desultory operations, conducted generally with more valour than science. Country-houses became fortresses, and sustained sieges, and in some districts the horrors of war were brought home to almost every village and every individual.

Devonshire was one of the counties that suffered most in this way, but the picturesque aspect of such proceedings must not be sought in the records of the Quarter Sessions of the Peace. The gown had to yield to the sword, and the laws were comparatively silent in the midst of arms. The justices rode out a "colonelling," and the Clerk of the Peace himself became a man of war, like the hero of Butler :—

> Mighty he was at both of these,
> And styled of war, as well as peace,
> (So some rats of amphibious nature,
> Are either for the land or water).

Nevertheless, Sessions were held, and records were kept of them, though more brief and imperfect than those of peaceable times. And from these records we may be able to extract a few memoranda, helping to illustrate the history and literature of the period.

It is evident that neither King nor Parliament could afford to let the justices stand as an independent authority. Each party in turn sought to govern the counties by select commissioners of their own appointment rather than by the whole body of magistrates, though certain matters of routine were left to the care of the latter, such as the trial of petty offences, the management of hospitals, the repair of bridges which were often pulled down by the troops, and the duty of providing pensions for the rapidly increasing numbers of "maimed soldiers," recommended by "Prince Maurice, his highness," and others.

At Epiphany, 1642-3, the Sheriff was fined 100*l*. for neglect of duty in not making arrangements for the sessions, and the next evidence of disturbances that we find is a change in the place of meeting. The Castle of Exeter was too important a post to be left in the hands of the civil power. It was fortified and garrisoned for the Parliament by the Earl of Bedford, Lord Lieutenant of Devon, and entrusted to the command of the Earl of Stamford. At Midsummer, 1643, the Sessions were opened at Tiverton. But the armies approached Tiverton, and the Sessions were adjourned to Topsham. Little business was transacted, but we may notice that John Gove, who had been bound over, was excused, "because oath was made that hee is in service in the King's Army under the command of Captayne Gidley."

The gaol was kept at Ottery St. Mary, instead of

Exeter, in the house of Mr. Vaughan (Clerk of the Peace). John Searle was committed to it for not paying his weekly assessment towards the payment of his Majesty's Army, and also on a more serious charge. James Bishopp, constable of Buckerell, deposed that

"John Searle, of Buckerell, the day that the King's army "came into Tiverton and took that town, being at the town "or village of Buckerell, did incite and persuade this depo- "nent, being then constable, to put himself and others of "the parishioners in arms, which he said that he would do "also, and said that he had six men's arms in his custody, "with which he would arm men, and that neighbouring "parishes would join with them to withstand the King's "army from coming that way, and said that if there were "but one hundred did come, he doubted not but that he "would withstand them."

At the same sessions we find an order that four men who had been wounded in the last expedition "by the forces under the command of the Earl of Warwick against Topsham" should have forty shillings apiece paid them by the Treasurers for maimed soldiers. There is also mention made of a weekly rate for the maintenance of His Majesty's Army in these parts. And Henry Oldinge, "who was taken for an espy," was committed "to the prison in the Shipp" at Topsham.

The parishes of Sidmouth and Salcombe were discharged for not attending the commands of the Sheriff for the *posse comitatus* "in respect of the daunger of the enymye latelie attendinge the coasts borderinge upon the aforesaide parishes."

Soon afterwards we have long lists of persons indicted for neglecting or refusing to attend the Sheriff, Sir Henry

K

Cary, when he called out the *posse comitatus* to suppress the rebellion, and especially for the siege of Plymouth. It appears that all able-bodied men between the ages of sixteen and sixty were called out. The bills were sometimes ignored, but generally found true. The difficulty of enforcing punishment must have been soon found insuperable.

On the 4th of September, 1643, Exeter was surrendered to Prince Maurice, and the Michaelmas Sessions following were again held in the accustomed place. But the Castle of course continued to be garrisoned, and soon after we find arrangements made for holding the sessions " in gardino prope Castrum," or " apud le Gaole Garden,"—the garden attached to the prison, which was outside the walls of the castle.

The mansion of Great Fulford, the seat of the ancient family of that name, certainly from the time of Richard I., and probably before the Conquest, had been sacked in the troubles, and the court made an order for the constables of Crediton, Moreton Hampstead, Newton St. Cyres, Sandford, and St. Thomas the Apostle, to make diligent search for "divers goods and chattles which are Sir ffrauncys ffulford's, knight," and which had been "taken out of his house at ffulford by persons unknown, and conveyed secretly into diverse houses in the severall parishes."

Master James Style, clerk, complained to the bench that, as he was travelling towards the chapel of Petton, in Bampton, "to officiate his duetie there" one Sunday morning, certain persons did take from him his horse, saddle, and bridle. It is not stated that the horse was "requisitioned" for the public service, but we may suppose it was from the order that follows close afterwards :—

" Whereas we be ready to obey his highness and the

"officers in chief of His Majesty's army, and the several
"governors of towns within our county, and to execute all
"reasonable warrants from the Master of the Ordinance,
"the Quarter-Master General, the Waggon-Master General,
"and the Provant Master, but are unwilling that the county
"should be subject to the extravagant and illegal commands
"of inferior officers, or the violence of common soldiers. It
"is therefore ordered, That if any officer of the king's army
"whatsoever, except some or one of the foresaid parties,
"shall grant any warrants for the taking away of any man's
"horses, arms, or goods within this county, or if any man
"whatsoever (except as aforesaid) shall grant any warrant
"for the free billetting of any soldier within this county, that
"it shall be lawful for each man to deny any obedience to
"any such inferior warrant. And whosoever shall here-
"after take or steal horses, or any other thing from any
"man within this county, shall be pursued, apprehended,
"and tried according to the laws of the land. And who-
"ever shall offer any violence and injury to any soldier
"within this county, shall be severely punished for the
"same."

The tone of these records during the war is almost invariably loyal, but there are one or two exceptions, such as the information of Thomas Rosemond, of Otterton, against John Austen, of Sidmouth, which must have been laid before some Puritan justice. It has preserved for us a political conversation of the year 1642, such as Sir Walter Scott might have introduced into a novel.

"The said Thomas Rosemond saith that on Tuesday last
"he, meeting with the said John Austen at Greenway Lane,
"in Sidmouth aforesaid, the said John Austen asked him
"whether his master had paid the rate, who answered, yes.

"Austen replied, and said that none but a few Puritans had
"paid. Thomas said again, all the parish of Otterton had
"paid, and his master did go at Exon and pay it in. To-
"morrow, Austen said, they would wish for their money
"again, for the ship-money was bad, but this was worse, and
"that he had not paid, nor would not pay it, for the King
"had set out a proclamation that it should not be paid, and
"that if the constables did distrain, he would make them
"bring it again, and that they that would not obey the pro-
"clamation were traitors and rebels against the King; and
"said that Parliament would have new tricks and new laws,
"contrary to that was before in King James' and Queen
"Elizabeth's days, and would have this money to maintain
"wars against the King and amongst ourselves, and the
"Parliament were all Puritans, for the Protestants were all
"gone away from them to the King, and there were none
"left but a few Puritans; and said that if it came to, he
"would fight against that sect. The said Thomas asked the
"said John Austen if he had not taken the protestation,[1] he
"told him yes, but if it were to doing again, he would never
"do it; and said further, the Puritans should be the first he
"would fight against.

"Also Austen said that Richard Clapp, of Sidbury, had
"played new tricks, but now the Parliament had sent a
"warrant for him and for Mr. Searle also, and they must
"appear at London, and must new christen the child again.

[1] The "Protestation" was framed by a Committee, of which Maynard was chairman, and was taken by the two houses, May 3, 1641, and afterwards tendered to all persons throughout the country. It was a solemn vow to maintain and defend the Protestant religion, the king, the power and privileges of Parliament, and the lawful rights and liberties of the subject.

"And that Mr. Babbington, because he would not say the
" Epistle and Gospel, was fast enough, but he did think he
" was not in prison, but he could not come home, and had
" sent private letters, that if any were sent for, they should
" not appear in person, but by an attorney ; and Mr. Bab-
" bington was a *whither-witted* man and a *turnecoat*, and had
" preached (when the Bishops were up) against those who
" would not pay to the organs, but now he was turned
" another way ; and said also that there was such another
" *coxcombe foole* at Newton that would not say the Epistle
" and Gospel, nor the Common Prayers."

A learned friend assures me that the phrase " a whither-witted man " is invaluable, and well deserves to be revived. In an age of ecclesiastical disputings, it may be useful to restore to the language a convenient term of opprobrium, such as Cromwell may have flung at Laud, or Falkland at Hugh Peters.

> Obscurata diu populo bonus eruet, atque
> Proferet in lucem speciosa vocabula rerum,
> Quæ priscis memorata Catonibus atque Cethegis
> Nunc situs informis premit et deserta vetustas.

It seems probable that the spelling in the text is correct, and that "whither-witted" means one whose wits are gone " whither" no one knows. But it is so excellent a word that no spelling comes amiss to it, and it would "make sense" if it were spelt whither, weather, wether, or whether.

At Easter, 1644, the constables of Southmolton were accused of having directed certain soldiers the wrong way, when they ought to have sent them to Exeter. Many complaints were made of unjust assessments for the weekly taxes "towards the maynteynance of his Mat"' army, in these westerne partes." It was the habit, in those times, to levy all rates weekly, and those who have no love for the visits of the modern collector may imagine how large an amount of friction and annoyance was caused by such a practice.

One at least of the ladies of the county distinguished herself on the side of the rebels. Complaints were made by the constables of Kenton, " that they having arrested the body of *Archillis* Slapton by order of his Mat"' Commissioners, the Lady Elizabeth Martyn, wife of Sir Nicholas Martyn, Knight, did beat and abuse the said Constables, and by herself and others whom she incited thereunto rescued the said Slapton from the custody of the said constables." It was therefore ordered

" That the said constables of Kenton shall apprehend and " take the body of the said Lady Martyn, and her safely " bring before some one of His Majesty's justices of peace " of this county, next unto the place where she shall be " apprehended," &c. &c.

It seems improbable that the constables succeeded in arresting a lady who was so capable of defending her friends, even though " all his Majesty's officers and loving subjects " were required to be aiding and assisting the said constables in the due execution of these presents. Sir Nicholas Martyn, of Oxton, was a man of very large property in those days. He was knighted in 1624, and was sheriff of Devon in 1640. He was proclaimed a traitor by the King in November, 1642, and was excepted from the offer of a general pardon, together with Sir George Chudleigh, Sir John Northcote, and Sir Samuel Rolle. He no doubt gained popularity by the spirited conduct of his wife, for he

Quarter Sessions during the Civil War. 135

was elected knight of the shire in June, 1646. He died in 1653.

At Michaelmas, 1644, Peter English of Bradninch got into trouble for his too great readiness to fight upon both sides. It is recorded that he,—

"In the beginning of the rebellion having taken up arms "on the rebels' part against the king, did after the battle at "Stratton, as a trainer for the king under the command of "Captain Sainthill, and while he served a soldier for the "king, he did associate and help some troopers which "abused and wounded Mr. Peter Warren, a constable of "Bradninch. And upon the Earl of Essex his coming into "these parts, the said English voluntarily went over into "Essex his army, and there served and went with him into "Cornwall. And coming now to be fined upon an indict- "ment for his not appearing at the sheriff's *posse* in Novem- "ber last, is by order of the Court committed to the gaol "of this county. And it is further ordered that he be at "the next sitting of the Comm^t. of Oyer and Terminer in- "dicted for High Treason."

Whether "the said English" was ever tried, or when the next sitting of Oyer and Terminer took place, does not clearly appear. The crime of treason, like the prisoner himself, shortly afterwards changed sides, and the power of Government "went over into Essex, (or rather Fairfax,) his army."

The Queen, and afterwards the King, were in Exeter in 1644, but no notice is taken of them in the proceedings of Sessions. The Court was much occupied with "the greate necessitie of releeveinge of the Late maymed souldiers whose wounds are yett bleedinge," and, finding that the rates were not sufficient to relieve both them and the old pensioners, they proceeded to inquire whether the old ones were not "able to subsist without further payment of their pensions formerly assigned to them."

In 1645, the records are very scanty, and at Epiphany and Easter following there are none at all. Their absence is more expressive than many words. At that time Fairfax, Cromwell, and Waller were driving the Royalists before them throughout Devon and Cornwall.

Exeter was besieged for several months. The country seats round the fair city, from which the peaceable Justices had been wont to trot in to attend Quarter Sessions, Powderham, Canonteign, Fulford, Peamore, Barley, Stoke, Columb John, Poltimore, Bishopscourt, Nutwell, were all occupied by garrisons, which were no doubt employed in cutting off the supplies destined for the Queen of the West. Each of these houses is conveniently situated for commanding one of the roads leading to Exeter; and Powderham (Lord Devon's), and Nutwell (now Sir F. Drake's), also command the estuary of the Exe. A letter has been preserved, written by the Puritan officer in command of the garrison at Peamore, in which he expresses his dislike of Devonshire for two reasons, the sour cider and the bad preaching, and concludes with the pious hope that, if ever he returns home, he may in future be more thankful for the great blessings of sound doctrine and wholesome liquor.[2]

[2] The letter was written to Lenthall from Chudleigh, which is called Chidley, after the manner of the Devonshire dialect. The writer's name is not given, but the date is Feb. 2, 1645. The conclusion runs thus :—

"I pray commend me to all our Friends; tell them I am (thanks be to God) in health, and want only two things respecting my inward and outward condition; the one, a Preacher like Mr. *Stirry*, the other, a

Quarter Sessions during the Civil War. 137

At last, on April 9, 1646, the City and Castle of Exeter were surrendered to the Parliamentary Army.

At Midsummer, 1646, the Sessions were held at Crediton. The names of the Justices who attended are not recorded, but it may be hoped that they were not the same as those who were present the year before. The tenor of their orders veered completely round. Parliament was the only lawful authority, and the Justices were shocked at the rebellious conduct of the royalist faction, now distinguished as "malignants."

"Whereas by sad experience it appeareth that divers
" Constables of Hundreds and Petit Constables have been
" very active for the Cavaliers, and evil instruments to the
" State, and that divers of them do yet continue in their
" said offices, to the retarding of the service of the country
" and encouraging of the Malignant party. It is therefore
" ordered, and the Justices in their several divisions are
" desired, where they shall find any such Constables, to dis-
" miss them, and swear others in their stead of trust and
" credit."

It appeared necessary also to take order for the settling of poor persons belonging to the County of Devon, "whose houses had been burnt or puld downe by the *crewell enemy*." And orders were made for the payment of church rates, "forasmuch as it appeareth that diverse Churches within this Countie are very much decayed for wante of

cup of *London* Beer. There is a scarcity of the former here, and the latter not to be had, only a little sowre Syder. If ever I return to *London* again, I shall (through the Grace of God) indeavour to have an higher esteem of those precious opportunities which are there. Thus committing you to the Protection of the Almighty, I rest."

reparacon by reason that the people have forboren the paiment of their Church Rates."

Five pounds were voted to Joane Ellery of Hemyock, "wydowe," because "the inhumane and barbarous carriage of the lord Paulett did soe appeare against Henry Illerie her husband, by executing him for that he was in the Parliament Armie." If we had Lord Paulet's version of the affair, we should probably hear some equally strong remarks on the "carriage" of the besiegers of Basing House.

The Puritans immediately proceeded to improve their victory by suppressing "the Multiplicity of the Alehouses" in the county, and the "daylie abuses and disorders kept and suffered in such Alehouses, especiallie on the sabboth Dayes, whereby the service of Almightie God is much hindered."

They also rejoiced after the fashion of those described by the satirist:—

> That with more care keep holyday
> The wrong, than others the right way;

as may be seen by the following order:—

"Whereas this Court is informed that the last Wednes-
"day in every month, which is appointed a day for solemn
"fasting and humiliation over the whole kingdom, is not
"observed and kept as it ought to be by divers persons,
"and in many places within this county, and also that the
"Lord's day, likewise appointed to be kept holy, is pro-
"faned by many lewd people, and not kept and observed
"in many places as it ought to be; It is therefore ordered
"by this Court that if any person or persons hereafter shall
"not observe and keep the said fast day, or shall profane

"the said Lord's day, that then the next Justice of the Peace upon complaint to him made, shall bind over the said person or persons so offending to the next Assizes to answer his contempt. And all constables and other officers are hereby required to take especial care to see this order performed, as they will answer the contrary, and from whom this Court will expect a good account of the performance thereof."

It may be remembered that Sir Simonds D'Ewes, according to his autobiography, used to observe one day in the month as a fast in his family. This was probably the private practice of the Puritans before the war, and it was now established by public authority.

Five persons of Chudleigh were summoned to appear and answer for working upon the last fast day, "in contempt of the ordinance and officers' reprehension."

The Court was scandalized by receiving information that there was great preparation for divers Revels to be shortly held in the county, and especially one at Cheriton Fitzpaine, "which kind of assemblys, for that they commonly produce noe good but the dishonor of Almightie God and the breach of the peace by excessive drinking, quarrelling, and other disorderly carriadges, hath occasioned diverse Orders both from the Sessions and Assizes for their restraint and suppression." It was therefore ordered that all justices, constables, and other officers should use their best endeavours against such disorderly courses and unlawful meetings, "especially in these times of troble and so great Contagion." And any persons who were found remiss or refractory in execution or obedience of this order were to be proceeded against as "Enemyes to the Comon pease and weale of the Kingdome."

The Court seems to have had no objection to receive written certificates, even of mere rumours, instead of oral evidence. Here is a specimen, relating to the prosecution of a spiritualist of the period :—

"Wee, whose names are heere under written, doe testifye
"that to our knowledge this Maudline Clap hath many
"tymes wronged and abused this poor woman Thomasine
"Smith, threatning to kill her, breaking open her doores
"upon her, plucking downe her garden Hegge, and laying
"it open to the highway, and taking away her herbes, or
"spoyling them. Shee is a woman of wicked life and con-
"versation, a great swearer, a drunkard, and then in that
"case given to railing and slandering of her neighbours.
"Besides, shee is vehemently suspected with burning the
"Church House, for shee sayd the night before it was
"burnt that shee had power to burne them all out. Shee
"hath also some tymes disguised herselfe in the night,
"*faining herselfe to be a spirit*, and in a strang forme
"endevoured to break open her neighbours doores. There
"are many other complaints against her by her neighbours,
"but this we know to be true, and wilbe ready to testifie
"the same upon our oathes at any tyme."

"Given under our hands att Clist Saint Lawrence, this
"10th day of January, 1647.
  "Nicholas Bickleigh.
  "Thomas Bussell."

On the other hand, as might be expected, Maudlin Clapp produced a certificate signed by five persons, to the effect that Thomasine Smith was a woman "of very lewd life and conversation."

An immense number of entries of course relate to the

pensions for maimed soldiers, and the rates imposed on the county for their relief were doubled, although the allowance to an individual was generally no more than forty shillings.

Many petitions were received respecting losses in the war. "Sheepe" and horses were the objects most in request. The parish of Up Lyme had lost 3000 sheep "in the troubles when Lyme was besieged." Joseph Hall, of Teignmouth, was bringing a horse to Exeter, "but coming on Haldon Downe did there unhapily meete with sixteen of the Cavaleere Troopers, who owned the said horse, and did beate and abuse your petitioner, taking not only the said horse from him (wch they said was taken out of their troope by stealth half a yeare then before), but also robed yor pet^r of his mony and other things about him, and soe cruelly used him that he was in greate daunger of his life, and inforced to keepe his bead a long tyme after in the greife and paine thereby sustayned."

However pleased the justices might profess to be with the new government, they were not unnaturally anxious to get rid of the burden of a standing army, especially as they were suffering much at the same time from dearth and pestilence. They appealed to Fairfax, and received the following characteristic reply.

As Cromwell wrote of him after Naseby: "the General attributes all to God, and would rather perish than assume to himself."

"*Gentlemen,*—I have received yours of the ninth instant, wherein you were pleased to begin with such acknowledgements as I wish may always be directed to God, the Author of your peace and blessings, and not to myself otherways than as a weak instrument in His hand, who shall expect or wish no return from you, but that, as I presume you are constant to the interest, which God hath so owned, so you would be careful that those whom He hath likewise so eminently owned to make them the chief instruments of His work to yourselves and the Kingdom may meet with no unworthy requitals. As to the business of Major Perkins his troop, I confess I did (not?) before understand what you now write concerning the appointed disbanding thereof, and I thank you for the friendly information. I shall now leave it to be accordingly disbanded by you, desiring only that (if possible) they may have the encouragement of three weeks' pay and your certificates for what further arrears may be reasonably due unto them, and that you would use the same hand towards what other troops of Salary Horse you have belonging to your county, to disband them likewise, since they can none of them come within the establishment now resolved on by the Parliament. And so doing I assure you that I shall not continue to any of them any order or countenance from me to be longer in a body to the terror or trouble of your county, but do hereby revoke what order they had from me for their quartering in your county. I have one request to add in behalf of the Governor of Exeter Castle with the other officers and foot belonging thereto, that they, being to be continued and brought under the establishment of the 18,000 now resolved on by the Parliament, so as there will be very shortly order taken for their constant pay, you would for the present take care and effectual order that they may be supplied for their subsistence with either money, provisions or convenient quarters nearest to their place of duty, which you will shortly have power to discharge out of the assessments of your county. I shall not

trouble you further at present, but remain your very assured friend, THO. FFAIRFAX.
"Turnham Green:
"19th of *October*, 1647."

It may perhaps be doubted whether the conduct of the Puritan army was as much admired by its contemporaries as it has been by certain modern historians, and whether the warlike saints trained by Cromwell and Fairfax were all distinguished by their "austere morality and fear of God," and their respect for "the property of the peaceable citizen and the honour of woman." The Devonshire justices, at any rate, were not disposed to give them such a character. On the receipt of Fairfax's letter they immediately passed the following resolution:—

"Whereas Major Perkins his troop of Horse were by
" order of the standing committee of this county to disband
" for divers months since, and paid according to an order
" of the committee of the Lords and Commons for the
" safety of the West, yet have ever since in contempt and
" disobedience to the said order continued together and
" taken free quarter, to the great grievance, oppression, and
" terror of the country, and being questioned at the last
" Session of this Court for so doing, they pretended an
" order from General Sir Thomas Fairfax for their quarter-
" ing, but upon notice given unto him that they were
" formerly ordered to be disbanded, revoking all former
" orders by him made for their quartering, hath left them
" to be disbanded by the Justices and Committees of this
" county. It is now, therefore, according and in pursuance
" of the said former orders, ordered that the said troop do
" forthwith disband, and are hereby disbanded, and repair to
" their several homes and places of abode, whereof the Cap-

"tain, Officers, and Troopers, and all belonging to the said "troop are, upon notice hereof, to conform and give obedi- "ence, as they will answer the contrary and expect to be pro- "ceeded against and dealt with according to law and justice. "And it is also hereby declared, according to the desires of "His Excellency, that if the said officers and troopers will "repair to the Committee they shall have their arrears "audited and certificates thereupon."

Barebone's Parliament, some years afterwards, made an enactment that marriages should be solemnized before the justices of the peace. An entry at Michaelmas, 1648, shows that some difficulties had already arisen in this matter. Robert Searle, clerk, promised in open court, that if it should appear henceforth "that he doth unduely marry any parties," he should be bound over with very good sureties, or in default committed to the gaol. And a general order was to be made "against all ministers for unduely marry- ing of people," but of this there is unfortunately no copy.

During all this time, and up to within three weeks of the King's execution, the Sessions were held in the name *Domini nostri Caroli nunc Regis Angliæ.*" All public busi- ness appears to have been nominally carried on, as usual, under the King's authority. We know that Sir Thomas Fairfax, when he met the captive King on his way to Holmby House in February, 1647, instantly got off his horse, and humbly kissed the Royal hand. I have found an original commission of the Peace dated July, 1647, in which the King is represented as addressing among others his dearest cousins the Earls of Northumberland, Pembroke, Manchester, and Say (*sic*), and his trusty and well beloved William Lenthall, Speaker of the House of Commons, and as appointing Edmund Prideaux Custos Rotulorum. The oath of allegiance was retained as a means of persecuting the Roman Catholics, and in August of the same year we find William Rose committed to prison for refusing it. John Kite met a similar fate in October for speaking dangerous words against the *King and Parliament*, as well as for "offering to abuse the Countery, &c., by cheating them under pretence of aucthority from the Earle of Northumberland." Such entries serve to explain the bitter sneer of Butler,—

> For, as we make war for the king
> Against himself, the self-same thing,
> Some will not stick to swear, we do
> For God and for religion too.

It is easy to explain such proceedings by a charge of gross hypocrisy, but it may be doubted whether they ought not rather to be attributed to the love of Englishmen for even the outward forms of established institutions, and to the conservative spirit which has been conspicuous even in our revolutions.

The Clerk of the Peace fell at the same time as his royal master. In January, 1648-9, there was a "full hearing of the difference between Mr. John Vaghan, and Mr. Nicholas Rowe touching the office of Clerk of the Peace." The result was thus entered, probably by the victor:—

" The truth of the Order was this ;
" Mr. Rowe claims the place of the office of Clerk of
" the Peace in Devon by a Commission under the hand
" and seal of Edmond Prideaux, Esq., *Custos Rotulorum*,
" dated 28 March, 1648. Mr. Charles Vaghan, being in
" possession of the place, and a member of the Parliament,

L

"shews an order of the House of Commons made in
"January, 1642 (1643), whereby he is enjoined and
"appointed to take the Custody of the Records of the
"County of Devon, and execute the place of Clerk of the
"Peace of the said County until the House take further
"order, the former Clerk being taken in levying War
"against the Parliament, and thereupon committed. And
"upon hearing the title on both sides, thereupon a Letter
"was formerly written to the Speaker by the Bench to
"desire the sense of the House, which was never read in
"the House, and now, after the delay of three Sessions,
"Mr. Rowe being in Court (and Mr. Vaghan, who is bound
"by his order to execute the place, and hath not the power
"to make a deputy, being absent, and relinquishing the
"place). It was upon the vote of the Bench (the Court
"being full) declared that Mr. Rowe should be reputed and
"taken for Clerk of the Peace, and that for this Sessions
"Mr. Inglett should officiate and account for the profits to
"Mr. Rowe, and pay them over to him, who is to be
"responsible for them."

Mr. Charles Vaughan had held the post in the time of James I. He sat in the Long Parliament as member for Honiton. Mr. Hugh Vaughan, probably his son, was restored to the place in the reign of Charles II.

If we had the minutes of the proceedings of the "Standing Committee for Compounding with Delinquents," or rather for sequestrating their property, those records might probably be more interesting than the Sessions' Books of this period. In their absence, we are not altogether without means of tracing the action of the victorious republicans towards the vanquished Cavaliers—an action which is summed up by Mr. Carlyle in the characteristic exclamation, "Poor Royalist squires, riddle the last due (?) sixpence out of them!" A few original letters and memoranda in the possession of Sir Thomas Acland, which he has kindly allowed me to examine, enable us to form some idea of the weight of the Parliamentary yoke.

Sir John Acland, the first baronet of that ancient family, was a Cavalier resembling the hero of Mr. Browning's ballad :—

> Kentish Sir Byng stood for his King,
> Bidding the crop-headed Parliament swing ;
> And, pressing a troop unable to stoop
> And see the rogues flourish, and honest folks droop,
> March'd them along, fifty score strong,
> Great-hearted gentlemen, singing this song.

Sir John served as sheriff for the King during the war. He raised at his own cost two whole regiments for the King's service. For the same cause he sacrificed his plate, his horses, cattle, sheep, corn, hay, and so forth. His house at Columb John was fortified, and was the last detached garrison that held out for the King in the West. After it was taken, it was occupied successively by Cromwell and Fairfax, and both it and his other house of Killerton were "ryfled and spoyled" of whatever remained in them Their gallant owner seems to have escaped into Exeter, and stood the siege there. After that city capitulated, Sir John Acland, as one of the garrison, and also as a freeman of the city, claimed the benefit of the moderate articles which had been agreed upon. He also obtained a letter from Fairfax to Speaker Lenthall, recommending him "for a moderate composition." His claim was at first admitted, and his fine was fixed at the sum of 1727*l*., which was estimated to be the tenth part of the value of his estate.

He managed to raise and pay one half of this, and gave security for the remainder. But he had enemies, and especially one Richard Evans, a brewer of Exeter, and one of the committee for that city, who professed to have been "ruined by the invetterate mallice and cruell comands of John Acland." No doubt the cavaliers had in their time been active enough in requisitioning horses and cattle for the army of the King. Sir John's conduct having been represented to the Commissioners, his fine was raised to one-third of the value of his land, which he was of course unable to pay. His estate was sequestered, and the "surplusage" granted to Richard Evans. He himself was obliged to hide away, being probably in danger of his life. The negotiations for the reduction of the fine were carried on through his wife, a daughter of Sir F. Vincent. There are copies of piteous letters from her to various influential people on behalf of her husband. Among others is one she wrote to Colonel Cromwell, reminding him of the favour he showed towards her "When you were pleased to quarter at my house."[3] Still more pitiful is a letter to her servant Charles Knight, written from Exeter in July, 1646, sending 600*l.* which she had scraped together, probably towards the payment of the fine, and describing the sad condition of herself and her little "boyes," destitute of almost every-

[3] In an account of plunder at Killerton, we find that eight oxen were valued at 50*l.*; eleven kine and two bulls at 70*l.*; two coach-horses at 35*l.*; one bay mare at 20*l.*, 55 sheep and 15 lambs at 35*l.*, and six horses and colts at 60*l.* The silver plate was sold at 58½*d.* an ounce. In a list of gold coins 70 angels were valued at 11*s.* 6*d.* each; 16 *Spurryalls* at 17*s.* 6*d.* each; one double pistole at 1*l.* 10*s.*; one gold noble at 13*s.* 4*d.*; one Treble Sovereign of Q. Elizabeth's reign at 1*l.* 15*s.*; another of the same at 1*l.* 18*s.*; and a double sovereign of King Edward at 1*l.* 3*s.*

thing, and yet having eight soldiers and their horses quartered on her. Sir John died not long afterwards, probably of a broken heart. Sir Walter Scott in *Woodstock* represents him as aiding in Charles the Second's escape after the battle of Worcester, but that is only a poetic licence. The poor lady renewed her petition to the "Standing Committee of Devon" for her jointure. She was at last allowed to have one fifth of the income of her husband's property. It is satisfactory to know that the family recovered their lands at the Restoration, and that the descendants of poor Sir John Acland have since flourished greatly in the three western counties.

QUARTER SESSIONS UNDER THE COMMONWEALTH.

THE King was dead, the Parliament was fading away, and the sword was now the lord of England. But Quarter Sessions continued to be held as usual, and the Court issued its orders on the usual subjects, though the number of justices in attendance appears at first to have been very small, and on one occasion did not exceed five.

At Easter, 1649, we hear of a collection made on a thanksgiving day appointed "for a victory over the Irish rebels obtained by the Lord Inchiquin." That nobleman was fond of fighting on any side, and was so unfortunate as to take the King's part just before Cromwell landed in Ireland.

On the same occasion an order was made to restrain the conversion of barley into malt, " forasmuch as by reason of the extremity of winter it is much to be feared that there will be a scarcity of corn at harvest, and that God will punish our excess and abuse of His creatures by the want of them, the poor everywhere complaining of their necessities, and all sober people abhorring the multitude of ale-houses, and protesting against the unreasonable quantity of barley turned into malt, which is wantonly and wickedly spent in such houses."

At Midsummer and Michaelmas the chief business, as we may well believe, was the arrangement of the pensions to be allotted to the "maymed souldiers." They were not excessively liberal, and rarely exceeded 40*s*. a year. Some unfortunate men were dismissed with a gratuity of only 5*s*. Widows were sometimes allowed a small gratuity, never a pension. Thirty-two poor widows, "whose husbands were slain in the Parliament's service in defence of Plymouth," were to receive 20*s*. a piece, but the ordinary allowance was no more than half that sum. The widow of a captain killed in action received 40*s*., " and she to trouble the Court noe more." It is mentioned that " Walter Yolland, a faithful soldier of the Commonwealth, was starved to death in the prison at Lydford by the inhumane dealing of the enemy." Altogether the rates for this purpose were double what they had been before 1648.

The King's name had been retained in matters of public business as long as he was alive. But it was now necessary to alter the style of the Government, and we find that recognizances were said to be due "Custodibus Libertatis Angliæ Auctoritate Parliamenti." Soon afterwards the English language was adopted in legal documents, and thenceforth we hear of "the Keepers of the Liberties of England by Authority of Parliament." The sentences on prisoners, the conditions of recognizances, and other similar entries, are for the first time written in English. Even the familiar "*posse comitatus*" becomes "the power of the county," and the bills of indictment are endorsed by the Grand Jury, " wee know not," instead of *Ignoramus*.

The first English Commission of the Peace that I have met with bears date the 9th day of March, 1651, and commences thus :—

" The Keepers of the Liberty of England by Authority " of Parliament to William Lenthall, Speaker of Parliament

"and Master of the Rolls, Oliver Cromwell, Captaine
" Generall of the Armies, Bulstrode Whitelocke, Richard
" Keble, John Lisle, Lords Commissioners of the Great Seal,
" John Bradshawe, Chancellor of the Dutchy of Lancaster
"and Chief Justice of Chester, Algernon Earl of Northum-
" berland, William, Earl of Salisbury, Henry Rolle, Chief
" Justice of the *Upper* Bench, John Wylde, Chief Baron
" of the *Publique* Exchequer, Robert Nicholas, one of the
" Justices of the Upper Bench, Edmond Prideaux, Attorney
" Generall of the Commonwealth."

These official personages amount to twelve, and then follow the names of sixty-eight baronets, knights, and esquires, mostly of well-known county families. It is evident that there was very little of the modern democratic ideal about this revolution. Any nobleman or gentleman who was believed to be not ill-affected to the new government was included in the Commission ; and we meet with the familiar names which have been seldom absent from Devonshire Commissions of the Peace—Drakes and Rolles, Davies, Yonges, and Fortescues, Poles, Quickes, Dukes, Carews, Coplestons and Woollcombes. With these are joined " John Disbrowe and Phillipp Skippon," and one or two others who may have belonged to the army. " The said Edmond Prideaux " is assigned as " Keeper of the Rolles of the Peace " in the said county.

A Commission dated September 26, 1653, begins, " The Keepers of the Liberty, &c., to Oliver Cromwell, Captaine Generall," &c., Mr. William Lenthall having evidently become of much less importance than formerly. And under date of March 4, 1653, we have a Commission commencing thus :—

" Oliver, Lord Protector of the Commonwealth of Eng-

"land, Scotland, and Ireland, and the Domynions thereto belonging."

The dates might puzzle a reader unacquainted with the fact that the English year then began on March 25, and that March 4 was therefore six months later than the September of the same year.

"The Keepers of the Liberty" and Mr. William Lenthall had their turn again in the Commission of July 8, 1659. On that occasion "John Desbrowe" was appointed Keeper of the Rolls in the county of Devon.

The squires who acted as justices under the Commonwealth appear to have been obliged to "sue out their pardons" at the Restoration, and no doubt had to pay heavily for them. One of these pardons is preserved in the family of John Quicke, Esq., of Newton St. Cyres. It is headed by a finely engraved portrait of Charles II.

We should require the records of assizes, and also of the proceedings of the major-generals commanding the districts, to form a complete idea of the administration of justice under the Puritan Government. But the glimpses we get of it in the Sessions-books are curious enough, and enable us to see something of the state of the country in what the cavalier poet called

> Those gospel-walking times
> When slightest sins are greatest crimes.

The laws against swearing were strictly enforced, and with the largest possible interpretation against the accused. We are reminded of the reproof that Sir Walter Scott put into the mouth of Cromwell—"What can it avail thee to practise a profanity so horrible to the ears of others, and which brings no emolument to him who uses it?" Every oath was counted. For a single oath the fine was 6s. 8d., but the charge was reduced to 3s. 4d. each "on taking a quantity." Humfrey Trevett, for swearing ten oaths, was committed till he pay 33s. 4d. to the poor of Harford. John Huishe, of Cheriton, was convicted for swearing twenty-two oaths and two curses at one time, and four oaths and one curse at another time. Of course, the greater number of these cases were disposed of at Petty Sessions without being sent for trial. One justice returned the names of ten persons whom he had convicted of swearing since the previous sessions.

We are not left without examples of what was considered swearing in those days. Wm. Hearding, of Chittlehampton, for saying two several times in Court " Upon my life," was adjudged to be within the act of swearing, for which he paid 6s. 8d. Thomas Butland was fined for swearing " On my troth." Gilbert Northcott had to pay 3s. 4d. for saying. " Upon my life." Thomas Courtis was fined for swearing in Court " God is my witness," and "I speak in the presence of God." Christopher Gill, being reproved by Mr. Nathaniel Durant, clerk, " for having used the oath, God's Life, in discourse," went and informed against the minister himself for swearing!

Words appear to have been considered of great importance at this time. The Cavaliers, beaten in the field, seem to have sought the small consolation of abusing the Government, and annoying the ministers who had been intruded into the parish churches. The ladies occasionally distinguished themselves in this way. Mrs. Hawkins, the wife of a clergyman who had probably been "sequestered for delinquency," and Alice Brooke, single woman, were to be apprehended " for their lewd behaviour and scandalous conversation," and also "for certain heretical and damnable opinions by them vented and maintained to the great dishonour of Almighty God, the reproach of the Gospel of Jesus Christ, and the offence of all good Christians."

Agnes Davie said that Mr. Hopkins, minister of Sandford, "went up into the pulpett with God in his mouth and the devill in his heart;" and, worse still, that Mrs. Hopkins "was a Leger in Gorin's Troope," whatever that may have been. Goring's troop, if I remember right, was the corps of "child-eaters" to which Captain Wildrake belonged.

William Langdon, of Brixham, was so unfortunate as to get into collision with two of the learned professions. He was convicted for saying, "The divell take such a sheppard, and the lawer too!"

We are shocked to learn that, though the committee of the county had placed Mr. Edward Hunt, "a godly and able minister," in the church of Ashcombe, to preach there, and also to receive the tithes, duties, and profits belonging thereunto, "yet the churchwardens and other disaffected persons of the said parish, in contempt of authority, do keep away the key of the said parish church, and do constantly disturb and interrupt him in the exercise of his ministerial function."

At Diptford, Thomas Hingston and Nicholas Bastard "do most unjustly detain the church Bible from Mr. Walplate, the minister there, and will not permit him to make use thereof in the congregation." At Widworthy, John Hutchins was said to have "embezelled the carpett of the pulpitt."

George Haybeard, blacksmith, was indicted for saying that "Mr. William Collings, Vicar of Modbury, had a necke as bigg as a Bull, and that he was a *Patterroone* to his Kinsman Thomas Shepheard."

At Loddiswell the vicarage was forcibly entered and the minister turned out. Something of the same kind happened at Inwardleigh, where Hugh Northleigh, Silvanus Hurst, and Alexander Luke "into the said church with the appurtenances with force and arms did enter, and him, the said Thomas Bridgman, out of the same with a strong hand did disseize, eject, and expel," and "him so expelled and ejected with a strong hand and with might, power, and force did keep out," &c. Even so Nehemiah Holdenough complained, "I was forcibly expelled from my own pulpit, even as a man should have been thrust out of his own house, by an alien and an intruder, a wolf, who was not at the trouble even to put on sheep's clothing."

At Berry Pomeroy, Andrew Curtis was committed for abusing Mr. Randall, minister in the church, and for saying that "hee did preach lyes and errors whereby to bring men to the divell." In fact, these cases of disturbing ministers were very numerous throughout the county.

Nor were the lay authorities much more popular. Robert Worth was fined 100*l.* for seditious words, and put in the pillory for an hour "with a paper in his hat." Similar sentences were by no means uncommon. An order for "keeping watch and ward," in 1651, declares that "by reason of the late distractions in this Commonwealth it is observed that, among other inconveniences that have happened, the number of sturdy beggars, rogues, and wandering idle persons is greatly increased; and although there have been excellent good laws made for the punishment of them, yet by the remissness of some inferior officers they have not been duly executed, so that *such vermin do every swarm*, not only to the terror of honest and well-affected people, but to the great dishonour of the nation. And now

Quarter Sessions under the Commonwealth. 157

many persons disaffected to the present Government do secretly meet together to disturb the peace of this Commonwealth," &c.

It may be worth while to quote one or two proceedings for speaking slanderous words. The "Keepers of the Liberties" evidently allowed none to be taken. Here is the indictment against William Worth, of Tavistock, tailor, who

"Being a dangerous and seditious man, evil affected unto, "and disliking the Governors and Government established in "this Commonwealth of England, and intending to vilify and "to bring into hatred and contempt with the people of this "Commonwealth the Parliament of England now sitting at "Westminster, on June 20, 1652, having conference and dis- "course with one Richard Kingdon of and concerning the "people of the Scottish nation, maliciously, advisedly, and "seditiously, these seditious, malicious, and dangerous words "with a loud voice did utter and speak, viz., that he (the "said William Worth meaning) did hope to have a King "again (of England meaning), and that he (the said William "Worth also meaning) should have the carrying of the "Roundheaded Rogues to gaol. In great contempt of the "Parliament and the members there sitting, and to the great "damage of the people of this Commonwealth, and to the "evil example of others in the like kind offending."

He was fined 10*l.*, and pilloried for one hour.

Still better is the following indictment for speaking slanderous words against the Parliament. It may be considered a gem of legal composition :—

"DEVONSHIRE.—The Jurors for the Keepers of the "Liberty of England by authority of Parliament do present "upon their oaths that Hillary Renell of Oakhampton in the "county aforesaid, *Tayler*, being a dangerous and seditious

"person, not only imagining, devising, and maliciously and
"seditiously intending the peace, tranquillity, and felicity of
"the good people of this Commonwealth and free State of
"England to disturb, but also to move, stir up, and raise
"discord, rebellion, and insurrection amongst the good
"people of England aforesaid, and the honest, godly,
"and religious persons then assembled in Parliament at
"Westminster, the then supreme authority of this nation,
"with the people aforesaid to cause to be in little regard
"and esteem, and their just and right actions in contempt,
"disgrace, hatred, and disdain with the said people of Eng-
"land to bring, the 28th day of March, 1653, at Oakhampton
"aforesaid, in the county aforesaid, having certain speech
"with one Robert Sprage, He the said Hillary Reynell, then
"and there of his devilish mind and wicked imagination
"these malicious, horrible, and seditious words following,
"falsely, seditiously, maliciously, advisedly, and directly,
"then and there spoke, published, and with a loud voice
"uttered (that is to say) I (meaning him the said Hillary
"Reynell) will approve that there are none but blood-thirsty
"and murderous and treacherous rogues that bears power
"now in putting the King to death (the aforesaid honest,
"godly, and religious persons then assembled in Parliament,
"the then supreme authority aforesaid meaning) who had
"lately by the laws of England caused Charles Stuart, late
"King of England (whom the said Hillary Reynell then
"meant) to suffer death as a traitor, To the evil and dan-
"gerous example of all others in the like case offending and
"against the public peace.

   "(Endorsed.)
 "Witness—Robert Sprage, sworn.
 "This bill is true."

William Harding told Arthur Featherstone that he had bribed Justice Wollocomb, and said further "I wish that Wollocomb had him att the Bench when I was called; itt should have sounded badly to his credit, but hee was att a Sermon, *hee is one of the new Sett*, and his Clarke is fitter to be a justice than he is."

At Midsummer Sessions, 1649, Gawen Sexton, baker, was committed for marrying his brother's wife, and preferring a petition containing heresy. The petition has been preserved, and, if it was really written by the accused, seems to prove that he was a preacher as well as a baker. It begins by stating that the petitioner is too unlearned to answer for himself, and too poor to hire an attorney to plead for him. Then, utterly ignoring the laws of England, he plunges into a Scriptural argument, supported by a formidable array of texts, and intended to prove that his matrimonial arrangement was not contrary to the law of Moses, and further, if it were so contrary, that the ordinance in question was a part of the ceremonial law, and that Christ had made us free from that yoke of bondage.

The commonest cases tried at Quarter Sessions during the Commonwealth related to those sins which most legislators have been unwilling to rank among crimes punishable by law. I have seen literally hundreds of such indictments of this period. The offences in question were no doubt punished in the time of Elizabeth, at least occasionally, but the law seems to have lapsed into desuetude under the Stuarts. Under the Puritan rule it was revived with a vengeance. The authorities seem to have taken an austere delight in raking up all the arrears of the past years of laxer morality. An order was made in Devonshire that every woman who had ever had an illegitimate child should be committed for trial, unless she had been previously punished. Married women were actually indicted for misconduct with their own husbands before marriage. The sentence was sometimes "to be whipt," as in the preceding century, but it was more generally three months' imprisonment, and to find sureties for good behaviour. At a single sessions there were twenty-two such cases.

Breaches of the Seventh Commandment were treated as capital crimes, and were not tried at sessions. The calendars of the assizes are not entered in the books, but we find persons committed on such charges, and orders respecting the disposal of children whose mothers had been executed. Advocates of women's rights may have their opinions confirmed by observing that the law was executed with gross partiality. Probably less than five per cent. of the indictments on these subjects were directed against individuals of the male sex.

If we deduct these cases, the calendars of Sessions appear short, but we do not know how many cases may have been disposed of by the Judges of Assize, or by the Major-Generals. In January, 1653-4, the witnesses are first spoken of as being "on behalf of his Highness the Lord Protector." In July following Thomas Nynoe was sentenced to remain until he paid 500*l*. "for a fyne for speaking trayterous words against the Lord Protector." And in the next year Mellony Farye (a woman) was fined 5*l*. for the same offence.

In 1656 John Huishe was committed to the assizes for saying that my Lord Protector was a rogue, and that he "did hope to live so long to see him hanged or burnt very shortly." He was admitted to bail, himself in 1000*l*., and two sureties in 500*l*. each! I suppose there can be little doubt that this was the father-in-law of Cromwell's mutinous Adjutant-

General Allen, who was arrested by Captain Unton Crook and the High Sheriff "at his father-in-law Mr. Huish's house in Devonshire," in January 1655.[1]

In October, 1658, one William Bowles, constable of Tavistock, was dismissed from his office and bound over to the assizes for saying since the death of Oliver Lord Protector that he was now free of his office, and that it was against his conscience to act for this Protector, *being he was a Cavelleire*, and farther said that he did believe or hope he should shortly act as a constable under another Government. He probably got his wish, for the next year was the one in which Mr. Pepys's friend boasted that he had managed to serve eight different Governments.

"Sabbath-breaking," we need hardly remark, was severely punished under the Commonwealth. Persons were sent for trial for travelling with a horse on the Lord's Day, for "shooteing in a gunne on the Lord's Day," for "prophaning the Sabbath and beating of ye said Thomas Tanner on ye last Lord's Day," for "not frequenting the ordenances, and driveing of horses on the Lord's Day."

"Unlawful meetings at cock-matches" were of course repressed with a strong hand. The Court was shocked by being informed that "certaine daies called Revell daies are yet observed in diverse parishes, which hath beene heretofore the unhappy occasion of much profanenes and wickednes in letting out the corruptions of men into all manner of disorder, as drunkennes, swearing, fighting and playing at games expressly against the Word of God and contrary to the statute." The constables were straitly charged to "forbid all meetings and concurse of people wheather strangers or others in publike or private houses," and to

[1] Carlyle's "Cromwell," ii. 315.

bring all offenders before the justices, "to bee dealt withall according to their demeritts."

The game laws were by no means repealed by the Parliament. An order to all constables was issued by the "Keepers of the Liberty of England," reciting the penalty of 20*s.* imposed "by law for spoyling and distroying of every feasant, partridge, hare, mallard, pigeon, and such like games, with any guns, netts, crosbowes, or other instruments or engyns, and alsoe for spoyling and distroying of every egg of phesant and partridge, and likewise for killing and distroying of hares with harepipes, cords, or other engyns." And likewise the sum of 40*s.* was imposed on any person keeping greyhounds or "setting doggs," except such as had an estate of inheritance of 10*l.* per annum, or an estate for life of 30*l.* yearly, or the value of 200*l.* in goods or chattels. "Nevertheless," the order goes on to say, "of late yeares the severall games above menconed have beene more excessively spoyled and distroyed then hath beene in former tymes, especially by the vulgar sort of people and men of small worth imploying most parte of their tyme in taking the said games, thereby bringing themselves the rather to poverty." And the constables were enjoined to arrest such offenders without warrant.

Democracy, as I remarked before, did not gain much by the Puritan Revolution. The doctrines then called levelling, in modern language socialist or communistic, never attained any considerable power. It was a hundred and forty years before the volcanic force of Sansculottism, as Mr. Carlyle would say, emerged from the abysses. The working classes were probably worse off under the Commonwealth than at any other time. I have met with an original table of the rates of wages settled by the Justices at Exeter, on April 4, 1654. They show only a small advance on those current in the reign of Elizabeth, sixty years before.[2] When we consider the diminution in the purchasing power of money which had certainly taken place, it cannot be doubted that such rates must have caused much suffering. The wages of masons, carpenters, and others employed in the building trade were actually the same as those fixed in 1594.

Omitting some superfluous verbiage, the following are the rates of wages voted by the Justices in 1654.

1. No bailiff of husbandry, hind, or miller to take above 4*l*. a year and livery, or 8*s*. 4*d*. instead.

2. No common men servants of husbandry from the age of 16 to 20 to take above 40*s*. a year, and above the age of 20 not above 53*s*. 4*d*.

3. No woman servant under 14 to take any wages but meat, drink, and clothes. From 14 to 18 not above 16*s*. and livery, or 6*s*. 8*d*. instead. From 18 to 30 not above 23*s*. 4*d*. and livery, or 6*s*. 8*d*.

4. Husbandry labourers.—From Allhallowtide until Candlemas not above 3*d*. a day, with meat and drink, and the rest of the year not above 4*d*. Without meat and drink, not above 10*d*. a day. When mowing corn and grass they might have 6*d*. a day with meat and drink, or 12*d*. a day without.

5. Women "labouring at hay," not above 2*d*. a day with meat and drink, or 6*d*. without. In corn harvest 4*d*. or 8*d*. At other work 2*d*. or 5*d*.

6. "Master carpenters," masons, plumbers, &c., having servants or apprentices, and able to take charge of the work, not above 6*d*. a day with meat and drink, or 12*d*. without.

7. "All labourers at husbandry at task as they can agree."

[2] See "Quarter Sessions under Queen Elizabeth."

8. Other masons, carpenters, &c., not above 5d. a day with meat and drink, or 11d. without. Apprentices and boys not above 2d., or 6d.

9. A pair of sawyers not above 12d., or 2s.

10. Weavers 2½d. or 8d. a day.

11. Spinsters not above 6d. *by the week* with meat and drink, or 16d. without.

12. All weavers and spinsters (if by the Greate) as they can agree.

In 1657 an order was made that all "masterless persons should take masters within one month."

Certain butchers, cordwainers, and others were indicted for "exercising or using an art, mistery, or manuall occupation, not having byn brought upp in the same by the space of seaven whole yeares at the least as an apprentice."

The restrictions on building were continued, and one man was fined 58l. for erecting a cottage without a licence.

Religious toleration was, of course, at this time considered impossible by all "practical men." Cromwell declared in Ireland that the Mass would never be permitted in any dominions under the power of the Parliament of England. But it does not seem clear at first why the zeal of the Puritans should have been particularly directed to the persecution of Quakers. Perhaps the "Levellers," or Communists, were included under that denomination. An order of September 1656, against rogues and vagabonds, goes on to say:—

"And now lately divers other persons styled by the name "of *Quakers*, disaffected to the present Government, do "wander up and down the country, and scatter seditious "books and papers to the deluding of many weak people, "undermining the fundamentals of religion, denying the

"Scriptures to be the word of God, and the godly ministers "of England to be the true ministers of the gospel, so as "many heresies and blasphemies are by them vented and "broached abroad, to the great dishonour of Almighty God "and grief of all pious and religious people, and to the dis- "turbance of the peace of the Commonwealth."

It was therefore ordered that all constables should cause good watches and wards to be kept for the apprehending of all beggars, rogues, vagabonds, wandering, idle, and suspicious persons, "and that they likewise apprehend all such persons as travel under the notion or name of *Quakers* without a lawful certificate testifying from whence he came and whither he is travelling, or shall have or do scatter, publish, or own any such seditious books or papers as aforesaid, or shall interrupt or disturb any minister in the congregation or otherwise." And all such persons, together with such books and papers, were to be brought before some Justice of the Peace to be dealt with according to law.

A similar order respecting Quakers was issued in October 1658, at the beginning of the Protectorate of Richard Cromwell. And all Quakers' books found in the gaol were to be burnt, especially those in the custody of Thomas Courtis, a Quaker, and now a prisoner. This was probably the same Thomas Courtis who was convicted of swearing, a curious offence for a Quaker. What he said was merely "God is my witness," which he probably considered something very different from an oath.

We get the titles of two Quaker books in an examination apparently of a lady of fortune. Mary Erberie, being arrested with Joane Ingrum, her servant, and John Browne, whose name seems appropriate for a footman, said that she was going to Launceston to visit some prisoners there, and that "shee owneth those people that are by the world scornefully called Quakers." She also admitted having two books, one intituled "To all that would know y[e] way to the Kingdome, &c.," and the other "Certaine papers w[ch] is y[e] word of the Lord, as was moved from the Lord by His servants to several places and persons, that they maie bee left without excuse, and God maie bee cleare when Hee judges and justified in His judgements."

I have not met with many of the curious Scriptural names supposed to be characteristic of this period. No Stand-fast-on-High Stringer, or Kill-Sin Pimple, appears in Devonshire. Abigail, Rhoda, Sampson, "Precilla," do not seem very extraordinary. Now and then we notice Elnathan, Archelaus, Mephibosheth, Sarepta, "Belshazer," John Baptista, and so forth. "Pentecost" was a name before the Civil War, and Christopher, Bartholomew, Christian, were always common. Armonell, Petronell, Wilmot (female), Hannibal, Scipio, Sibilla, Melior, are not Biblical. The name "Alpha" was probably given on the principle on which Mr. Bumble named the foundlings in the workhouse, and "Elevant Stoodley" was no doubt a nickname. "Iago" seems to have been not very uncommon as a surname. "Brute" was an unpleasant English form of Brutus. "Welthian" and "Damerne" were Christian names of women. Their derivation is a riddle which I give up.

An instance of the Protector's assumption of more than regal power occurs in connexion with the Castle of Exeter. The Assizes and Sessions for the county had been held there for generations, and the Justices had laid out large sums in erecting within it "houses, places, and seats of judicature." But in 1655 they had to appoint Colonel Robert Shapcote "to attend Generall Disbrowe for the

Quarter Sessions under the Commonwealth. 167

obtayning of a grant of the said Castle of Exon, and the said howses and places of Judicature from his highnes the Lord Protector, to and for the use of this county, according to his highnes gratious promise in that behalfe."

General Disbrowe, otherwise Desborough, was the major-general commanding the western district. Colonel Shapcote was one of the members for the county.

At last there came a time when the Justices of Devon thought themselves called upon again to come to the front in public affairs. The great Protector had been laid among his royal predecessors in the chapel of Henry the Seventh. His son had succeeded him as quietly as a Prince of Wales generally succeeds his father, but within few days he had passed away, neither in anger, nor in battle. The times were out of joint. It seemed almost certain that the country would become a prey to anarchy and confusion, and the eyes of all men were turned to him upon whom the weight and fate of England appeared to hang—the Devonshire gentleman who held the command of the Army of the North.

Many years had passed since old Sir Thomas Monk (or Mouncke, as the Clerk of the Peace delighted to write his name), of Potheridge, in North Devon, having kept his house too open to his friends, found himself compelled to keep it shut against his creditors. Being summoned to attend the King on his visit to Devonshire in 1625, he applied to the under-sheriff for immunity from arrest on that occasion. That functionary was, perhaps, one of those described by the Privy Council of James as "bred in nothing but in craft, extortion, and corruption." At any rate the request was granted, and the knight proceeded to Exeter, where he was taken by the bailiffs, and lodged in the debtors' ward. He had left at home his younger son George, a lad of seventeen, waiting for his commission in the army. This energetic young gentleman, hearing of the breach of faith of which his father had been the victim, rode straight to Exeter, caught the under-sheriff in the Castle, and caned him publicly in a way which would probably have been described in one of his own indictments as "verberavit, vulneravit, et maletractavit, ita quod de vitâ maxime desperabat." How he got away from the javelin-men, hue and cry, *posse comitatus*, or whatever force the man of law could dispose of, does not appear. Had he been caught he would no doubt have had to stand in the pillory with a paper in his hat signifying "This is the fellow that beat the under-sheriff." It may be feared that his conduct was avenged on his father, for poor Sir Thomas appears to have died in the sheriff's prison two years afterwards. Certain it is that George Monk quitted Devonshire, joined the army at the Isle of Rhé, and soon learned to conduct himself with equal valour and greater discretion. From that time he saw whatever service was to be seen, in the Low Countries, in Northumberland against the Scots, in Ireland against the rebels. The commencement of the Civil War found him in command of a regiment, but he had the luck to be taken prisoner by Fairfax, and kept in captivity until the end of the war in England. Towards the end of 1646 he took the Covenant, joined the army of the Parliament, and served with the highest distinction in Ireland and Scotland. He was not so gifted as some of the "warlike saints" in expounding Scripture or spouting politics, but probably he was not less valued by his chief. The great general and statesman of 1650 was himself very far removed from the fanatical Captain Cromwell of 1642, and could appreciate a trusty officer who knew perfectly how to do his duty, and also how to hold his tongue. In the words of Mr. Carlyle, Monk is "a taciturn man; speaks little; thinks more or less; does whatever is doable here and elsewhere."

After the pacification of Scotland, Monk obtained the command of a fleet, with which he succeeded in beating the great Admiral Van Tromp. And now, in 1659, having held for five years the chief command in Scotland, he was marching south with a well-disciplined army of 8000 veterans, to bear his part in the settlement of the Commonwealth.

The gentlemen of Devon, seeing that one of themselves had risen so high, thought it a good opportunity to impress their opinions on the authorities. They forwarded the following address "to the Right Honourable William Lenthall, Esq., Speaker of the Parliament," by the hands of Mr. Bampfield, who had been member for Exeter, and Speaker of Richard Cromwell's House of Commons:—

"We, the gentry of the county of Devon, finding our-
"selves without a regular Government (after your last
"interruption), designed a public meeting to consult reme-
"dies, and which we could not so conveniently effect till
"this week of our general Quarter Sessions at *Exon*, where
"we found divers of the inhabitants groaning under high
"oppressions, and a general defect of trade, to the utter
"ruin of many, and fear of the like to others, which is as
"visible to the whole *County*, that occasioned such disorders
"as were no small trouble and disturbance to us, which, by
"God's blessing upon our endeavours, were soon suppressed
"and quieted without blood; and though we find, since our
"first purposes, an alteration in the state of affairs, by your
"re-establishment at the helm of Government, yet conceive
"that we are but in part redressed of our grievances, and

"that the chief expedient will be the recalling all those
"members who were secluded in 1648, and sat before the
"first force upon the Parliament, and also by filling up
"vacant places, and all to be admitted without any oath, or
"engagement previous to their entrance, for which things, if
"you please to take a speedy course, we shall defend you
"against all opposers and future interruption, with our lives
"and fortunes, for the accomplishment whereof we shall
"use all lawful means, which we humbly conceive may best
"conduce to the peace and safety of the nation."

This address was agreed on at the Epiphany Sessions of 1659-60. It was signed by more than forty of the principal gentlemen of the county, among whom were five of the secluded members of the Long Parliament, viz., Sir Francis Drake, Sir John Northcote, William Morrice, Ellis Grimes, and — Vowel.

A similar letter, or a copy of this one, was sent to General Monk. It reached him while he was on his way from Scotland. Whether he had at this time determined to play the part of a king-maker, or whether he was more inclined to the part that Cromwell played before him, or to the part that Washington played long afterwards, no man can tell. He was now a very different character from the impulsive boy who caned the under-sheriff. He was impenetrable as William the Silent of Orange, or President Grant of America. Probably he had no fixed determination at all, and was calmly watching the course of public opinion. What is most certain is that he had no intention of having his hand forced by the Justices of Devon, though he paid them the compliment of answering their address. He wrote to them from Leicester, on January 21, 1660, the curious letter which may be read in Harris's *Charles II.*, in which he argued against their proposals, and pointed out the danger that the secluded members might attempt to restore the Monarchy. He reminded them that many vested interests had sprung up since the war; that, in ecclesiastical matters, the Presbyterians, Independents, Anabaptists, and other sectaries, had acquired rights which they could not be expected to relinquish; that, in civil affairs, the estates of the King, Queen, bishops, and deans and chapters had been sold, resold, settled on marriages, &c. He showed that a King would be bound to overturn these arrangements, both civil and spiritual, and that therefore the attempt to restore Monarchy would certainly produce a fresh war, in which all these interests, and, above all, the army, would be decidedly in favour of the Republic. It was, therefore, his opinion that such a government "in the way of a commonwealth" should be established as might be comprehensive of all interests both spiritual and civil, "to the glory of God, and the weal and peace of the whole."

Yet it seems by no means impossible that this demonstration made by his native county may have had some effect in influencing the resolution of the general, especially if, as we are assured, it was the original precedent which was shortly followed by most of the counties and boroughs.

Monk was elected to the Convention Parliament as Knight of the Shire for Devon, his colleague being Sir John Northcote, a lineal ancestor of the present Chancellor of the Exchequer.

The events that resulted belong to general history. All that concerns our story is that the younger son of an embarrassed squire, who fled from his home in sore danger of a prosecution, returned to it at last as Duke of Albemarle and Lord-Lieutenant of his native county.

QUARTER SESSIONS UNDER CHARLES II.

PART I.

THE records of Quarter Sessions are in one respect not unlike the records of geology. In that science we find certain fossils, like the nautilus, existing with little modification in a number of different formations. We find other fossils, like the ammonite, specially characteristic of certain formations, and very rare, or entirely absent, in others. So, in the county records, we find entries on certain subjects which are common to all, or at least to many, reigns. We find other entries which are so limited, or so nearly limited, to particular periods, that they may be considered characteristic of the reigns in which they occur, and may be as confidently referred to that time as the fossils of the geologist may be referred to his so-called epochs. Orders relating to bridges and settlements, and appeals in cases of affiliation, are common in every reign, from that of Queen Elizabeth to that of Queen Victoria. Entries respecting "purveyance" and "privy seals" distinguish the reign of the Virgin Queen. Prosecutions of "Popish recusants" are most frequent under James I. The Civil War overshadows everything else in the reign of his son. Indictments for profaneness and immorality are characteristic of the Commonwealth. The entries which especially distinguish the reign of Charles II. are, as might be expected, of a very different character. They relate to the persecution of Protestant Nonconformists, and to the imposition of the hearth tax.

The Acts, however, which we shall find illustrated by these proceedings did not come into operation during the first two or three years after the Restoration. The first business was to undo as much as possible of what had been done by the preceding Government. While the authorities in London were occupied with hanging the surviving regicides, and digging up and insulting the bodies of the dead ones, and turning the officials of the late Government out of the public offices, the justices in Devon proceeded to take away the pensions of the unfortunate "maimed soldiers" of the Parliament, and to bestow them upon those who had received their wounds in defence of the "Royal Martyr," to whose memory the new church at Plymouth was at this time dedicated.

In October 1660 the Court passed a resolution that no pensions should be paid without fresh certificates. A committee was appointed to take an account of the maimed soldiers, and, as it was neatly expressed on a subsequent occasion, "to examine their indigency, impotency, and loyalty."

At Epiphany the committee brought up a list of eighty-seven persons, who were to receive pensions amounting altogether to 241*l.* 3*s.* 4*d.* At Easter fifty-six more were added. It is expressly mentioned that a maimed soldier of the time of Queen Elizabeth was to have his pension as before, as if there were anything wonderful in a pensioner living to receive his stipend for a period of sixty years.

The triumphant Cavaliers, in the midst of their gratitude to their old soldiers, preserved a more frugal mind than might have been expected. The pensions very seldom amounted to as much as 4*l*. 10*s*. per annum, and sometimes did not exceed 1*l*. 10*s*. The average was scarcely 3*l*. All maimed soldiers were ordered to appear at the next Sessions, and to be examined by two " chirurgeons." The latter word is in one place spelt " cureurgent," which would not be a bad title for the medical profession to adopt.

Besides the surgeons' certificates it was necessary to produce " certificates under their field officers' hands," or other sufficient proof to satisfy the Court " that they were maymed in his Ma^{ts} service, and that they were never in armes against him," and also certificates from two justices as to their character and poverty.

Notwithstanding all these precautions, the number of claimants was so great that it was found necessary to increase the rates. The rate for this purpose in the time of Charles I. had been 188*l*. 9*s*. 4*d*. It had been doubled in the time of the Long Parliament, and was now trebled, so that it amounted to 565*l*. 8*s*. Reference is made to a recent Act " for the releiffe of poore and maymed officers and soldiers who have faithfully served his Matie and his Royall father in the late wars." Even this rate was not found sufficient in 1664, but after that the expenditure seems to have declined.

A sum of 4*l*. was granted to Honor Deyman because her husband, "at the tyme of the risinge of Colonell Penruddick," was sent to gaol for twelve months, " and afterwards sent beyond the seas, where he died." This is a reminiscence of the abortive Royalist insurrection at Salisbury, and of Cromwell's transportations to Barbadoes. These

Quarter Sessions under Charles II. 175

last were so frequent as to produce a new verb—to *barbadoes* a man. Colonel Penruddock was beheaded at Exeter, May 16, 1655.

Jane Knott, widow of a "levetenant" slain in the late King's service, was presented with 5*l*. Grace Battishill, whose husband was a soldier, and "was hanged for his loialty," received 6*l*. 13*s*. 4*d*. Elizabeth Radford, widow of an ensign was to have 20*s*. "in full of all pensions." A major had a pension of 4*l*., and 4*l*. gratuity. Captain Cockayne, "formerly muster master of the county," was allowed 8*l*. 14*s*. 4*d*. for arrears from November 30, 1642, to the surrender of Exeter in April 1646.

In 1664 it was mercifully provided that the maimed soldiers should no longer be obliged to come to Exeter to receive their pensions, but might be paid by the constables. But mistakes would happen, and the Court was shocked to learn that four men had got pensions who had been wounded in serving against the king. But, as both parties were in the habit of pressing soldiers, it might have been argued that serving against the King was not a conclusive proof of disloyalty. In one case a maimed soldier was deprived of his pension "because he went *voluntarily* into the Parliament service."

The pensions seem in all cases to have been granted with reluctance, and reduced rather than increased. Frequent orders were made for lists of maimed soldiers, and for their inspection. Although the number of applicants was increased by the Dutch war, we find the rates reduced by one-third part in 1674. The number of pensioners was at that time 203, and only 376*l*. was raised for them. The burden seems to have been gradually shifted on to the parishes. A pension of as little as 20*s*. was sometimes voted, and the unfortunate recipient commended to the overseers of his parish. A lieutenant got only 30s. In 1683 the justices went so far as to resolve that no maimed soldiers should have pensions until they had been relieved by their respective parishes. From this time we hear very little more of this subject, which had been at one time almost the chief business of Sessions.

The feelings which had produced the restoration of monarchy prompted men to take a pleasure in recurring to the smallest details of the ancient order. The leaders of the Commonwealth had introduced the use of the vernacular language into the "tortuous ungodly jungle of English law." The officials of Charles II. restored the custom of employing what they were pleased to call Latin.

In July 1660 Sessions were said to be "in the yeare of the raigne of our Soveraigne Lord Kinge Charles II. over England, &c., the twelveth." But at Michaelmas the old Latin heading reappears.

Quarter Sessions were again "sessio quarterialis," and "tenutus apud Castrum Exoniæ in et pro Comitatu predicto," &c. Again the unhappy vagrant was informed that he was "convict. essendi rogus incorrigibilis." Again orders were made about "fiat warrantum ad comprendum," and offenders were again "tradit. pro bene gerendo usque ad prox. Assisas." Again they were indicted in this style: "Quod vi et armis unum saccum valoris quatuor denar. et septem mensuras Avenarum (*Anglicè, pecks of oates*) valor quatuor solidorum, &c. &c., ad tunc et ibidem felonicè furat. fuit cepit et asportavit,' &c. &c.

When a farmer set his dog at a neighbour's cow, we find the fact translated into an indictment "quod Thomas Mingo agricola apud Stokenham quendam Canem Molossum Anglicè *A Mastive Dogg* ad mordendum quandam vaccam pretii quatuor librarum de bonis et cattallis cujusdam Elianor Deary ad tunc et ibidem vi et armis illicite et malitiose excitavit persuasit et procuravit contra pacem dicti domini Regis nunc Coronam et dignitatem suas."

Even when a dog bit a pig without having been "excited, persuaded, and procured" to do so, his owner was indicted in this fashion: Thomas Stove "quendam Canem Molossum (*Anglicè, one biting Mastive Dogg*) color *Dunne* (faucibus suis non ligatis) scienter malitiose et illicite habuit et custodivit et ad largum ire permisit. Qui quidem Canis Molossus quendam porcum pretii duodecim solidorum, &c.—ad tunc et ibidem, violenter et graviter incursavit et momordit, ac etiam in tanto lesit ita quod porcus præd. et alia averia præd. multipliciter deteriorat. devenerunt," &c. &c.

It is time to turn to more important matters. When Mr. Pepys recorded in his diary the fact of his having been sworn a justice, he went on to say, "With which honour I did find myself mightily pleased, though I am wholly ignorant in the duties of a justice of peace." His cousin Thomas Pepys, being troubled with a conscience, confided to him that he was unwilling to be a justice, because he did not feel free to exercise punishment according to the Act against Quakers and other people for religion. "Nor do he understand Latin, and so is not capable of the place as formerly, now all warrants do run in Latin."

The two qualifications, then, esteemed necessary for a justice under Charles II. were intolerance and Latin. Of the latter we have seen a few specimens. Of the former it will not be difficult to give a sample.

The Conventicle Acts made it a crime for any five persons, not of the same household, to join in an act of religious worship differing from the forms of the Church of England. At first this crime seems to have been punishable only by imprisonment, and, for the third offence, by transportation. A subsequent Act enabled, or rather enjoined, every justice to inflict penalties, which were divided into three parts—one-third to be paid to the King through the Court of Quarter Sessions, one-third to the poor of the parish in which the offence was committed, and one-third to the informer, or such persons as had been diligent and industrious in "the discovery, dispersing, and punishing of the said conventicles." Any person preaching in a conventicle incurred a penalty of 20*l.* for the first offence, and 40*l.* for the second. And if the preacher could not be caught, or was unable to pay, the sum due from him might be levied on any persons who were present. A single justice was authorized to convict. The only appeal allowed was to the Court of Quarter Sessions, and any offender appealing, and failing in his appeal, was to be condemned in treble costs. Justices were directed to break open any house where a conventicle was supposed to be held, and might call upon a military force to help them. The Act was to be "construed most largely and beneficially for the suppressing of conventicles, and for the justification and encouragement of all persons to be employed in the execution thereof." And any person neglecting to perform his duty in enforcing the Act was liable to a penalty amounting in the case of a constable or churchwarden to 5*l.*, and in the case of a justice of the peace to 100*l.*

The latter penalty does not seem to have been much needed. The justices were now almost all Cavaliers and Churchmen, many of whom had suffered for their political and religious opinions, and were only too eager to inflict similar sufferings on their vanquished foes. The Puritans had had their day, and had used their power with little reluctance or remorse. The Churchmen now had their innings, and were ready to play the same game with at least equal spirit.

As early as March 1661 the grand jury of Devon made a presentment desiring that the laws might be put in force against Popish recusants, "who, with the sectaries, *Tub Preachers*, Quakers, &c., are the most pernicious enemies and subtil underminers of the established religion."

The offences for which persons were imprisoned or transported are seldom mentioned. We are therefore unable to judge from these records how many were punished for religion in that manner. But, under the Act imposing fines, one-third of every penalty was to be paid in at Quarter Sessions, and we thus have some record of the amounts collected by the active justices of the period.

In 1665 we only find that "Roger Muckle, for being at a conventicle, was fyned x^s, wch he refusing to pay, is com. for one moneth." But soon afterwards the Act comes into full play. We have a "conviction of conventiclers" given at full length, probably as a precedent. It relates to William Frade, tanner, Thomas Mapowder, gentleman, Samuel Sheeres, ironmonger, Westcote Doble, mercer, James Liverton, tanner, and William Harrison, tanner, all of the parish of Holsworthy, who were indicted for that they, on a certain Sunday, "apud domum Manconalem cujusdam Thomæ Mapowder assemblaverunt et illicite congregaverunt et quilibet eorum assemblavit et illicite congregavit sub colore exercendæ religionis in alio modo quam allocatum est per liturgiam aut usum Ecclesiæ Anglicanæ contra pacem domini Regis nunc et contra formam statuti," &c. &c. They were convicted and committed to gaol—Frade for one month, Mapowder and the others for ten weeks—unless they paid certain fines, varying from 5*l.* to 1*l.*

At the same Sessions we notice a list of unusually heavy fines. Daniel Northern was fined 100*l.*, Anthony King and Elizabeth May 500*l.* each, Peter Oxenham, John Huish, and Christopher Pearse, 100 marks each. But the reason for imposing these penalties is not stated.

On another occasion twenty-three persons belonging to the city of Exeter were summoned for being at a conventicle in the house of Mr. Barton at Netherexe, in the county of Devon. Five persons living in the county were also summoned at the same time.

At Midsummer, 1670, several magistrates brought into Court sums of money, being one-third part of the fines they had levied since the last Sessions upon persons present at assemblies, conventicles, or meetings.

At Michaelmas in the same year there is a long list of these cases, which may be taken as a specimen of many entries in subsequent Sessions.

George Reynell, Esq., paid in 9*l.*, being one-third of a sum of 27*l.* levied upon divers persons for being at a seditious conventicle in Kingsbridge.

Francis Fulford, Esq., paid in 13*l.* 18*s.* 4*d.*, being one-third part of 41*l.* 15*s.* levied for a similar reason at Moreton Hampstead.

William Bastard, Esq., brought 13*s.* 4*d.* from the parish of Sherford.

John Tuckfield, Esq., brought 15*l.* 16*s.* 8*d.* from persons meeting in the house of Catharine Northcote in Crediton.

Francis Drewe, Esq., brought 8*l.* 16*s.* from a conventicle held in the *parish church* of Sheldon.

The Mayor of Dartmouth brought 11s. 8d.

Francis Drewe and William Walrond, Esqs., brought 5l. 13s. 4d. from the parish of Halberton.

John Beare, Esq., brought 8l. 11s. 8d. from the parish of Malborough.

Sir Thomas Hele, Bart., brought 10s. from Modbury.

The ayor of Bideford brought 7l. He had also imposed a fine of 20l. upon Sarah Dennis, but this conviction was reversed upon appeal—a very rare occurrence.

At Culmstock 5l. apiece was levied on several persons *for a preacher unknown*, and at Silverton 6l. 15s. 4d. apiece for a similar reason; but these convictions were quashed because the preacher was not convicted.

Robert Collings, of Ottery, was fined 20l. for preaching in his own house, and 20l. more for permitting a conventicle to be holden there. He appealed to the Sessions, failed to get his sentence reversed, and was ordered to pay treble costs—amounting to 20l. more.

As all magistrates at this time were sworn champions of Church and King, an appeal to the Sessions was not a very hopeful undertaking; and as the treble costs were always inflicted, appeals soon ceased to be attempted.

A constable was fined 5l. for negligence in detecting a conventicle. We do not find that it was ever necessary to impose a penalty on any justice for his remissness in this business, but it is evident that some were far more active than others. One brought in as much as 28l. at a single Sessions. These proceedings go far to explain certain epitaphs of the period, wherein we find it recorded, among the other virtues of the deceased *Irenarcha*, that he was "Ecclesiæ Anglicanæ vindex acerrimus."

In 1661 Sampson Larke, refusing to take the oath of allegiance, was "put out of the King's protection, and his lands, goods, and cattle forfeit to the King, and is imprisoned and ransomed at the King's will." His name, being rather an uncommon one, attracted my attention, and I observe that he is entered in every calendar for ten years, as remaining in prison "for *præmunire*." Several others remained nearly as long. Sampson Larke was a Nonconformist preacher. He was liberated in 1672, and afterwards lived at Lyme. He joined Monmouth, and was hanged by order of Jeffreys. His execution is described at length in the " Bloody Assizes."

Two counsellors were to have 20s. each " for their paines as counsel for his Matie against the Dissenters on several traverses."

The county of Devon, like the rest of the country, was kept in a state of terror and excitement by rumours of plots and counterplots, Papists and Exclusionists, Oateses and Dangerfields. The feelings of the public are reflected in the proceedings of our Court.

At Epiphany, 1681, the justices thought it right, " as good Christians and faithful subjects," to issue the following public order :—

" Forasmuch as religion is the foundation of civil govern-
" ment, and whilst faction and schism is allowed and per-
" mitted in the Church we can never expect peace and quiet
" in the State ; and observing at this time (as we have here-
" tofore by sad experience found) that those that dissent
" from us in our established religion, of what persuasion
" soever, though at seeming variance and difference among
" themselves, yet agree in their wicked attempts upon the
" Government and their traitorous plots and designs against
" the King's sacred Person—We therefore think ourselves
" obliged, in discharge of the trust reposed in us (as good

"Christians and faithful subjects), to put the laws effectually
"in execution against all Dissenters, whether Papists or
"Sectaries, and do unanimously resolve, agree, and order
"that the laws following through every division of this
"County shall be put in due execution.

"*Imprimis.* We think the King's sacred Person (whom
"God long preserve) and the Government cannot be safe
"and secure unless all persons who are of due age be re-
"quired to take the oath of allegiance. We therefore order
"and appoint that the oath of allegiance be duly tendered
"to all persons through every subdivision of this County,
"according to the statutes made in the third and seventh
"years of King James, and that all refusers be prosecuted
"as the said laws appoint.

"*Secondly.* We order and appoint that the laws made in
"the first of Queen Elizabeth and the third of King James,
"requiring all persons of the age of sixteen years and up-
"wards to resort to their parish church, and there to abide
"soberly and orderly during the whole time of Divine service,
"under the penalty of twelvepence for each neglect, &c., be
"duly put in execution. And the Justices are desired to
"meet in their several subdivisions of this County once every
"month to take the presentments of all head constables,
"petty constables, tithing men, churchwardens, and others,
"all which said several officers of the respective parishes
"they are to require to attend them and make true present-
"ments of all absenters from church as aforesaid. And the
"Ministers, Parsons, and Curates of the respective parishes
"are desired to be aiding and assisting to the said parochial
"officers, and to inform the Justices if they shall observe any
"of them to be negligent or remiss in their duties.

"*Thirdly.* And those whom this gentler discipline will not

"correct and reform, we do order and agree shall be prose-
" cuted, according to the directions of the statutes made in
" the third year of King James, as recusants. And the said
" presentments, for as many months as they shall absent
" from church, shall in due form be returned into this Court,
" so as there may be such proceedings thereon as the law
"appoints. And those whom we find yet more incorrigible
" and dangerous we resolve to prosecute and punish accord-
" ing to the directions of a statute made in the thirty-fifth
" year of Queen Elizabeth, entitled an Act against Seditious
" Sectaries, &c.

"*Fourthly.* Forasmuch as the great danger that at this time
" threatens the Government flows from Corporations and
" Boroughs, who are the Nests and Seminaries of faction and
" disloyalty, where, notwithstanding and in contempt of a
" law made in the seventeenth year of this King, entitled an
" Act to Prohibit Nonconformists from Inhabiting in Cor-
" porations, we find that in some of our boroughs and cor-
" porations in this County several of those dangerous and
" disloyal persons inhabit and reside, taking the same sediti-
" ous methods they did in the late rebellion of drawing the
" people from their allegiance and duty—That we may there-
" fore prevent the mischiefs that may flow from such prac-
" tices, we order and agree that the aforesaid law be duly
" put in execution through every part of this County.

Fifthly. We likewise order and agree that a statute made
" in the two-and-twentieth year of this King, entitled an Act
" to Prevent and Suppress Seditious Conventicles, be care-
" fully and duly put in execution. And all Constables, Church-
" wardens, and Overseers of the Poor, in whose parishes any
" such unlawful meetings shall be held, are to take notice
" that they give due information thereof to the next Justice

"of the Peace, so as they may be suppressed; otherwise the "penalties in the Act mentioned will, with all severity, be "inflicted on such of the said officers as shall be found negli-"gent or remiss in their duties. And, that faction may have "no encouragement, we order and agree that all Church-"wardens and Overseers of the Poor, that from and after the "first day of March next ensuing, in their contribution to "the poor, shall give and allow any relief to such as are able "of body and not repair every Sunday to their parish church "and there abide soberly and orderly during the whole time "of Divine service, no such contribution in the passing their "account shall be allowed.

"And that all people may have notice of this our Order, "and avoid the punishments of the aforesaid laws by a "regular conformity, charitably believing that some may "be ignorantly misled, we desire that all Parsons, Vicars, "Curates, of the respective parishes within this County, will, "some Sunday before the said first day of March next, in "their parish churches publish this our Order.

"And we would have all men seriously consider the "gentleness of our laws and the wonderful goodness and "clemency of our present King, who, till provoked by un-"sufferable affronts and traitorous plots against his sacred "Person, would not turn the edge of those laws towards his "subjects, but try the effects of kindness and indulgence. "But, to the eternal infamy of those people, he hath proved "the experiment that not kindness, but the Rod and Disci-"pline, must keep them within the bounds of duty and "allegiance."

This order was signed by Arthur Northcote, Coplestone Bampfield, Peter Fortescue, John Rolle, and twenty-three others. Several persons were committed at these Sessions for *præmunire*, or refusing the oath of allegiance.

The disloyalty of corporations seems to have been deeply impressed on the minds of the justices. At one time it was the practice to adjourn Sessions to Clovelly, Dartington, Ermington, Stonehouse, Totnes, Ashburton, &c., and this was probably done to give people in various neighbourhoods an opportunity of taking the oath of allegiance. In 1681 it was resolved that Sessions should not be adjourned for taking the oath, "except for loyal gentlemen, and not for any Corporations."

An address was presented to his Majesty in 1681 by the justices, officers of militia, and freeholders of Devon. We have not the text of it, but no doubt it was about Nonconformists and "Absenters," as recusants were commonly called. John Lambert was indicted because he

"illicite et injuriose dixit propagavit et asseruit hæc falsa "scandalosa opprobriosa et seditiosa Anglicana verba sequ- "entia, viz: *They are all knaves or fooles that signed the* "*Addresse* (humillimam aplicaconem prædictam innuendo). "In manifestum contemptum dicti domini Regis, in magnam "depravaconem et scandalizaconem præfat. justic. officiar. "militiæ, liber. tenent. et al. person. præd. qui humillimam "applicaconem præd. signaverunt et subscripserunt."

When the justices spoke of the "wonderful goodness and clemency of our present King," they were probably alluding to a letter which had been sent from the Council some years before:—

"After our hearty commendations. His Majesty's con- "stant desire for the ease and happiness of his people hav-

Quarter Sessions under Charles II. 187

"ing, amongst other things, put him upon enquiry into the
"gaols and prisons of this Kingdom, and having received
"information that in many of them there are objects as well
"fit for clemency as justice, both which he is willing to dis-
"pense in such manner as bold offenders may receive no en-
"couragement, whilst his Majesty extends mercy to unwary
"and seduced persons whom there may be any hopes of re-
"claiming—His Majesty hath therefore, in order to his clearer
"information in this affair, thought fit to command us to
"write these our letters unto you the Justices of the Peace of
"the County of Devon, to be read at the next Quarter Ses-
"sions to be held for the said County, charging and requiring
"you to examine and certify unto this Board, at or before
"the 20th day of January next, the names, time and causes
"of commitment of all such persons as shall then be in custody
"in any gaol or prison of that County, and particularly of
"that sort of people called *Quakers*, with your opinion con-
"cerning them respectively, who of them may be fit objects
"of his Majesty's mercy, and who are Ringleaders of
"faction in contempt of the laws; and hereof you are
"not to fail at the time aforesaid. And so we bid you
"farewell.

"From the Court at Whitehall, the 10th day of December,
"1667.

"Your loving Friends,

"GIL. CANT,   "ARLINGTON,
"LAUDERDAILL,   "THO. INGRAM,
"CARLISLE,   "ANGLESEY.
"LINDSEY,   "BERKSHEIRE,
"BRIDGWATER,   "WILL. MORICE,
"CRAVEN,   "W. COVENTRY,
"CARBERY,   "JOHN NICHOLAS."

We have here a list of the Council at this period. Most of them are mentioned by Pepys, and nine of them were present when he was called before "a large Committee of the Council" on June 19, 1667.

The justices were so pleased with the effect produced by their order of 1681, that they proceeded in the same direction in the following year, being of opinion that the corporations within the county would be the better for their advice, and that the Dissenting preachers might probably like to know what they thought of them, and might enjoy a pun upon the word "minister."

"Having found so good an effect of the order and resolu-
"tions agreed on last sessions for the putting the laws in
"execution against Dissenters, it having wrought so great a
"reformation and (in those parts of the County where it was
"observed) reduced most of those wandering people into the
"bosom of their mother Church, whom they had undutifully
"forsook, we are encouraged and resolve cheerfully to pro-
"ceed in the method we have begun. And we hope all those
"whom his Majesty hath entrusted in the Commission of the
"Peace in this County will heartily concur with us, and show
"their zeal for our established religion and their love of the
"King in the punishing those people who have declared
"themselves enemies to both.

"And though we will not take upon us to advise, yet we
"heartily recommend the putting those laws in execution to
"the Chief Magistrates within the several Corporations of
"this County, inasmuch as, unless that be done, we can never
"hope to reform the country. And we would desire you all,
"gentlemen, seriously to consider the great and more par-
"ticular obligations you have received from the King, who,
"upon his happy restoration, was graciously pleased to con-

"firm to you all your ancient privileges, and hath since
" given you so many testimonies of his great grace and kind-
" ness as should raise you to the highest pitch of loyalty.
" And we hope (when you have throughly considered it) you
" will not think it agreeable with the rules of loyalty and
" gratitude to shelter and protect from justice any of those
" people who are professed enemies to the King and his
" Government, but will inflict such punishments on them as
" the laws direct. But more particularly we desire you would
" deliver up to us those *ungrateful Monsters* (Nonconformist
" *Ministers*, we mean) who in the late rebellion preached up
" sedition and treason. And though the King, out of his
" wonderful grace and mercy, hath since been pleased to
" pardon them, yet we have reason to believe they take the
" same methods and endeavour to debauch the people with
" the same doctrines still."

Some ungrateful monsters had probably remarked that the Cavaliers were a drunken, dissipated, and swearing party, and that they were far more ready to fight for their Church than to be guided by the common precepts of Christian morality. Although nothing but virtue could flourish under a monarch who had issued a proclamation against vice and immorality, the justices were not, perhaps, free from some uneasiness in their consciences, and the rest of their order runs thus :—

" And because it is a common objection that profaneness,
" debaucheries, and irreligion are countenanced or never
" punished by us (which yet those Zealots who raise this
" Scandal are as much guilty of, though they hide it under
" the Vizard of hypocrisy, and of pretended sanctity) we de-
" clare that (according to the precepts of our religion, which
" teach us obedience, temperance, and the strictest rules of

"virtue, and according to the directions of his Majesty's
" Royal Proclamation, 1660) we will endeavour with as much
" zeal to suppress all profaneness and debauchery. And
" we do resolve, agree, and order that the several Laws fol-
" lowing shall with all severity be put in execution in every
" part of the County.

" We will with all diligence, according to the direction of
" the Statutes made in the One and-Twentieth year of King
" James and Third of King Charles, punish all profane
" Swearers and Cursers, which give so great an offence to
" religion, and which we acknowledge to be the Common Sin
" of our Age. And because Disorderly Alehouses are most
" commonly the *rendezvouz* of profane, debauched, and lewd
" persons—

" We do therefore order and agree that all such Ale-
" house-keepers as shall permit or suffer any such profane or
" lewd persons to sit tippling in their houses shall be care-
" fully suppressed in every part of the County. And we do
" resolve that in the licensing and allowing Alehouses we will
" strictly observe the directions of the Laws made in the
" fifth year of King Edward the Sixth, and the first, fourth,
" and seventh of King James.

" And we do further order and agree that no persons shall be
" permitted to keep Alehouses that shall not every Sunday
" repair to their parish church and there abide orderly and
" soberly during the whole time of Divine Service, and shall
" not likewise produce a certificate that they have at least
" twice in the year last past received the Sacrament of the
" Lord's Supper according to the usage of the Church of
" England.

" And we do further order and agree that at all our monthly
" meetings we will strictly require all Constables, Church-

"wardens, and Tithing Men to present unto us upon oath all "Drunkards and such as shall remain tippling in Alehouses "at unreasonable times, according to the Directions of the "Laws made in the One-and-twentieth and Fourth years of "King James.

"And we would have those Schismatical factious people "who upraid us with the countenancing debauchery and "lewdness to look back upon the late times, and they will "find it was their Schism and Rebellion which was prologued "with such an entry as this too, which first weakened and at "last broke down the banks of Government, and let in upon "us a deluge of profaneness and irreligion; and though "they call themselves now the Sober party, it is evident they "take the same methods again, and would (if it were pos- "sible) bring us into the same confusion."

This order was signed by Edward Seymour, Coplestone Bampfylde, Arthur Northcote, H. Acland, and eleven others. The four whom I have mentioned bore the names of families known beyond the narrow limits of Devonshire. The representative of one of them is the present leader of the House of Commons. Another occupied a similar position two hundred years ago. We all know how Sir Edward Seymour of Berry Pomeroy, member for the city of Exeter, stands out in the brilliant picture of Macaulay, "looking like what he was, the chief of a dissolute and high-spirited gentry, with the artificial ringlets clustering in fashionable profusion round his shoulders, and a mingled expression of voluptuousness and disdain in his eye and on his lip." His eloquence, knowledge, and habits of business, had caused him to be the first country gentleman who was elected to the chair of the House of Commons, a post that had been usually reserved for a trained lawyer. He was long the head of the

Parliamentary party called the Western Alliance, and afterwards the leader of the whole Tory party. The order I have quoted, which was, in fact, a political manifesto, is in some respects characteristic of his fierce and haughty temper. If it was not written by his own hand, there can be little doubt that its terms were settled in accordance with his suggestions.

The orders of the Court at this period are somewhat long, yet it may perhaps be allowable to quote another. It is not without historical interest to know what a large body of country gentlemen thought of the state of public affairs at an important crisis. The discovery of the Rye House Plot in 1683 brought the rage and panic of the dominant party almost to a state of rabidity. The sectaries were denounced in language like that sometimes applied to the modern Turks, as the enemies of the human race. The laws were declared to be too gentle to admit of such creatures being dealt with according to their deserts. The justices were shocked to hear that people who were fined for not going to church were depraved enough to go there "only to save their money," and not to join heartily in the service. The holiest mystery of the Christian religion was degraded into a mere political test. The present generation can hardly realize the fact that it continued to be so used until the days of our fathers. The county record rooms are full of "Sacramental Rolls,"—certificates that soldiers and sailors, and persons of all ranks and degrees, had received the Sacrament according to the forms of the Church of England.

Here is the order of Michaelmas, 1683 :—

" We have been so abundantly convinced of the Seditious
" and rebellious practices of the Sectaries and *Phanaticks*,

Quarter Sessions under Charles II. 193

"who through the course of above one hundred years since
"we were first infested with'em have scarce afforded this
"unhappy Kingdom any interval of rest from their horrid
"Treasons as that we must esteem 'em not only the open
"enemies of our established Government, but to all the com-
"mon principles of Society and Humanity itself. Where-
"fore, that we may prevent their horrid conspiracies for the
"time to come, and secure (as much as in us lies) our most
"Gracious King and the Government from the fury and
"malice of'em, we resolve to put the severest of the Laws
"(which we find too easy and gentle unless enlivened by a
"vigorous execution) in force against'em.

"*First.* We agree and resolve in every division of this
"County to require sufficient Sureties for the good Abearing
"and peaceable behaviour of all such as we may justly
"suspect, or that we can receive any credible Information
"against, that they have been at any Conventicles and un-
"lawful meetings, or at any factious and seditious Clubs,
"or that have by any discourses discovered themselves to be
"disaffected to the present established Government either
"in Church or State, or that have been the authors or pub-
"lishers of any Seditious Libels, or that shall not in all
"things duly conform themselves to the present established
"Government.

"*Secondly.* Because we have a sort of false men and
"more perfidious than professed *Phanatiques*, who, either
"wanting courage to appear in their own shape or the better
"to bring about their treasonable designs, privately associate
"with and encourage the Seditious Clubs of the Sectaries,
"and with them plot heartily against the Government, and
"yet, that they may pass unsuspected, sometime appear in
"the church with a false show of Conformity, only to save

O

"their money and the better to serve their faction—That
"we may (if possible) distinguish and know all such dan-
"gerous enemies, we will strictly require all churchwardens
"and constables at all our monthly meetings to give us a
"full account of all such as do not every Sunday resort to
"their own parish Churches, and are not at the beginning
"of Divine Service, and do not behave themselves orderly
"and soberly there, observing all such decent Ceremonies
"as the laws enjoin ; and that they likewise present unto us
"the names of all such as have not received the Holy Sacra-
"ment of the Lord's Supper in their own parish churches
" thrice in the year.

" *Thirdly*. Being fully satisfied, as well by the clear evi-
"dence of the late *Horrid Plot*, as by our own long and sad
"experience, that the Nonconformist Preachers are the
"authors and fomenters of this pestilent faction, and the
"implacable enemies of the established Government, and
"to whom the execrable treasons which have had such
"dismal effects in this Kingdom are principally to be imputed,
"and who, by their present obstinate refusing to take and
"subscribe an Oath and Declaration that they do not hold
"it lawful to take up Arms against the King, and that they
"will not endeavour any alteration of Government either in
"Church or State, do necessarily enforce us to conclude
"that they are still ready to engage themselves (if not
"actually engaged) in some rebellious conspiracy against
"the King and to invade and subvert his Government—
"Wherefore we resolve in every parish of this County to
"leave strict Warrants in the hands of all Constables for the
"seizing of such persons. And as an encouragement to all
"officers and others that shall be instrumental in the appre-
"hending of any of them so as they may be brought for

"justice, we will give and allow forty shillings as a reward
"for every Nonconformist Preacher that shall be so secured.
"And we resolve to prosecute them and all other such
"Dangerous Enemies to the Government, and Common
"Absenters from Church and frequenters of Conventicles,
"according to the directions of a law made in the five-and-
"thirtieth year of the reign of Queen Elizabeth, entitled an
"Act for the Keeping her Majesty's Subjects in due Obe-
"dience.

"*Lastly*. That we may never forget the infinite mercies
"of Almighty God in the late wonderful deliverance of our
"gracious King and his Dearest Brother and all his Loyal
"Subjects (who were designed for a Massacre) from the
"horrid conspiracy of the *Phanatiques* and their Accomplices,
"and that we may perpetuate as well our own thankfulness
"as their Infamy, that the Generations to come may know
"their treachery and avoid and never trust men of such
"principles more, and also that we ourselves may perform
"our public Duty to Almighty God before we enter upon
"the Public Service of our Country—We order, resolve, and
"agree, with the advice and concurrence of the Right
"Reverend Father in God our much-honoured and worthy
"Lord Bishop, to give and bestow for the beautifying of the
"Chapel in the Castle of Exon, and for the erecting of
"decent Seats there, Ten Pounds; and we will likewise give
"and continue Six Pounds to be paid yearly to anyone of
"the Church of Exon whom the said Lord Bishop shall
"appoint to read the Divine Service with the prayers lately
"appointed for the day of thanksgiving on the ninth of
"September last, and to preach a Sermon exhorting to
"obedience in the said Chapel on the first day of every
"general quarter sessions of the Peace held in the said

"Castle, to begin precisely at eight of the clock in the "morning.

"And may the mercies of Heaven (which are infinite) "always protect our religious and gracious King, his Dearest "Brother, and every branch of that Royal Family, and may "all the treasonable Conspiracies of those rebellious Schis- "maticks be always thus happily prevented."

It was scarcely complimentary to the Nonconformist preachers to offer as little as forty shillings a head for their apprehension. But surely it was not much more flattering to Church and King to vote ten pounds as a thank-offering to the former for the preservation of the latter, and at the same time to devote the said thank-offering to providing comfortable pews for the justices at the chapel in the Castle, which pews were also to serve as a perpetual monument of the infamy of the Dissenters. Nor were the justices disposed to rush into excessive extravagance when they allotted 6*l.* for four services and sermons on the duty of obedience. They made the most of this grant, and at each Sessions formally voted a sum of 30*s.* to one of the prebendaries "for his excellent and *apposite* sermon preached this day at the Chappell in the Castle of Exon."

If the Dissenters thought they were going to escape punishment by coming to church and squatting when they ought to have knelt, and sitting down when they ought to have stood, they were very much mistaken. The justices had their eyes on them, and were determined to make them "serve God in the beauty of holiness." If they brought a horse to the water, they were resolved to make him drink.

Macaulay tells us that great numbers of persons who had been accustomed to frequent conventicles repaired to the parish churches; but "it was remarked that the schismatics who had been terrified into this show of conformity might easily be distinguished by the difficulty which they had in finding out the collect, and by the awkward manner in which they bowed at the name of Jesus." This statement is well illustrated by the following order:—

"The good effects which our former orders and resolutions
"have had, enforcing the Laws against Dissenters and
"suppressing factions in this County, doth encourage us to
"proceed till we have made, if it be possible, a thorough
"reformation according to the established Laws, and
"reduced all our Dissenters to a perfect conformity. And
"because we have received frequent Informations, as well
"from the respective Ministers as from the Churchwardens
"and Constables of the several parishes within this County,
"and also by our own observation, that although almost all
"our Sectaries do now resort to their parish churches, yet,
"as it appears by their rude and disorderly behaviour here,
"it is no kind of their duty, but only to save their money
"and avoid the penalty of the law, they behaving them-
"selves with all imaginable irreverence and ill demeanour
"in time of Divine Service, contemning at once both
"the laws of God and man, and giving just offence to all
"devout Christians, and intimating by their rude Carriage
"that though they be enforced to come to church yet they
"scorn to communicate with us in our solemn offices of
"religion—We do therefore, by the advice and with the
"concurrence of the Right Reverend Father in God our
"much-honoured and worthy Lord Bishop, order and
"resolve in every division of this County strictly to require
"all Constables and Churchwardens carefully to present
"unto us at our monthly meeting all such as do not kneel

"at the prayers of the Church, stand up at the repeating
"of the Creed and in giving glory to the Blessed Trinity
"and at other hymns of the Church, and observe all other
"decent ceremonies as they are enjoined by the Rubric,
"which is allowed and confirmed by several statutes. And
"because we are afraid that some may offend through
"ignorance, not knowing their duty, we do therefore desire
"the Lord Bishop of this Diocese to admonish the
"respective ministers of every parish to instruct their
"parishioners either in their sermons or in catechising to
"understand the directions and orders of the Church, by
"which means in a short time we hope they will come to a
"sense of their duty, and we shall all of us with one accord
"serve God in the beauty of holiness."

This violent enforcement of conformity goes far towards explaining the cause of the enthusiasm with which the middle and lower classes of the West of England greeted the arrival of Monmouth in 1685, and of William of Orange in 1688.

Incumbents of parishes were required from the beginning of the reign to come into Court and take an oath of passive obedience. The form is given in the cases of the Rector of Denbury and the Rector of Woodley:—

"I, Richard Bickle, and I, Richard Binmore, doe sweare
"that it is not lawfull upon any pretence whatsoever to
"take armes against the Kinge, and that I doe abhorre
"that traiterous position of taking armes by his authority
"against his person or against those that are commis-
"sionated by him in pursuance of such commissions, and
"that I will not any time endeavour any alteracon of
"government either in Church or State."

Richard Saunders, clerk, formerly beneficed, "and being

lately taken preaching in the corporation of Tiverton," and refusing to take the oath, was sent to prison for six months.

Richard Sparke, clerk, "for depriving (depraving?) the Booke of Common Praire," was fined 100 marks, and 2*l*. for an assault.

Even the County Treasurer, a gentleman who had for many years done good service to the shire, and had been repeatedly complimented by the Court, and presented with sums of money in token of their approbation, was by no means safe from an accusation of nonconformity. At Michaelmas, 1682, it appears that the Duke of Albemarle recommended John Hutchingson, Esq., for the office of Treasurer in the room and place of Mr. Henry Fitzwilliams, who was "charged for nonconformity and other neglects." But a *locus pœnitentiæ* was left, and it was ordered that if Mr. Fitzwilliams did receive the Sacrament before the next Sessions at his own parish church, and did also prove that he had received it within twelve months before the present Sessions, he might be continued in his office, " but otherwise to be discontinued." This notice seems to have been disregarded, and at Epiphany in the following year a more formal and elaborate warning was recorded :—

"Informations being given unto this Court that Mr. "Henry Fitzwilliams, Treasurer of the Stock of this County, "hath heretofore and of late neglected to yield due "obedience to the Laws and Statutes of this Kingdom in "Causes Ecclesiastical—This Court doth think fit and "order that if the said Mr. Henry Fitzwilliams shall not at "the next General Sessions of the peace for this County "prove his due and full conformity to the Laws and "Statutes of this Realm by frequenting the ordinances of "the Church by being usually present at the beginning of "the Divine Service, and demeaning himself there as the "Law directs, at his own Parish Church, and receiving "the holy Sacrament, That then the said Mr. Henry Fitz-"williams do attend this Court at the said next Sessions "with a full account of his receipts and disbursements, to "the end the same may be adjusted, and *a more conformable* "*person* placed in his room."

This order seems to have had its effect, for Mr. Fitzwilliams retained his office until his death in 1689.

QUARTER SESSIONS UNDER CHARLES II.

PART II.

I MENTIONED in a former paper that the entries in the Sessions Books characteristic of the reign of Charles II. relate to the persecution of Nonconformists and to the hearth-money or chimney-tax. With the former subject we have already dealt at some length. The latter will not require any long notice, although it occupies in the records a far larger space than the former.

It was in 1662 that a tax of two shillings a year was ordered to be levied on every chimney in the country, "as a constant revenue for ever to the Crowne." About three months afterwards Mr. Pepys noted in his diary, "much clamour against the chimney-money, and the people say they will not pay it without force."

It is often difficult for a statesman to foresee what kind of tax will be most disagreeable to the public, and this is a very strong argument against attempting to impose any burden of a nature to which people are unaccustomed. A tax which is borne with tolerable cheerfulness by one nation may be peculiarly hateful to another. In France people submit to a tax on furniture, but are indignant at the very idea of an income tax. In England we bear an income tax, but will not stand a tax upon matches. In America a tax upon matches is paid by the descendants of the men who immortalized themselves by rebelling against a duty upon tea.

Of all the many taxes which have been imposed on this country, not even excepting the window tax, there has perhaps never been one more unpopular than the hearth-money. Nor was this unpopularity without good reason. Macaulay, writing of it a hundred and sixty years after its repeal, uses language almost as strong as that which he might have employed in attacking an existing grievance from the Opposition benches:—

"The discontent excited by direct imposts is almost "always out of proportion to the quantity of money which "they bring into the exchequer; and the tax on chimneys "was, even among direct imposts, peculiarly odious; for it "could be levied only by means of domiciliary visits; and "of such visits the English have always been impatient to "a degree which the people of other countries can but "faintly conceive. The poorer householders were frequently "unable to pay their hearth-money to the day. When this "happened, their furniture was distrained without mercy: "for the tax was farmed; and a farmer of taxes is, of all "creditors, proverbially the most rapacious. The collectors "were loudly accused of performing their unpopular duty "with harshness and insolence. It was said that, as soon "as they appeared at the threshold of a cottage, the chil- "dren began to wail, and the old women ran to hide their "earthenware. Nay, the single bed of a poor family had "sometimes been carried away and sold. The net annual "receipt from this tax was two hundred thousand pounds."

We now turn to the proceedings relating to this impost

in Devonshire. It appears that at first the constables had to make returns to Quarter Sessions of every chimney (which they always spelt *chimley*) in their parishes. At Midsummer, 1662, complaint was made to the Court by divers petty constables that they were "soe straitned in tyme as they could not make soe exact and due retorne of the fire-hearthes and stoves within this county as by the Act of Parliament was required." They therefore besought the Court "for a further daie for the doeinge of the same, and that they might receave some further instructions from this Courte for their proceedings herrein."

The Court consented to adjourn the Sessions until August 26, in order to receive the returns, and in the mean time ordered the unfortunate constable to observe certain "direccons," under penalties which must have been rather alarming.

In the first place, they had to require every inhabitant in their respective parishes to give in "a perfect list of all his fire-hearthes and stoves under his hand which are in his possession."

Secondly, they had to "informe themselves by their owne viewe of the truth and certenty herrein." In case of failure they were to forfeit 5$l.$ for every week's neglect, and in case of a false return they were to forfeit 40$s.$ for every hearth or stove "soe falsely returned or omitted."

Thirdly, persons who by reason of poverty were excused payment of poor-rates were to be exempt from payment of the hearth-money. Other persons claiming exemption were to obtain a certificate under the hands of the church-wardens and overseers, or one of them together with the minister, "and the same to be allowed by the two next justices."

Fourthly, the petty constables were to make their returns to the chief constable of the hundred, and he was to return them to the adjourned sessions. "And that the hearth of each chimney wherein is any oven, dry kilne, or furnace, be onely and singly charged."

The Justices felt it their duty to make these stringent orders, but symptoms may be observed showing that they had no great love for the tax. They had before them one of the ladies spoken of in the old ballad :—

> There is not one old dame in ten, and search the nation through,
> But, if you talk of chimney-men, will spare a curse or two.

Elizabeth Codner, being convicted "for assaultinge of the collector of His Mat's revenue of hearth-money," was committed *for one day*, "and discharged afterwards." This sentence can hardly have been encouraging to the prosecutor, and we do not hear of many such cases being brought to the sessions, nor of further orders to the constables. There are, however, many cases of assault in which the circumstances are not mentioned.

It seems that the powers of distraint were exercised directly by the collectors and their agents. But the Justices in Quarter Sessions retained the power of excusing or reducing the tax in cases in which it was certified by the minister and churchwardens or overseers that the number of chimneys belonging to any person had been reduced. As time went on, these applications became more and more frequent, and the entries relating to them take up a very considerable part of the books in the latter part of the reign. The tax may have had a good effect in one way, for the general "demolition of fire-hearths" which seems to have taken place must have checked the wasteful consumption of fuel for which our country is still remarkable. The tax was so unpopular that persons to whom a few shillings more or less can hardly have been of much importance demolished some of their chimneys and applied for a reduction, as people used to take steps to avoid the unpopular burden of the window-tax, and as they now sometimes try to avoid the scarcely less unpopular turnpike-toll.

Humphry Gilbert, Esq., of Compton, the representative of the family so famous in the days of Elizabeth, "having formerly twenty chimleys and fire-hearthes in his house at Greenway," proved that "tenne of them are since totally demolished," and was discharged from the payment of hearth-money for the said ten fire-hearths.

Sir William Morrice, Secretary of State, demolished seven fire-hearths in his house called Mount Wise at Stoke Damerel, near Plymouth.

Sir William Courtenay had ten fire-hearths in Ilson or Ilton Castle, and demolished six of them. (In the following sessions it appears that he demolished eleven out of thirteen in the same place.)

Sir Walter Yonge, Bart., "had formerly in his Capitall Mancon howse of Mohun's Ottery fourteene Chimneyes," but he demolished four of them and was discharged from paying for them.

Pepys tells us that it was at one time proposed in Parliament that people should be permitted to buy off the chimney-money at eight years' purchase. The King refused to part with it, and Sir W. Coventry told the Duke of York "that whoever did advise the King to that did as much as in them lay cut the King's throat, and did wholly betray him."

The truth of this was seen at the Revolution. The

hearth-tax was especially associated with the restoration of the Stuarts, and passed away at their final expulsion. In 1689 it disappears completely from our records of sessions. We turn to Macaulay for an explanation, and we find that as soon as William of Orange landed at Torbay, and along his whole line of march to London, he was importuned by the common people to relieve them from the intolerable burden of the hearth-money. He was so much impressed by the public opinion of this grievance, that he introduced the subject at one of the earliest sittings of the Privy Council. He sent a message respecting it to the House of Commons, and the tenth Act of the first year of William and Mary declared the chimney-tax to be a badge of slavery, and abolished it for ever.

The government of Charles II. was probably the most prodigal and reckless, in proportion to its resources, that ever existed in Europe, until the Turks discovered that they had almost unlimited powers of borrowing from Christians. It is scarcely possible even now to read without shame and indignation how English soldiers and sailors were left to starve, or to desert to the Dutch, while the money freely voted by Parliament for their maintenance was devoted to the profligate extravagance of Lady Castlemaine and Barbara Palmer. We might have expected that the county finances would have been administered as carelessly as those under the control of the "Merry Monarch." This, however, was by no means the case. Economy, with many other more important virtues, when expelled from the court, took refuge in the country. The contrast resembles that noticed by Mr. Pepys, when he left for a day or two the wigs, and wickedness, and wantonness of Whitehall, and saw upon the Downs what he calls "the most pleasant and innocent sight that ever I saw in my life;—a flock of sheep, a shepherd, and his little boy reading, far from any houses or sight of people, the Bible to him."

It would appear that the expenditure of the county of Devon at this time was most frugal, not to say parsimonious. We have already seen that the pensions granted to the " maimed soldiers " were very scanty, and that the cost of their maintenance seems to have been gradually shifted from the county on to the parishes. We have also seen that when the justices voted a thank-offering for the escape of the King and the Duke of York from the Rye House Plot, the amount of their offering was no more than ten pounds, and even that was appropriated to erecting seats in their own chapel. A similar policy seems to have prevailed during the whole reign. One of the first orders made after the restoration was that all treasurers and constables who had held office since March 25, 1642, were to account to the Court for their receipts. This order, no doubt, served a double purpose, as saving the imposition of new rates, and also as affording a convenient way of inflicting penalties on the unfortunate members of the Roundhead party. The accounts, as we may imagine, were found to be in considerable confusion, and constant orders were made upon the subject.

All arrears of rates between 1642 and 1660 were enforced as far as possible. It is mentioned that the Judges had decided that these arrears had not been pardoned by the Act of Indemnity. Mr. Henry Fitzwilliams, who had been Deputy Clerk of the Peace in 1658, was appointed Deputy Treasurer (the treasurers being justices, who were generally changed every year), and was allowed 2s. in the pound on

all arrears that he succeeded in collecting. In 1663 he
reported that he had collected 967*l.* 6*s.* 11*d.*, and that
there remained about 2100*l.* unpaid. Afterwards we find
that he was allowed 2*s.* 6*d.* in the pound for all arrears that
he should collect. He had only " 20*l.* standing sallery for
auditing and taking all the publique accompts of the
county." By 1666 we find that he had collected altogether
1433*l.* 9*s.* 1*d.* for arrears.

We find a summary of the treasurer's accounts entered
pretty regularly in the books during this reign, which had
never been done before. In 1667 the total rates imposed
on the county were :—

	£	s.	d.
" For the Gaol	164	14	10
" For the Hospitals	167	14	4
" For the Maimed Soldiers	565	8	0

It may not be of much general interest to dwell on the
subject of county accounts, but our prison reformers may
contemplate with admiring despair the "utilization of
prison labour" during the reign of Charles II. The work
on which the prisoners were employed was, no doubt,
weaving, the staple manufacture of the West of England at
that time and long afterwards. Justices committing any
person to gaol were " to express under the *mittimus* whether
such person be of ability to maintain himself, or else to
receive relief from the county." The allowance from the
county, which was seldom granted, did not exceed three
half-pence a day. The court was so liberal as to vote
twopence a day for some Dutch prisoners of war.

Prisoners confined in the workhouse or Bridewell at St.
Thomas were not only to maintain themselves by their

work, but also their wives and children; and the governor was ordered to detain part of their wages for this purpose. Perhaps one of these orders may be worth quoting at length, in the hope of a good time coming when similar orders may be possible:—

" Whereas this Courte is informed that some persons who
" have wives and children, & formerly have been sent to y^e
" house of correccon or workehowse at St. Thomas Appos-
" tle's, who are able to gett whilest they are there more
" than sufficient for their owne releife & maintenance, yet
" spend & consume all their gettings & send none to y^e
" reliefe of their families: The Governor of the said howse
" is therefore hereby ordered not to give nor allow unto
" such persons (as have a charge to maintaine) out of their
" worke more than in his discretion shall be thought fitt
" for their owne releife and maintenance whiles they are in
" ye said howse, and for what any person can gett over and
" above it is to be paid towards ye reliefe of ye wives and
" children of such persons as have any."

They had an opportunity of "consuming their gettings," as beer was sold in the gaol, "but not above twelve shillings to the hogshead."

A chaplain was provided by allowing Mr. Reynolds, the minister of the parish, 30*l.* a year for officiating at the House of Correction. The Governor had 60*l.* a year, and must have been well worth it. The charge on the county for this purpose went on diminishing. (In our time no charges ever diminish.) In 1675 the rate for the gaol, which was 164*l.* 14*s.* 10*d.*, was reduced to one-half. In the next year it was again reduced one-half, so that the whole rate was only 41*l.* 3*s.* 8½*d.*, "and no more," as the Clerk of the Peace exultingly adds. It was at this time that Sir John Maynard's gift came in aid of the rates. In 1678 the actual cost of the gaol was only 27*l*. 8*s*. 5*d*.,—less than the cost of a single prisoner two hundred years afterwards—a result which may well be commended to the notice of the Social Science Association.

Six prisoners, in gaol for want of sureties for good behaviour, were allowed to visit their families from Monday to Saturday. It may be hoped that their offence was not wife-beating.

Debtors were kept in a separate prison—"the Sheriff's Ward." In 1682 the Justices, in a fit of liberality, appointed Master George Smith "curate of the Sheriff's Ward, at a salary of four pounds a year." But this was too good to last, and the order was rescinded next year.

In 1671 there was a new Act "for releife and release of poore distressed prisoners for debt." The Justices were empowered to act as Bankruptcy Commissioners; and, after examining a number of debtors and their creditors, ordered "that the foresaid severall and respective prisoners shall be forthwith discharged and sett at liberty according to the directions of the said Act (if ymprisoned for the causes aforesaid and noe other) without paying anything for ffee or Chamber Rent."

In the case of John ffawkener three of his creditors declared themselves not satisfied, and desired that he should remain in prison. They were thereupon ordered to pay the sum of one shilling weekly towards his maintenance, "for soe longe time as they shall desire hee may soe remaine in prison, and for default thereof the said John ffawkener is to bee sett at liberty." No more than 6*s*. 8*d*. was allowed for the burial of each prisoner who died in gaol.

The Justices saw no use in keeping a man who was going to be hanged. They resolved that "condemned persons were a great and constant charge to the county," and directed Thomas Carew, Esq. (*Judge of the Sessions*), "to move the Judges at the next Assizes how the county may be eased of this burthen." Symon Kent, the hangman, was committed for contempt of court in not performing his duty.

One head of county expenditure, familiar enough under James I. and Charles I., but which disappeared when Cromwell was dictator and Blake was his admiral, reappears with the restoration of the Stuarts. This was the charge for liberating English subjects from "Turkish captivity." It was not to be expected that a Government which could not keep the Dutch fleet out of the Thames could protect its subjects from the attacks of the Barbary corsairs. Some attempts were made, both by diplomacy and by naval expeditions, with ill-success in both cases. Mr. Pepys records the information he received from Captain Mootham and Mr. Dawes, who had both been slaves at Algiers, of the manner of life of the Christian captives, how they were allowed nothing but bread and water; and, at their redemption, were forced to pay for the water they drank at the public fountains during their time of slavery :—

"How they are beat upon the soles of their feet, and
"bellies, at the liberty of their *padron*. How they are all
"at night called into their master's *Bagnard*, and there they
"lie. How some rogues do live well, if they do invent to
"bring their masters in so much a week by their industry
"or theft; and then they are put to no other work at all.
"And theft there is counted no great crime at all."

The Devonshire Sessions books abound in entries respecting these cases. But, true to their economical practice, the Justices no longer took the initiative, or subscribed largely towards making up the ransom required. Fifty shillings was the usual grant, and it was only in special cases that the Court went so far as to vote five pounds. Here is the order of Michaelmas, 1673:—

"This Courte taking into consideracion the great misery
"and slavery that many poore English Christians suffer
"under the cruell tyranny of the Turkes, being there kepte
"captives, and that it will be a greate peice of Charity to
"extend their compassion towards their Redemption : It is
"therefore ordered that all such as are captives in Algier
"who presented their petitions to this Courte att last Sessions, and all such others as shall present their petitions
"unto this Courte att this Sessions, that are captives in Algier
"shall have fforty shillings a peece given them out of the
"County Stocke towards their Redempcon. And all others
"that are prisoners in *Tituan* or other places in Turky
"who presented their petitions att the last Sessions or shall
"present their petitions to this Courte att this Sessions
"shall have ffive pounds a pcece given them out of the
"County Stocke towards their Redempcon out of Slavery as
"aforesaid. And this Courte doth desire Sʳ Thomas Carew,
"Knight, to take care the money be not parted with but
"upon certainty of their Redempcon, or if it be parted with
"before they be redeemed, that then the money be repayed
"againe for such as shall not be redeemed, within one yeare
"after."

This order is accompanied by a list of the names of the captives. Seven were in *Salley*, four in *Tituan*, and two in *Algier*.

At the next sessions the Court voted five pounds a-piece for two captives at *ffez*, one at *Sally*, and one in *Tituana*, "upon satisfaccon given to S⁺ Thomas Carew, Knt., that there is course taken for their redempcon."

On another occasion we have a list of ten captives in *Sally*, and one in *Tituan*, who had 5*l*. a-piece; and one at *Algiere*, who had 40*s*. It is mentioned that the ransom of one captive cost 58*l*. 10*s*.

The economical management of the county finances may, I suppose, be attributed in great measure to Sir Thomas Carew of Barley, who was "Judge of the Sessions" during a great part of the reign, and Member for Exeter in 1681. Mr. John Northcote was Clerk of the Peace at first, and was succeeded by Mr. Hugh Vaughan.[1]

It is satisfactory to observe that our countrymen do not appear to have avenged the "Turkish Atrocities" on the Mohammedans that fell into their hands. The epithet applied to them is exactly the reverse of that appropriated in our days to their compatriots in Bulgaria:—

"Whereas it appeareth unto this Courte that there is now "*one naturall turke and fower moores* in the workehouse of "this County, sent thither by the Major of Dartmouth, being "taken upp on the Sea neere the Coasts of Barbary: This "Courte doth thinke fitt and order in pursuance of his "Matie⁺ pleasure, signified by one of the Lords of his "Matie⁺ most honourable privy Councell, That the said five "persons be forthwith returned att Dartmouth aforesaid, "there to have reasonable accomodation as well as

---

[1] The office was in the gift of the Lord-Lieutenant, the Duke of Albemarle, who, as George Monk, had been Sir John Northcote's colleague in the representation of Devonshire in 1660. Mr. John Northcote was probably a son or nephew of the Baronet.

"Security, and where they may be putt to reasonable labour for gaining something towards their better Subsistance, and suffered to straggle abroad untill the first opportunity of any vessell bound from those westerne partes for Tangier or the mediterranean, and then the said five men are to be putt on board of it, and landed upon the Barbary coasts in any place neere their own country, his Matie being further pleased to signifie as aforesaid that his Matie being att amity both with the Emperor of Morocco and with the Governments of Argeir, Tunis, and Tripoli, its his Matie's pleasure to have them used friendly without any hardshipp."

Other foreign personages besides "turkes" and "moores" occasionally appear on the scene. Three "ffrenchmen" were treated with much consideration. A committee was appointed to inquire "how longe they were kept at Topesham to Charity Tomling's there," and to order Mr. Fitzwilliams to pay her "after the rate of six shillings a weeke at seaven dayes to the week for each of the said ffrenchmen for the time they soe remained there for their meate, drinke, and lodginge."

Moses Aberdena, "formerly a professed Jew," had since his coming into the county been "converted to the Christian faith and growne very poore and necessitous." The Court kindly voted him "the sume of fforty shillings towards his present reliefe and more comfortable subsistance."

A still more mysterious individual appears on another occasion, and induced the Justices to combine their charity with a taste for Biblical archæology. The treasurer was ordered to pay 5*l.* to Mr. John Reynolds, minister of St. Thomas the Apostle, "for the use of *Kas Isa,* a Caldean minister, who lately lived in *Mosul*, a greate citty neer the place where old *Nynivee* stood, whose wife and children are taken into captivity in Turkey." And the said 5*l*. were to be remitted to Mr. Thomas Hyde, "Publique Library Keeper in Oxford," according to the desire of the said Kas Isa. The Justices would evidently have appreciated Mr. Layard. Their treatment of a Chaldæan minister is in strong contrast to that applied to Nonconformists.

It is not often that a county excites in its children those feelings of patriotism which so often induce people to bestow endowments on their town or parish. The county of Devon, however, has an endowment of about 186*l*. a year, arising principally from certain fee farm rents, the origin of which had been completely forgotten, but is entered at length in these records. It seems to deserve mention, as being connected with a man of considerable eminence. Sir John Maynard, Serjeant-at-law, who was a leading lawyer and member of Parliament during more than half of the seventeenth century, who prosecuted Strafford in 1641, and was a Commissioner of the Great Seal under William III., offered in 1665 to present the county with a thousand pounds, on condition that the Justices should meet it with a similar sum, and that the whole 2000*l*. should then be devoted to some public purpose for the benefit of the county. It was resolved that the sum should be laid out in lands for the maintenance of the workhouse at St. Thomas. After long delay, caused, as it would seem, by the difficulty of finding a suitable investment, this "noble worke of charity for the publique good of the county" was duly accomplished. The general Act of Parliament, 19 Charles II., c. 4, "for relief of poor prisoners, and setting them on work," is more than half occupied by regulations respecting this sum of 2000*l*., and other rules for the conduct of the gaol and workhouse for the county of Devon, which seems to have been held up as an example for other counties. The fee farm rents of the Manor of Dunkeswell, amounting to 54*l*. 4*s*. 4*d*., were bought of Peter Prideaux, Esq., in 1672, for 850*l*., or rather less than sixteen years' purchase. The bill of the attorney employed, Mr. Daniel Vinecombe, is given at length. "For his own paines and labour" he charged 6*l*. His disbursements amounted to 6*l*. 15*s*. 6*d*., besides 2*l*. 10*s*. for engrossing the deeds. He had to pay 1*l*. 1*s*. 6*d*. for a "Guiney" in gold to give to Sir William Jones for advising on the conveyance. It seems there was no duty on deeds payable to the Government at this time.

In 1674 fee farm rents, amounting to 108*l*. 4*s*. annually, and issuing out of various parishes in Devon, were purchased of Thomas Greene, of Throgmorton Street, London. The amount of the purchase-money is not mentioned, but it must have amounted to about 16 or 18 years' purchase, and the Justices must have provided more than the 2000*l*. It is recorded that Edward Yard, Esq., of Churston, wished to purchase the rent of 4*l*. 13*s*. 8*d*. out of the parish of Dean Prior at the same rate as that for which the county had contracted. The Court agreed to let him have it at 18 years' purchase. Perhaps he thought this too much. At any rate, the sale was not effected, and it is a good example of the permanence of English institutions that Lord Churston, the present representative of Mr. Yard, pays to the county at this day the annual rent of 4*l*. 13*s*. 8*d*. for the manor and rectory of Dean Prior, the living once held by the poet Herrick. The other rents paid in the year 1876 are also identical with those of 1676.

Mr. Daniel Vinecombe's bill of charges for this purchase amounted to 21*l*. 8*s*. 4*d*., and the Justices were so pleased that they voted him a gratuity of 20*l*. "for his extraordinary paines, care, and charges" in effecting the said purchase.

It is curious that so eminent a man as Sir John Maynard is not included in Prince's "Worthies of Devon." He was born at Tavistock in 1602. For anything that appears in the county records, the gift of 1000*l*. came from his own pocket. But this was not really the case. It came from the estate of Elize or Eliseus Hele, who left a very large property for "pious and charitable uses." Sir J. Maynard was one of his trustees, and founded schools and other charities at Exeter, Plymouth, and other places.

The difficulty of "supplying and furnishing His Majesty's fleets with able and sufficient mariners and seamen," which most deservedly perplexed Mr. Pepys and his colleagues, gave rise to a conscription not less rigorous than that of Germany. A letter was received by the Justices at the beginning of 1672, requiring them to direct all headboroughs, constables, tithing-men, and other officers within the county, to make exact lists of the names "of all such seamen as inhabit within their respective parishes and precincts, together with an account of their several ages." One copy of these lists was to be transmitted to the Lords of the Council, and a duplicate to the Vice-Admiral of the county or his deputy. And this process was to be repeated every year at the next Quarter Sessions after Easter. The letter bears the signatures of Craven, Bath, Ossory, Arlington, G. Cartaret, J. Duncombe, J. Bridgwater, Newport, Trevor, Thomas Chicheley, and Edward Walker. It is dated January 10, 1671-2, which is the first instance

I have found in these volumes of uncertainty as to the commencement of the year.

On one occasion we find that three men found wandering without a "let-passe" were to be "sent to the fleet to serve His Majesty."

There are other letters respecting the supply of seamen in the following year, written by the Lords of the Council to the Earl of Bath, *Custos Rotulorum*, by the Earl of Bath to Sir Thomas Carew, "Judge of the Sessions," and by Sir Thomas Carew to the Justices who were not present when the subject was brought before the Court.

How the business of pressing mariners for the fleet was carried on in the time of "the Merry Monarch" may be learnt from many parts of the journal of the excellent Clerk of the Acts, whose heart, to say the truth, was scarcely so hard as the organ that might have been expected to beat in the bosom of an official of that period. His pity, however, seems to have been mingled with his usual appreciation of a dramatic situation :—

"To the Tower several times, about the business of the
"pressed men, and late at it till twelve at night shipping
"of them. But, Lord! how some poor women did cry;
"and in my life I never did see such natural expression of
"passion as I did here in some women's bewailing them-
"selves, and running to every parcel of men that were
"brought, one after another, to look for their husbands, and
"wept over every vessel that went off, thinking they might
"be there, and looking after the ship as far as ever they
"could by moonlight, that it grieved me to the heart to
"hear them. Besides, to see poor patient labouring men
"and housekeepers leaving poor wives and families, taken
"up on a sudden by strangers, was very hard, and that

"without press-money, but forced against all law to be "gone. It is a great tyranny."

In another place Pepys describes men being pressed who were "wholly unfit for sea, and many of them people of very good fashion, which is a shame to think of." Even men employed in victualling ships for the fleet, and in the boats of the Admiralty and Ordnance Offices, were pressed, "so that for want of discipline in this respect I do fear all will be undone."

The only notice of the Great Plague occurs by way of precaution. At Easter, 1666, the chairman was directed to write to Sir Hugh Pollard, Baronet, Controller of his Majesty's Household, and Sir William Morice, Knight, Principal Secretary of State (both Devonshire M.P.s), "to acquaint them of the danger that threatens us by reason of the dispersion of the pestilence, which, should it break out in any parts of this county, our numerous poor people who are already too much inclinable to disorder by reason of the decay of trade, upon which their subsistence so much depends, we fear will run into greater confusions." The Justices, therefore, desire to have some instructions from the Privy Council "what course wee shall take upon such an occasion, which wee the rather desire because some doubte hath beene made of the validity of the lawes in that behalfe."

A reminiscence of the siege of Lyme appears in 1661, in an order that a certificate should be sent to the Right Hon. Edward Earl of Clarendon, Lord Chancellor of England, "of the great ruine of the town of Axminster by the armies in the late unhappy warrs."

Transportation now appears for the first time as a definite sentence. The usual course had been to enter in the book that a certain person had been convicted of felony, but judgment was respited on his consent to be transported.

Witchcraft, of course, was believed in, not only by the Bench, the jury, and the witnesses, but by the unfortunate culprit herself. The Court was informed that John Jermin, late of Woodbury, "lay languishing for the space of half a yeare and then dyed," and that Agnes Ryder of the same parish had confessed that she had bewitched him to death. A warrant was issued against the said Ryder, but the result does not appear, as she was probably committed to the assizes. In 1682 three witches were sentenced to death at Exeter. In the same year we find a breaking-up of a gipsy family bearing the famous name of Stanley. Three of the men were convicted of being dangerous rogues, and sentenced to transportation, and a woman was whipped and sent to her birthplace in Lincolnshire.

An extinct word may be noticed in the commitment of Robert Coad, who was convicted of "being a night-walker, and pilfering and *strubbing* in the night-time."[1]

The dawn of modern times appears in the New Highway Act of 1671, which was probably as great a plague to the country gentlemen of the period as its modern anti-type. The orders about the preservation of fish, too, are very similar to those issued in the reign of Mr. Frank Buckland. Even a "Conservator" was appointed for the rivers Exe, Bathon, and Barle, to look after the offenders who "doe keepe netts of less meash than two inches and halfe from

---

[1] A writer in the *Examiner*, noticing this passage, asserted that *strubbing* is merely a local way of pronouncing the word *disturbing*. Mr. Pengelly says (*Notes and Queries*, July, 1870) that the word was common in East Cornwall thirty years ago, and signified *stripping* or robbing, e.g. "To *strub* a bird's nest." It is still used in some places.

knot to knot, and therewith take and destroy the spawne and fry of fish, and *Towts* of lesse than eight inches in lengeth." He was also to "inform the names of all such persons as have any such hutches or engines at theire milltailes, and also to open, enlarge, and widen, alter, or destroy such straite and unlawfull weares and hutches, and in all things to do and act as a conservator of the said rivers."

Not so modern are the entries respecting servants. Evidence was given before the Court that Aaron Nightingale did, in the year 1655, with the consent of his friends, make a covenant with John Trankmore, of Topsham, to serve the said Trankmore for 40*s*. per annum and diet *for twenty years*, "if Mr. Trankmore would entertaine him soe longe att such a rate!" And in 1684 the Court took measures for "reforming the irregularities and illegal practices used in receiving, keeping, and putting away Servants," and for providing "that noe person may henceforth receive and entertain any Servant without a Testimoniall as the Law directs, and that the order of this Courte in pursuance of the Act of Parliament for assessing wages may be henceforth the better observed."

Very far, too, from modern ideas is the petition of certain inhabitants of St. Sidwell's, Exeter, in 1667, recommending an accused person to severity. They humbly beg that Peter Crosse, now a prisoner, may be transported, as he is "a terror to the City and Country, having committed many outragious Crimes, and is a Cheiffe Actor of mischeivious Actions." "And itt may please God this to be the meanes to save him from hanginge, which undoubtedly will attend him withoutt some wise prevention."

Since writing the previous part of this paper, I have been

favoured with a sight of the records of the county of Bucks, which commence in the year 1678. They are, of course, somewhat similar to those of Devon, but are not without some points of difference. The first three or four years show an active Protestant, if not Puritan, spirit among the authorities as well as the common people, as might be expected in the county of Hampden and Fleetwood. Some "conventiclers" and sectaries were of course indicted, as the law required, but the greatest severity was reserved for *Papales Recusantes*, Popish recusants, or, more briefly, *Po. Rec.* At Epiphany, 1678, 55 persons were indicted for this offence, and proclamation made that, if they did not "render their bodyes" to the Sheriff before the next sessions, they would be convicted as Popish recusants, and special process ordered to go out against them. Persons of good family, such as Sir John and Lady Fortescue, Sir Robert Throckmorton, and others, were indicted in a similar manner.

But about 1682 special attention was directed to Protestant "absenters from church." Many scores of such were indicted. An order was made that no constable was to be appointed without inquiry "whoe is ye most fittest person for that office, and particularly of his conformity to the Church." Another order directed all churchwardens, overseers, constables, and other officers, "to diligently inquire, observe, and take notice of all conventicles," and to present the names of all persons attending them. This order was to be read in every church once a quarter.

The Clerk of the Peace was directed to wait upon the Right Rev. Father in God, Thomas, Lord Bishop of Lincoln, "to intreat his Lordship's favour from this Court," that he might give positive directions to his subordinate officers, "that they for the future take special care there be good churchwardens in every parish in this county, that are good Churchmen and well affected to the Government."

At Midsummer, 1683, after the Rye House Plot, the Court ordered that an address be made to his Majesty from the Justices of the Peace, "to show their sincere joy for the preservation of his sacred person from a most wicked and horrid conspiracy against the precious lives of his Majesty and his royal brother James Duke of York, and to show their detestation and abhorrence to all plots, conspiracys, and associations whatsoever against his Majesty or his government, either in Church or State."

It was also ordered "that noe person or persons whatsoever but what are Loyall and well affected to the Government be lycensed to sell Ale, Beer, &c."

Many more persons were indicted and fined for attending conventicles; and the gaoler, "Mr. Birtch," not only lost his place, but was fined 5*l.* for suffering some Quakers committed by the Court to go at large.

Whipping seems to have been a favourite punishment in the county of Bucks for many small offences. Perhaps this practice received an impulse from a certain Justice who is recorded to have acted at Beaconsfield, Sir George Jeffreys. His seat was at Bulstrode, now the Duke of Somerset's. The Clerk of the Peace seems to have taken a pleasure in carefully recording the details of the punishment. Here is a specimen of a whole class of entries. Kellham Hebbes and William Bates having been convicted of theft, it was ordered "that they and every of them be made fast to the breech of a cart, and stripped naked from the wast (*sic*) upwards this present fryday about one of the clock in the afternoon, and whipt from the Mercatt howse in

Chesham to the greate Elme att ye upper end of the street, and soe downe to the Mercatt place againe, untill their bodye be bloody, and soe to be discharged paying their fees."

The punishment sometimes exceeded the offence. At Midsummer, 1684, the Court received credible information that divers Scotch and other pedlars, or petty chapmen, did travel and wander about in the county "to the greate damage and hindrance of all shopp keepers and others his Ma$^{tie's}$ leige subjects." The Court passed a strong measure of protection, and ordered that the petty constables and tithing-men, whenever they saw or heard of a Scotch pedlar, or other petty chapman, should immediately apprehend and take the body of such person, and (apparently without taking him before a Justice), should strip him naked and whip him, or cause him to be openly and publicly whipped and sent away.

The farmers of the hearth-tax were not more popular in Bucks than they were in Devon, and met with even less support from the Justices. "Divers and sundry good subjects of our sovereign Lord the King did complaine of many and greate abuses to them lately done by the collectors of his Majestie's revenues ariseing by fire-hearths in this county by takeing extortively of them many summs of mony." Several bills of indictment were preferred against the delinquents, but "after a longe heareing of divers just complaints well proved in Court against them," they produced a *certiorari* to remove all proceedings against them into the King's Bench. Whereupon the Court determined to make an address to the King and Council against the farmers of the said revenue and their officers, "for the regulating such greate and greivous oppressione of the people."

QUARTER SESSIONS UNDER JAMES II.

THE days of James II. were few and evil, and the ordinary course of business was so similar to that which prevailed under the rule of his brother, that few remarks need be made upon it. But, though the reign was so brief, it was distinguished by two great events, both of which were closely connected with the county of Devon. The Duke of Monmouth landed within two miles of the boundary of Devonshire, and the course of his expedition for the most part lay not far from its eastern frontier. William of Orange landed in Torbay, marched through the heart of the county, and held his court in its ancient capital.

Of the latter of these events we find no notice in the records of Quarter Sessions. Of the former some brief reminiscences may be gleaned.

Monmouth had always been singularly popular in Devonshire. Five years before the death of his father he had been received in Exeter with royal honours, and more than loyal enthusiasm. Even to this day some oral traditions of his visit are preserved in the neighbourhood. He is said to have visited Topsham, the port of Exeter, and to have composed these doggerel lines, which may with more probability be attributed to some local poetaster:—

> Topsham, thou'rt a pretty town—
> I think thee very pretty,
> And when I come to wear the crown
> I'll make of thee a City!

A street in the favoured locality still bears his name, and a public-house boasts the sign of the Duke of Monmouth.

The Devonshire militia, called out under the Lord Lieutenant, the second Duke of Albemarle, to serve against the " Protestant Duke," promptly ran away, or deserted to the enemy. At the Michaelmas Sessions of 1685 we find an order that "diligent search should be made for the soldiers who had deserted from the Earl of Bath's regiment."

War was not very costly in those days. At the same sessions an order was made reciting that in the time of the late rebellion, "there being then great occasion for a great sum of money for suppression thereof, and that his Majesty's emergent and present Service might be prosecuted with all vigour," his Grace the Duke of Albemarle was pleased to require from the Treasurer of the county the sum of one hundred and ten pounds "for Suppressing the Rebbles." And the Reverend Dr. Annesley, " Dean of the Citty of Exon," and Mr. Robert Davyes, of Exon, goldsmith, were ordered to repay the said sum "out of the publicke money belonging to this County remaining in their hands."

The battle of Sedgemoor was fought on the 6th of July. The Sessions were held at Exeter eight days afterwards, and the Justices calmly made their usual orders about bridges, and fire-hearths, and parish constables. But we find a very long calendar of prisoners in the gaol, and three are specially mentioned as having borne arms in the late rebellion. The persecution of the Nonconformists had borne its fruit. It is certain that there were not a few Devonshire men among the Somersetshire peasants who, on the field of Sedgemoor, received the charge of the Life Guards with their scythes and pitchforks. Before the Michaelmas

Sessions "the famously Loyal Lord Chief Justice," as an enthusiastic Plymouthian called Jeffreys in 1684, had visited Exeter, and had left little work for the county Justices to do, except for Mr. Richard Coffin, of Portledge, who had the misfortune to be High Sheriff for that year. It was well that his house was far away from Exeter, or his wife might have been frightened out of her wits, like poor Lady North, by the hangman driving up to the front-door with a cart full of the heads and limbs of the rebels whom he had quartered, and calmly asking "his master" where he was to put them.[1] Mr. Coffin is mentioned by Prince, in the *Worthies of Devon*, as a right worthy and worshipful gentleman, of great piety and virtue, and, *for his quality*, of excellent learning. "He hath a noble library, and knows well how to make use of it."

Mr. Thomas Northmore, of St. Thomas, near Exeter, was his "Assistant Deputy Sheriff." The Sheriff himself was in an infirm state of health, which kept him at home during a part of the year, and necessitated much correspondence with his deputy. The letters of the latter have been fortunately preserved at Portledge, and have been most kindly entrusted to me by Mr. J. R. Pine Coffin, the representative of that very ancient family. They are of greater historical interest than the County Records of this period.

On the 1st of June, 1685, Mr. Northmore wrote to inquire about Mr. Coffin's health, and mentioned that "here hath been very little or no business." He says, "I had no great need of an employment, neither was I very fond of it, but shall dispose my duty to my King, and you as his Sheriff of this County."

[1] "Life of Sir Dudley North."

He little knew what was coming.

Before he had finished his letter, he had reason to retract his opinion as to the absence of business. Symptoms of insurrection had appeared at Taunton, excited perhaps by Thomas Dare, who had been sent in advance by Monmouth. " Since the writing above here is an express from Taunton with a letter from the Mayor there to the Mayor of this City (Exeter) whereof inclosed is a copy. The Militia here is up. I hope you will take care to give me order to raise the *Posse* if occasion."

The Mayor of Taunton had received two intercepted letters, "intimating an intention of an insurrection forthwith in the West." And a miller and his wife had deposed that above eighty horsemen, " supposed armed," passed near Taunton at four o'clock in the morning of that day (June 1) " by a way leading into the West of England."

On the 8th of June Mr. Northmore reported that the Duke of Albemarle had come to Exeter, and ordered his regiment to be raised. " It's thought it is on the supposition of an insurrection or rebellion here in the West, by reason of a ship which the " Tiger," one of his Majesty's frigates, lately took at sea and brought into Plymouth laden with arms and ammunition."

Monmouth landed at Lyme on the 11th of June. On the 12th Mr. Northmore wrote to the Sheriff:—

" Sir,—The Mayor of Lyme is come hither this morning, and since that another express to his Grace the Duke of Albemarle, with an account that the Duke of Monmouth landed there, and hath set up his standard, and is listing of soldiers under his service. We do not hear of above three or four hundred men that are yet landed, but it's thought there are many more embarked in four ships which lie before that place."

Macaulay mentions only three ships.

"I waited on the Duke of Albemarle this morning early, to know what service he had for you. He willed me to send an express to you, and thought he should have an occasion to raise the *Posse Comitatus*, but would not have it done till further order from him. However, that we may be in readiness, it's advisable to prepare warrants for raising the *Posse*, as I am now about to do. Pray order the like there" (in the northern division of the county).

"Foreign assistance may be doubted. The Duke of Albemarle directed me to write a letter to Sir Hugh Piper to secure the ships and ammunition in the harbour of Plymouth, and to search all suspected places for arms, and to secure all such persons as are thought to be disaffected to the King and Government, and withal to set forth as many ships as he could from that place well manned and armed, with provisions necessary, to be before Lyme with all speed, where his Grace intends to be in a few days, which letter I wrote, and his Grace did sign and seal it, and an express is gone to Plymouth with it.

"I think it necessary for you to send to Barnstaple and Bideford, and other port towns in the North to secure the Shipping, and Ammunition for his Majesty's service, and to seize the arms and persons of those which are suspected anywise to the Government, and to give notice to the Towns in your parts to be in readiness with arms and ammunition to attend your further Summons."

The next letter is apparently from Mr. Northmore's clerk. It differs slightly from the account of Macaulay, who says that the Duke of Albemarle had four thousand men actually assembled at Exeter when the news was brought by Gregory Alford, the Mayor of Lyme.

"Honoured Sir,—This day about ten in the morning his Grace the Duke of Albemarle went hence with a considerable company of horse and foot soldiers, and intended to lodge at Honiton this night, where will meet him the militia of the East part of the County. Those he carried with him from hence, and those that will meet him at Honiton, are computed to be three thousand five hundred and upwards. Besides these there are a great many who live in the remotest parts of the County that are expected to assist him speedily, together with the militia of Somerset and Dorset, which will be near 10,000. His Grace hath not yet given orders for the raising of the *Posse Com.*, there being no need of it as yet, for it's said that the Duke of Monmouth brought with him but 300 or 400 men, and since his landing hath listed about 800 (as it's here reported). This is the best account I can give. Enclosed is a copy of the precept for raising the *Posse Com.* I have made 34 copies of it, which is one for every hundred in the county, which I shall disperse as soon as I have orders from his Grace the Duke of Albemarle so to do. Thus, with the tender of my humble service to yourself, good Lady, and Branches, I rest—Your honour's most faithful humble servant,

"JACOB CLIFFE.

"St. Thomas, 13° Junii, 1685.

"My Master received yours, and gives you his humble service."

It may be doubted whether the *Posse Comitatus* of Devon has ever been called out since this occasion, except in that wild week of 1690, when a French fleet dared to anchor in

Torbay, and actually burnt the village of Teignmouth. Perhaps the form of the precept may be worth preserving.

"*Devon.*—Richard Coffin, Esq., Sheriff of the County aforesaid,

"To the Constables of the Hundred of —— and to every and either of them, Greeting.

"Whereas a great number of men in arms and warlike manner are landed at Lyme Regis in the County of Dorset, and have there set up their Standard and declared open war against his Majesty and Government, and it's vehemently expected that they design very speedily in a Traitorous and Rebellious manner to invade this County, and to disturb the King's peace by an open war therein. These are therefore in his Majesty's name, by virtue of his Majesty's writ of assistance and of my office, to will and require you that you forthwith on receipt hereof summon and warn all sufficient and able men within your hundred which are above the age of Sixteen and under Sixty (those which are in Holy Orders only excepted). That they be and appear at the Castle of Exon in the County aforesaid without delay, furnished with arms and ammunition fit and convenient to aid and assist me in his Majesty's service for the suppressing of all such Rebellions or Insurrections as are, shall, or may be committed or done within the County aforesaid during my office, on pain of being proceeded against according to law. And that you be there present to make return hereof. And this you are not to omit. Given under the seal of my office this — day of June in the first year of the Reign of our Sovereign Lord King James the Second over England, &c.—Annoque Domini 1685°."

On the 15th Mr. Northmore wrote that he had orders

from the Duke of Albemarle to direct the Sheriff to call out the *Posse Comitatus* at Exeter, and the Mayor and Dean of Exeter advised him to come himself with about 200 horsemen, " as well armed and provided as they may be, of the most able and loyal men." He says, "there is noe doubt of a ready complyance in all the loyall gentry and comonalty in this emergency to serve theire Kinge and country."

The latest news that he had received was that the Duke of Monmouth, with about 1000 men, was on the previous night at Bridport, "where they met with about 600 of the militia of Dorsetshire, who engaged them. There were about ten killed on each side (as it's said) and the Duke of Monmouth wounded, and that the Duke of Monmouth and his party retreated, and the militia followed them, and took some of their guns which were left in the flight. The Duke of Albemarle, with the King's forces of this county, intended to march this morning from Honiton towards Lyme. Colonel Lutterell, with the militia of Somerset, intends this day to join the forces of that county with these (*sic*) of our county (as it's said) and that the King's army will this day be 20,000 strong. It's talked that a Royal Regiment is also coming from London to assist the King's forces here, and that some of the King's ships will speedily be, if not already, before Lyme. So that I hope (by God's assistance) a few days will set an end to this Rebellion in Dorsetshire. . . . Pray give order and encouragement to the country to send hither corn, cattle, and other provisions for the King's forces here. You may assure them they will be paid ready money for the same, and have all freedom, *without any pressing of the men or horses.*"

On the 19th of June Mr. Northmore mentions a brush

which he had had with Mr. Wollocombe, Mr. Coffin's son-in-law. The gentlemen of the county had been summoned to appear at Exeter, and Mr. Wollocombe said at the Castle "that hee thought there was noe need thereof *unless it were to waite upon mee*, but said that hee and severall others would follow the campe." Mr. Northmore booked him at once, by reporting his name to the Deputy Lieutenants, "and I presume to-morrow hee will beginne his march."

The news was that the King's army was supposed to be at Wellington, about 20,000 in number. "His Majesty's Granadeers, with severall of his Royall Troopes and Dragoons, have given greate life to the army, and it's hoped that a few days will show a signall victory. The enemy is supposed to encampe in or about Taunton."

It was on the 20th of June that Monmouth caused himself to be proclaimed king in the market-place of Taunton.

On the 22nd there was a report from Taunton that Monmouth was at Bridgwater, with about ten thousand men, "rabble and all." The Deputy Lieutenants had only required each parish to provide one man, horse and arms for the *Posse*.

On the 25th Mr. Northmore complains of the great neglect of the constables. "Many parishes made no appearance, but their constables returned there was not a substantial man in their parishes, and swore to it, though every subsidy man is such." His Majesty's forces were following the enemy, who was reported to have been the previous day at Shepton Mallet. "This day I took the examination of one William Smith, a master of a ship of Topsham, on his oath before the Deputy Lieutenants, wherein he swore that he discovered yesterday, about four leagues off from the shore, between Dartmouth and Berry Point, eight or nine ships without flags, and that a pilot which he got there, and the fishermen there, did suppose them to be French men-of-war. This is sent to my Lord Sunderland, and another copy to the Duke of Albemarle. *I should write you more fully, but perceive by others that you are pleased to expose my letters to publique view.*"

He adds in a postscript, "We had this day an account that Argyle is taken, which is confirmed this post, which occasions much rejoicing here, and it's hoped we shall shortly hear of the like success on our domestic and intestine Enemies."

The Scots were still considered foreigners.

Inclosed in this letter is a copy of an order forwarded by Sunderland, the Secretary of State, to the Duke of Albemarle.

"JAMES R.

"Right trusty and right entirely beloved cousin and councillor, we greet you well. Our will and pleasure is, and we do hereby authorize and direct you to give order forthwith for seizing and apprehending all disaffected and suspicious persons, and *particularly non-conformist ministers*, and such persons as have served against our Royal father or late Royal Brother of blessed memory, and for sending them in safe custody to our Royal Citadel of Plymouth, to be secured there till further order. And for so doing this shall be your warrant.

"Given at our Court at Whitehall, the 20th day of June, 1685, in the first year of our Reign.

"By his Majesty's Command.
"SUNDERLAND.

"Our will and pleasure also is that you give order for

the seizing all the horses belonging to any persons which shall be so seized."

On July 2 the Duke of Albemarle had set out again towards Taunton with the whole army except two companies. The only news was that the enemy had been defeated in another skirmish, and was said to be coming back to Taunton. The *Posse men* were ordered to convey the disaffected persons from Exeter to Plymouth.

On the 4th my Lord Churchill and my Lord Feversham, with the King's forces, were said to be in pursuit of the enemy's army. There was a report that some of the enemy's scouts had reached Tiverton and Cullompton. It was conjectured that the design of the rebels might be to march off to some of the northern ports of Devonshire. " I question not but you have already sett good and strict watches att all the ports and creakes in your parts, as Appledore, Barnstaple, Biddeford, Combe Martyn, Ilfracombe, Clovelly, and other adjacent places, to view, search, and take an account of all ships and vessels that shall come in and go out at those places."

The battle of Sedgemoor was fought and ended before sunrise on July 6, and the news did not take long to reach Exeter.

On July 8, by order of the Duke of Albemarle, the Sheriff was advised " to send out scouts in your northern partes, to apprehend such as are scattered there. Some were examined here yesterday, who confess that about two hundred of them went towards Ilfracombe and dispersed, some one way some another, neere that place, and one of the witnesses saith *hee*, with Ferguson and about thirty others, went off in a boate at sea at Ilfracombe, but were driven back, seeing the King's shipping making toward them."

Whether "hee" meant Monmouth or the witness appears doubtful. Another part of the same letter says that the Duke of Albemarle had received information that the late Duke of Monmouth (as he was called in consequence of his attainder), and Lord Gray, had been taken by a troop of Sir William Portman's near Blandford, " the Rebel's Army being defeated and quite broken abroad in the fight at King's Sedgmoor on Sunday night last, when about 2000 of the Rebels were killed and taken prisoners, whereof my lord of Bath shewed me an account by letter." He mentions that " the *Posse* men " were coming in in swarms, and he was sending out expresses to stop them, but they were to be ready at an hour's warning " if occasion." The militia of the county were also discharged, except the Duke of Albemarle's own regiment. A Council of War was to sit next morning on some of the prisoners.

During the next month the Justices were fully employed in committing prisoners for trial.

On the 10th of August Mr. Northmore writes about the preparations for the Assizes. No day had yet been fixed. The Judges were to leave London on the 24th, and sit at Winchester on the 25th. It was expected that they would have to try about 1000 prisoners before coming to Exeter. It was thought that they would sit at three places in Somerset. " We shall be at great trouble and charge in removing of prisoners hence to Somerset and Dorset, in order to their trials where they entered into the Army. It's thought the greatest part of the prisoners will be removed. We have been troubled with new warrants every day for summoning a guard to secure the prisoners ever since the Duke went hence. . . . Sir Arthur Northcote giveth you his service ; he is now with me, and would have sent his coach, if occasion, and company."

Quarter Sessions under James II. 237

On the 17th of August he writes again about the Assizes. He had had to go to Axminster to wait on one Mr. Loder, but he only received information that the Judges would be at Dorchester on the 3rd of September. It was thought that most of the Devonshire prisoners would be removed to Dorset and Somerset for trial. " He told us that the Judges would expect very good juries, and that gentlemen of the best quality might serve on the petty jury under the degree of Justices of the Peace."

It was expected that the Judges would be in Exeter the week after the beginning of the Assizes in Dorset. " The expense of removing the prisoners will first lie on you. Some allowance will be given for the same on making up your account, which will be twelve months hence." The only news was that some writs of *Habeas Corpus* were being issued for the prisoners, and that " my lord Keeper was relapsed," which affected Jeffreys' hopes of promotion.

On the 26th of August the day for the Assizes was not yet certainly known. The difficulty and expense of removing prisoners was still pressing. " I will be as good husband for you as I can, and will endeavour to *put in on the Counyt*, but doubt that I shall not prevail, having never known the County to bear any of the charge for removing the prisoners, but the sheriff hath always done it." He was out of cash, and anxious for a remittance. " I shall render you a fair account of the profits of the office, and I wish it would tend more to your profit than it is like to do. I am well assured that what I wrote you formerly will prove too true. It hath been a year of more than treble the ordinary expense, charge, and trouble, and not half the profit of what hath usually been in a sheriff's year." The news was that " Newheasell " (Neuhausel) was taken, that the Imperialists had killed six thousand of the Janizaries, and that the remainder of the Turks' army was routed. The difference between those times and ours was not so marked in foreign as in domestic intelligence.

Mr. Coffin no doubt came to Exeter for the Assizes, and the correspondence ceases for a month.

We then have some evidence of the results of the Bloody Assizes.

On the 1st of October Mr. Northmore writes: "I ridd to Wells purposely to save you what I could of the extraordinary charge of whippinge and executinge the prisoners, wherein I gott some mitigation. However, the charge will bee very greate. The quarters of the rebells are to bee sent to the severall townes hereunder written. It hath been and will be a very chargeable and expensive year to you. . . . The Under-Sheriff is this day gonne to Coliton to execute those two prisoners that were to bee executed there, and on Saturday a Crediton man is to bee executed there; it had been done formerly, had wee knowne how to dispose of his quarters, and there was noe day assigned in the kallender or in the warrant for his execution. All the other executions will be done with all speed. I hope you will consider the great trouble and charge of it; brick cannot bee made without straw; paines and care shall not bee wantinge on my part, but the charge and expense you are to disburse. . . . Places where quarters and heads of rebells are to bee sent are Honiton, Axeminster, Coliton, Ottery, Crediton, Biddeford, Barnestaple, Torrington, Tiverton, Plymouth, Dartmouth, and Tottnes."

On the 12th of October he writes: "I was driven to ride to Wells, and there to tarry all the Assizes, for a mitigation of the whipping, and about disposeing of the quarters of the rebells. I acquainted my Lord (then Cheife Justice, now Lord Chancellor) that wee have many markett townes in our county, soe by Charter, that scarce retaine at this day the name of marketts, in some of which not many, in others not any, did resort to buy and sell, but as in other little villages where no markets ever were. To which my Lord answeared that the whipping should be onely in the greater and more generall marketts, &c. . . . On Saturday next, at Axminster, is the last execution to bee done, and one more then at Honyton, unles reprieved, endeavours being makeing per expresse, who is not yet retorned."

The one intended to be executed at Honiton may have been Edmond Prideaux, from whom Jeffreys extorted a bribe of 15,000*l.* The seat of the Prideaux family, Netherton Hall, is within a few miles of Honiton. It seems probable that Edmond Prideaux was a cousin of Mrs. Coffin. Her father and one of her brothers bore the same name. Another brother was the celebrated Humphrey Prideaux, Dean of Norwich.

"Three were executed at Honyton Saturday last. Quarters are already sett up at Colliton, Honyton, Ottery, Crediton ; others are brought hither to bee sent as above. The quarters are already *boyled and tarred;* warrants are to bee sent to the mayors to sett them up. I saved you considerably by my journey to Wells, and endeavour to save you what expences I can ; however, it is exceedinge chargeable and troublesome. *Another such yeere's trouble will I not undertake for* 500 *li.* . . .

" There were about 400 condemned at Taunton ; and 700 at Wells. It's thought about 100 are and wilbee executed ; the rest transported, unles perhaps a few may be pardoned. You fared better than the Sheriffe there."

Which last reflection was no doubt extremely true, as the Sheriff of Somèrset had to execute at least two hundred and thirty-three of the rebels.

The story of the Bloody Assizes has been told often enough, nor is it pleasant to dwell on the time when an English Chief Justice was more cruel than a leader of Hindoo mutineers, and an English colonel more brutal than an officer of Bashi Bazouks. It is probable that not more than twenty-six persons were executed in Devonshire, though the number has often been estimated as high as eighty.

After this business we are not surprised to find Mr. Northmore informing his principal that "it hath pleased God to visitt mee with a lurkeing fever." But people's nerves were stronger in those days, and it does not appear to have been caused by his work, as it had broken out "in diverse families in this parrish," and some who had "adventured abroad" too soon after it had lost their lives. We may, perhaps, suspect that an outbreak of typhus was caused by the mangled bodies of rebels, which remained suspended in some places even till the Revolution.

The remainder of the correspondence relates chiefly to the business of passing the Sheriff's accounts, which was not completed till the end of the following year.

To return to the County Records.

At the Michaelmas Sessions there was again a long list of prisoners in the gaol, many no doubt sentenced to be transported to the West Indies. The Justices ordered certain persons to be whipped and pilloried for seditious words. They granted Mr. Thomas Carew, "chirurgeon," the liberal remuneration of four pounds for receiving into his house a maimed soldier, curing him, and keeping him several months, by direction of the Duke of Albemarle.

At this time the Bishop of Exeter (Lamplugh) issued an order that the resolutions of the Justices in Quarter Sessions "against Sectaries, Phanatics," &c., should be published in all churches. The bishop's letter begins: "We think it our duty, after such an execrable Rebellion as we have lately had." The same prelate is said to have been the first, three years afterwards, to carry to King James the news of the landing of William of Orange. He obtained the Archbishopric of York as the reward of his loyalty.

At Epiphany, a sergeant in the troop of the Hon. Lord Cornbury, bearing the appropriate name of Symon Fferrett, was allowed a gratuity of twenty shillings for apprehending one Mr. Richard Evans, a Nonconformist minister, "a dangerous Rebble engaged in ye late rebellion." Macaulay describes the dissenting preachers who had joined Monmouth, and some of whom had probably fought in the great Civil War, as praying and preaching in red coats and huge jack-boots, with swords by their sides. Mr. Evans was tried before Jeffreys, and executed at Honiton.

Thomas Major, a soldier under the command of Captain (or General?) Churchill, was presented with three pounds for apprehending Mr. Vincent, another Nonconformist minister. And Mr. Robert Wolcombe, another minister, "formerly beneficed at Moreton Hampstead," was committed for residing there, contrary to the Statute.

. The Justices were much disturbed by seditious libels. It does not seem to have occurred to them that by burning such productions they were destroying the principal evidence against the culprits. Here is an order on this subject.

"Whereas by several former orders of this Court his

Majesty's subjects have been by promised rewards encouraged to detect and discover any person whatsoever that should raise, publish, or declare any seditious, factious, or scurrilous reports or libels against our gracious King or his Government or persons in authority under him. And forasmuch as one or more persons as yet unknown hath or have this present week by the Common Post sent unto Sir Boucher Wray a wicked, factious, scurrilous, and seditious printed paper sealed up and directed unto him. And forasmuch as the said Sir Boucher Wray did forthwith shew and communicate the said printed paper unto the Right Hon. John Earl of Bath, Lord Lieutenant of this County now present at this present Sessions, which his Lordship hath been pleased to communicate to the rest of the Justices of the Peace of this County, now in Sessions assembled. His Lordship with the rest of the Justices do order and command that the High Sheriff of this County of Devon do cause the common hangman of this County on Saturday, in this present Sessions week, to cause the said scurrilous printed paper to be burnt openly in the Castle of Exon. And this Court doth promise and order that in case any person or persons shall find out and discover the author, printer, or sender of the said printed paper, that such person or persons first finding out and discovering such author, printer, or sender of the said Libel, shall receive as a reward from this Court the sum of Twenty Pounds."

Nor were seditious words considered of less importance than writings. At the Midsummer Sessions of 1686, the jurors for our Lord the King on their oath presented that Nathaniel Harvey, of Membury, on April 13, " machinans et malitiose admodum intendens etiam serenissimum Regem nostrum Jacobum Secundum in contemptum et odium inferre, ac etiam regiam suam auctoritatem hujus regni Angliæ in disceptationem et dubium inferre, ac Ligeos suos a debita sua Ligeantia versus eundem Regem nostrum substrahere," &c. when talking with William Mayo, clerk, and others about the King, and being asked whether he would take the oath of allegiance, answered "in his seditiosis, opprobriosis, et contemptuosis verbis, viz. *Yes, if I did know the lawful heir; how do you know him* (serenissimum Dominum regem Jacobum Secundum nunc Regem Angliæ innuendo) *to be the lawful heir?*"

They also presented that John Butcher, of Combe Raleigh, worsted comber, having the same intentions as aforesaid towards the King, &c., when talking with one Katherine Sydenham concerning the King and his merciful proclamation of a general pardon, and concerning "horrenda illa rebellione et bello," lately levied against the King by James, Duke of Monmouth, and other "Inimicos nefandos domini Regis," then and there with a loud voice, "dixit, propalavit et asseruit hæc falsa, seditiosa, opprobriosa, et malevola Anglicana verba sequentia, viz. *I know of noe Rebellion there hath beene in the case;—a Gratious King! I know not where I have any King or noe, for I have not seene him this tenne days* (præfatum proditorem Jacobum nuper Ducem de Monmouth innuendo.)" And so on *usque ad nauseam.*

The state of the prisons had not improved. The poor prisoners in the Sheriff's ward in the parish of St. Thomas addressed a humble petition to the Right Worshipful John Beare, Esq., and the other Justices, declaring that they were "brought in a very low and sad condition," for it had "pleased the Lord to send his visitation among us, and for want of attendance we shall undoubtedly perish." Doctor Waterhouse and his apothecary had "taken a view," and said, "the decease is very dangerous." One prisoner was lying dead, and several "upon their Languishing Beds." Their keeper had been very free and liberal, and several gentlemen-prisoners besides, "to discharge and pay Doctor Waterhouse." And so they prayed the Court to "commiserate us poor prisoners' condition, that wee may not perish for want."

At Michaelmas, 1686, we have a glimpse of the practice of levying black-mail upon jurymen. The Court declared that it was "notoriously evident" that a great number of freeholders and others had for several years been much burdened and oppressed, and annual contributions had been exacted from them by the "subtill and uniust practices" of bailiffs of hundreds and liberties, upon pretence of exempting them from serving on juries of the General Sessions and elsewhere. And notwithstanding that the Court had inflicted exemplary punishment upon such bailiffs as had been prosecuted for such offences, "yet they are noe way reformed, and such extortive practices noe way forborne." The Court observed that the practice of the sheriffs had been to grant warrants to the bailiffs to summon four-and twenty substantial freeholders, without specifying their names, "but leaving the same to the election of the said Bayliffes whome to warne," so that the bailiffs had not only, through "ignorance and want of due apprehention," often warned people who were not freeholders, but had often taken occasion, by means of such warrants, to warn a far greater number, "and upon pretence of favour, had had and taken severall sumes of money," so that many persons were kept "under constant composicons and contribucons towards such Bayliffes, to their manifest oppression of such freeholders and owners of estates." The remedy, of course, was that the Sheriff should in future insert in his warrant, "the name, sirname, and place of habitacon" of every person to be summoned to serve on any grand or petty jury.

The practice, however, seems to have been "noe way forborne," as a similar order was issued in the reign of William III., and there are occasional rumours of such a system having survived even in the reign of Queen Victoria.

The authorities of the miniature borough of Bradninch stood up for their separate rights of local government, and obstructed the administration of justice, even as such petty jurisdictions have sometimes done within our own remembrance. It was declared to be "notoriously evident" that certain persons indicted for "trespasses, contempts, and misdemeanours," were residing and sojourning within the *vill* and parish of Bradninch. The Sheriff and his officers endeavoured to apprehend the persons so indicted; but "instead of being assisted therein by the officers of the said Burrough, they, by the encouragement of the Maior of the said Burrough, and other judiciall officers, did oppose the execution of such writts and processe, and the said Maior declared noe warrants should bee executed in his Burrough which came not from himselfe or other magistrates there, and soe, instead of promoting and assisting in the execucon of such writts and processe, imprisoned the ministeriall officer who brought the same, and suffered the offenders to escape." It was also manifestly proved "that the said Burroug of Bradninch is *a place of refuge for criminalls* to defend them from the reach of Justice, in contempt of the laws and statutes of this Kingdom," &c. The Court, therefore, determined to apply to the Court of King's Bench for a writ of *quo warranto* against the Mayor and Town Clerk of the borough of Bradninch.

The Court was troubled by the misconduct of certain

masters and employers of wool-combers and spinsters, who cheated their work-people by false weights, so as to make them comb and spin eighteen or twenty ounces of wool, while they only paid them for doing one pound.

In November, 1688, William of Orange was in Exeter, but, as no Sessions were held at that time, we are left to learn from other sources how the gentlemen of Devon assembled together on that occasion, and, under the guidance of Sir Edward Seymour, entered into their memorable association "for the defence of the Protestant religion, and for the maintaining of the ancient Government, and the Laws and Liberties of England, Scotland, and Ireland." They engaged "to Almighty God, to his Highness the Prince of Orange, and to one another, to stick firm in this cause in the defence of it, and never to depart from it, until our Religion, Laws, and Liberties, are so far secured to us in a Free Parliament, that we shall be no more in danger of falling under Popery and Slavery."

At the Epiphany Sessions of 1688-9 we may imagine that the Justices were somewhat puzzled. The King had fled on December 22, but the Clerk of the Peace nevertheless entered his name in the usual heading "*Anno regni Regis Jacobi Secundi nunc Angliæ, &c.*, iiii°." The Justices did as little as possible, and adjourned to February 6. At that meeting they did still less. The clerk omitted the King's name altogether, and the Court adjourned to February 27, when a new era began: "*Anno regni Regis et Reginæ Will' et Mariæ nunc Angliæ, &c., primo, Annoque Domini* 1688."

When we turn to the records of the county of Bucks, we find, as might have been expected, very slight allusions to

Quarter Sessions under James II. 247

the rebellion of Monmouth, although that movement probably commanded the sympathies of so Protestant a county. The Clerk of the Peace disbursed 30*l.* for "distributing the King's commands in relation to the late rebellion;" and David Stanley was committed to prison for asking Thomas Kent whether he would drink the Duke of Monmouth's health, and for declaring that "he had a son that lived with the Duke of Monmouth a long while, and that he believed him to be with the Duke at present."

A relic of the feudal system may be recognized in an order of Easter, 1688, which recites that "there hath beene, and still are, accustomed Homage Fees due to his Majestie's Ancestors' Servants, and his Majestie's that now are upon his passeing or journeying through any of his Maj$^{tie's}$ Countyes, corporations, or into any cathedrall or collegiate church within his said Maj$^{tie's}$ kingdomes of England upon the ffirst tyme next after his Maj$^{tie's}$ accession to the Crowne." These fees in Bucks amounted to 36*l.* 6*s.*, for which the Sheriff had been sued in the Court of Exchequer "by English Bill." The Justices were satisfied that the Sheriff was not personally liable, and ordered the amount to be paid by the "Receivers Generall" of the county.

Mr. Richard Brugis, of Edlesborough, who had been a commissioned officer in the civil war, and had been "highly eminent both for his loyalty and sufferings," and was greatly impoverished, "having, as he affirms, lost a considerable estate of the value of Five Thousand Pounds and upwards," was rewarded by having his pension increased from 8*l.* to 10*l.* per annum.

At the same time the Court was informed "that the daily concourse and great increase of Rogues, Vagabonds, and Sturdy Beggars is a great Grievance and Annoyance to the inhabitants of this County," and that they " are now growne soe insolent and presumptious that they have oft, by Threats and Menaces, extorted Money and Victualls from those who live in houses remote from neighbours, whilst theire Husbands and Servants have beene employed abroade in the Management of their Lawful Vocacons, and have put the people into a Generall Consternation or feare that they will fire theire houses or steale theire Goods." The Court therefore issued most elaborate and stringent orders for keeping watch and ward, and examining and securing all strangers or suspected persons. All rogues and wandering idle persons were to be " stripped naked from the Midle upwards, and openly whipped till theire bodyes shalbe bloody." They were then to be forwarded to their parishes with a " Passe or Testimoniall " certifying that they had been so whipped, and requiring the constables of the places through which they had to pass to give them necessary relief on their passage, the time of their journey being strictly limited. And the minister of the parish was required to register "every such Testimoniall."

There were also strict orders against harbouring any rogue or sturdy beggar, and any person arresting such a character was to receive a reward of two shillings.

The vicinity of the antique towers of Eton does not seem to have caused the Latin of Aylesbury to be more classical than that of Exeter.

Three men were indicted "pro piscacone in certo rivulo cum quodam Rete vocat. *a Shovenett.*"

Nine men were indicted "pro piscacone in certo rivulo cum diversis Retibus et al. Engin. ad capiend. pisces."

A farmer who neglected to do his share of work in mending the highways was indicted " pro non laboracone erga

Quarter Sessions under James II. 249

emendaconem altarum viarum Regiarum in Aylesbury pro spa. 6 dierum cum carrucis."

One who kept a disorderly beershop was accused "pro manutencon. dom. malegubernat. tipulator."

The offence of rabbiting was translated into "Riott. et transgressione in fracone Warrene Johannis Stiles et capcone et asportacone cuniculorum."

A "torment" was probably a gun, though it was more generally called a *bombarda*. Four men were indicted "pro habente et custodiente Tormentarum ret. et canibus contra formam Statuti."

At the Easter Sessions, 1688, the rates of wages allowed by the Justices of Bucks were entered in the records.

A "Cheife Bayliffe or Hyne in Husbandry" was allowed to receive 6*l.* a year "in the Chilterne," and 5*l.* 10*s.* "in the Vale."

Every other man-servant in husbandry, if above twenty years of age, 4*l.* 10*s.* in the Chiltern, and 4*l.* in the Vale. If under twenty and above sixteen, 3*l.* in the Chiltern, and 2*l.* 10*s.* in the Vale. Boys between twelve and sixteen might receive 1*l.* 13*s.* 4*d.* and 1*l.* respectively.

"Cooke mayds and Dary mayds" were to have 2*l.* 10*s.* a year. Other maid-servants not more than 2*l.*

"Mowers or reapers of corne or grasse" might receive 1*s.* 2*d.* by the day without meat or drink, or 6*d.* with meat and drink.

Mowers of grass by the acre were paid 1*s.* 2*d.*

Men haymakers had 10*d.* a day without meat or drink, or 5*d.* with meat and drink. Women haymakers, 6*d.* or 3*d.*

Mowers of barley, peas, beans, or oats had 1*s.* 4*d.*, or 8*d.*

Labourers at other times might be paid 8*d.* or 4*d.* from Lady Day to Michaelmas, and 7*d.* or 3*d.* from Michaelmas to Lady Day.

"Free Masons" might receive 1s. 8d. a day without meat and drink.

"Rough Masons, carpenters, plough-rights (*sic*), bricklayers, *playsters*, and tylers" were to have 1s. 2d. from Lady Day to Michaelmas, and 1s. from Michaelmas to Lady Day. If supplied with meat and drink they were to have 8d. all the year round.

Gardeners and thatchers were paid at the same rate; but a tailor got only 6d. a day with meat and drink, or 10d. without; and a "spinner" had only 4d. without meat and drink.

These rates appear to have remained without material alteration until the reign of George I.

QUARTER SESSIONS UNDER WILLIAM AND MARY.

IN a former paper a parallel was suggested between the records of Quarter Sessions and the records of geology—between the entries characteristic of particular reigns, and the fossils characteristic of the epochs of the geologist. The Revolution of 1688 may well be compared to that great break or change which has been traced, in the opinion of some scientific men, between the Mesozoic and Cainozoic periods. The reign of William the Third is the Eocene formation, the dawn of the new ideas, or rather of the new practice, which has gone on peaceably developing itself, without any considerable break, from that time to the present day.

The hearth-tax, as I observed before, disappears altogether in the first year of William and Mary. The legal toleration of Protestant Nonconformists comes upon the scene for the first time, and gives occasion to the entries which are peculiarly characteristic of the new reign.

As early as Midsummer, 1689, we find a memorandum "that at this present Generall Sessions it was certified unto this Courte that the house called the Chapple, in the towne of Honiton, the house of William Yeo, called Rydon, scituate in the parish of Wollborough," and thirteen other houses in various parts of the county, were "severally used for places of Religious Worshipp, according to a late act of this present Parliament, intituled an Act for exempting their Majesties' protestant subjects dissenting from the Church of England from the penalty of certain Laws."

At Michaelmas eight more houses were certified as places of religious worship. From this time such entries became very common. At Epiphany, 1690, "the house of John Bowering, in the Towne of Chulmeley," and twenty others in various places, were certified in the same manner. "John Bowering" was an ancestor of the late Sir John Bowring.

The duties of the Justices in this matter were merely ministerial, and must have been very distasteful to those gentlemen who had spent many of their best years in hunting down the "Conventiclers," and who now found it declared by Parliament that "some ease to scrupulous consciences in the exercise of religion may be an effectual means to unite their Majesties' protestant subjects in interest and affection." The Clerk of the Peace was compelled to register the names of such persons as took the required oaths on payment of a fee of sixpence " and no more."

In 1692, Mr. Stephen Moleines, a French Protestant minister at Stonehouse, is recorded to have taken the oaths mentioned in the late Act for abrogating the oath of allegiance, &c.

The Act of Toleration was not a very liberal measure, according to our ideas, but it was in fact the introduction of an enormous change in the policy of the Government of England. Though it was expressly provided by it that nothing contained in it should give any ease, benefit, or advantage, to any Papist or Popish recusant whatsoever, or any person that should deny in preaching or writing the doctrine of the Trinity, we find little or nothing from this time forward about the prosecution of any person in Devonshire for his religious opinions or observances. Perhaps the authorities thought it unfair to attack one class of Nonconformists and to tolerate others, and it is not improbable that many of the Justices may have liked a Papist better than a Protestant dissenter.

The entries respecting maimed soldiers become rather more frequent during the wars of William the Third. But the pensions rarely exceeded 40s., and sometimes a gratuity of only 20s. was given. "My uncle Toby" would have fared badly if he had been dependent on the Justices of Devon.

At Epiphany, 1695-6, Mr. William Martyn, of Heavitree, was appointed Clerk of the Peace, in succession to Mr. Hugh Vaughan. His appointment by the Earl of Bath, Lord-Lieutenant and Custos Rotulorum, was read in open Court, and he took the following oath in pursuance of a recent Act of Parliament:—

"I do swear that I have not nor will pay any sum or "sums of money or other reward whatsoever, nor given "any bond or other assurance to pay any money, fee, or "profit, directly or indirectly, to any person or persons "whomsoever, for such nomination or appointment."

Neither the old nor the new Clerk of the Peace made many entries in his books during this reign, except the necessary routine business concerning constables, settlements, rates, apprentices, affiliation cases, bridges, highways, and the like. In those dangerous times of foreign war and domestic disaffection, it was the custom in some counties for the Justices in Quarter Sessions to pass loyal addresses of condolence or congratulation on the state of public affairs. No such resolutions appear in the records of Devon, nor is it likely that any such were passed, There can be little doubt that the country gentlemen of the West were for the most part staunch Tories. The objects of their veneration were the Church and the Monarchy. A foolish King had insisted on compelling them to choose between their Church and him, and they had preferred the former. The Earl of Bath, who had been sent by James to influence the West, reported that all the Justices and Deputy-Lieutenants of Devon and Cornwall, without a single dissenting voice, declared that they would put life and property in jeopardy for the King, but that the Protestant religion was dearer to them than either life or property. "And, sir, if your Majesty should dismiss all these gentlemen, their successors will give exactly the same answer."

Under the pressure of James's tyranny, and under the guidance of their oracle, Sir Edward Seymour, they had slowly and reluctantly joined in welcoming William of Orange. In 1690, after the disaster off Beachy Head, when they saw a French fleet riding in Torbay, and their homes were in immediate danger of foreign invasion, they had stood bravely forward in support of the new Government, even as their ancestors, a hundred years before, had supported Elizabeth against the Spanish Armada. As in those days, the beacons were kindled throughout the shire from Dartmoor to the Black Downs. "Early the next morning, without chief, without summons, five hundred gentlemen and yeomen, armed and mounted, had assembled on the summit of Haldon Hill. In twenty-four hours all Devonshire was up. Every road in the county, from sea to sea, was covered by multitudes of fighting men, all

Quarter Sessions under William and Mary. 255

with their faces set towards Torbay. The lords of a hundred manors, proud of their long pedigrees and old coats of arms, took the field at the head of their tenantry—Drakes, Prideauxes, and Rolles, Fowell of Fowelscombe and Fulford of Fulford, Sir Bourchier Wrey of Tawstock Park and Sir William Courtenay of Powderham Castle." Narcissus Luttrell mentions in his diary that he heard from Exeter that the militia and *posse* of the county amounted to at least 40,000 horse and foot, "very resolute, hearty, and unanimous to oppose the French."

But when the immediate danger was passed, and the country became comparatively safe and prosperous, the majority of the gentlemen of Devon, like the ancient Israelites, murmured against their deliverer, and, still under the guidance of Seymour, relapsed into opposition, if not into active Jacobitism.

Far different is the tone of the records of the county of Bucks. That fair shire had long been famous as the stronghold of the Roundheads, and afterwards of the Whigs, and was raised to glory by the Revolution of 1688. Nearly fifty years before, Bucks had returned to the Long Parliament the most popular politician in England. He had been attacked by the Stuart King, and four thousand yeomen of his county had ridden up to Westminster to defend him. Under the later Stuarts, the sons of Hampden's constituents had returned the statesman who carried up the Exclusion Bill to the House of Lords, and all the efforts of James, and Jeffreys, and the servile sheriff whom they had nominated, had been exerted in vain to oppose him. The county was still under the influence of the families of Hampden and Russell, and Algernon Sidney had been member for Amersham. The Fleetwoods, Ingoldsbys, and Maynes, were among the old Buckinghamshire families, and several of the Cromwells had resided within its boundaries. At Dinton, too, was still living that mysterious hermit, of whom ran the tradition that his was the hand that had struck off the anointed head from the royal shoulders. More important than all, at this time, was the influence exerted over the county by the house of Wharton.

Philip, Lord Wharton, was a Covenanter after the most straitest sect of that religion. He had commanded a regiment against Charles I. at Edgehill. Under Charles II. he had been known as a distributor of Calvinistic tracts, and a patron of Calvinistic divines. He founded a charity which still furnishes Bibles to the poor of the parishes with which he was connected. His son Thomas inherited his father's politics, though he renounced his father's religion. He was the most dissolute man of the most dissolute age of England. But he was the fiercest and most determined leader of the whole Whig party. He was the greatest electioneerer that had ever existed. In the course of a long life, it is said, he expended on Parliamentary contests about eighty thousand pounds, a sum equivalent to more than three hundred thousand pounds in our time. He was so popular in Bucks that "his journeys to the Quarter Sessions resembled royal progresses. The bells of every parish through which he passed were rung, and flowers were strewed along the road." Besides his other successes, he boasted that, as the author of Lillibullero, he sang a King out of three kingdoms.

In the old register of the parish of Amersham may still be read the opinion of the Reverend Benjamin Robertshaw, rector in the early part of the eighteenth century, on some of his neighbours. He noticed that, during the Protectorate, Paul Ford had been elected registrar, and sworn in by Francis Russell, justice of the peace. To this the rector appended the following note :—

"This Francis Russell lived at Chalfont St. Giles, on the "confines of this parish,—he was one of Oliver's justices, "*and a fit man for ye times*. I knew his son, *a kind of* "*Non-con.*, who came to poverty and sold ye farm. General "Fleetwood lived at ye Vache, and Russell on ye opposite "hill, and Mrs. Cromwell, Oliver's wife, and her daughters, "at Woodrow High House, where afterwards lived Captain "James Thomson ; so ye whole country was kept in awe "and became exceedingly zealous and very fanatical, *nor* "*is ye poison yet eradicated. But ye Whartons are gone and* "*ye Hampdens agoing.*"

He might have added that Frances, the youngest daughter of the Protector, was married to Sir John Russell. A splendid collection of family portraits and other relics of the Cromwells is still preserved in the beautiful mansion of Chequers.

It cannot, then, be a matter of surprise if we find among the records of Bucks some traces of the great political changes introduced by the Revolution of 1688. Even the formal entries are made at much greater length than those of Devonshire, as if the writer delighted to expatiate on the effects of the new settlement. The county had suffered, not only under James as King, but also under Jeffreys as his Lord Lieutenant.

At the Midsummer Sessions of 1689 we find long lists of persons who took the oaths and brought in the certificates required by the acts "for removing and preventing all

S

Questions and Disputes concerning the Assembling and Sitting of this Parliament," "for abrogating the Oaths of Supremacy and Allegiance, and appointing other oaths, &c.," for "preventing Papists from sitting in Parliament," and for "exempting their Majesties' Protestant subjects dissenting from the Church of England from the Penalty of certain Laws." These lists seem to comprise all the justices, all the clergy, and all the nonconformist ministers in the county, besides many other individuals. The sheriff at this time was William Fleetwood, a descendant of the Parliamentary general, whose seat was in the parish of Chalfont St. Giles.

An immense number of dwelling-houses were at the same time "certified to be public meeting-houses for Religious Worship."

At Michaelmas a number of meeting-houses were certified for religious worship "for the People called Quakers."

Entries of this kind are very frequent in the following Sessions. But no toleration was extended to "Popish Recusants," who continued to be presented, though not in very large numbers. Some of them were gentlemen of position in the county, such as Sir Robert Throckmorton, Sir Edward Longueville, John Webbe, and Charles Dormer, esquires, of Great Missenden. The two latter were formally convicted, but the sentence is not recorded, and in the next year a warrant was received from the Attorney-General, directing the Clerk of the Peace to enter a *cesset processus* upon their conviction.

At Michaelmas, 1691, however, twelve "Popish Recusants" were fined 40*l*. each, and two others 20*l*. each. And at the following Sessions sixteen persons were fined 20*l*. each for the same offence.

I do not find that any "person of quality" applied to have his dwelling certified for religious worship, except Philip Lord Wharton, who registered his "Mancon House at Woburn." We have mentioned him before as an old Covenanter. Wooburn, the famous seat of the Whartons, is now the property of Mr. Gilbey.

The Court was informed that certain persons, under pretence of being Dissenting Preachers, "had presumed to disturb and inveigh against the Church of England," and had "kept night assemblies, and imposed oaths upon persons that they had received into their Church or Communion to oblige them not to depart from their principles," especially in the parish of Olney.

At Michaelmas, 1690, an additional sum was voted for the militia, as they had been called out for more than a month for "the most necessary defence of this Realm" during "the late Invasion of the French." This of course referred to the landing at Teignmouth.

Great complaints were made of the oppression practised by the gaugers and "under officers of Excise." The justices caused proceedings to be taken against them before the Courts in London, and on a subsequent occasion we find a vote of thanks passed to the Right Hon. Richard Hampden, Chancellor of the Exchequer, and to the Right Hon. Thomas Wharton, Comptroller of the Household, for their great care in "preventing the oppression of their Majesties' Subjects in this county."

The rates for the carriage of goods by land were settled by the justices as well as the rates of wages. No carrier or waggoner was allowed to charge more than seven pence "for every five score and twelve pounds weight of goods for every ten miles within the Chiltern parts of this County," and ten pence within the Vale. From September till May, however, they might charge twelve pence for the same service.

At Epiphany, 1693, "divers poor distressed prisoners in the gaol presented a petition to the Court," showing "that by reason of the dearness of corn the County allowance of three halfpence per diem for bread is become so small that it will not keep them alive," and praying that the Court would save them from perishing by famine. The allowance was thereupon increased to three pence a day. In 1695 it was reduced to two pence, but it was soon found necessary to raise it again to three pence.

A new Act seems to have come into operation in 1695, "for the more effectuall suppressing prophane curseing and swearing." The convictions of swearers were registered in a separate list, stating the number of oaths. The fine for each oath was 2s., and 4s. if the party had been previously convicted. A certain carrier was convicted of swearing "Twenty several Oaths."

The vernacular language was now gaining ground upon the law Latin, but not without a struggle.

It seems to have required a great number of words to translate "keeping a skittle alley" into Latin. Peter Horton was indicted "pro illicitè tenendo custodiendo et manutenendo certum locum Jaciendi Globos ad ludum, necnon custodiendo malam regulam in Domo suâ contra formam Statuti."

Stealing horses' hair was "felonicè furando secando capiendo et asportando Jubas et Caudas equorum."

Refusing to join in a hue and cry was "negligendo et recusando portare Hutesam et Clamorem."

Keeping disorderly alehouses was "Custodiendo quasdam popinas perturbatas, et permittendo otiosas et dissolutas personas existere et remanere in eisdem, et vendendo et utterando cervisiam et potus tipulat. absque Licenc. Justic."

Edward Cannock, yeoman, could hardly have used worse language than that in which he was indicted. He was declared to be a "communis Barrectator, pacis Perturbator, necnon communis Objurgator, Pugnator, Calumniator, et Litium et Discordiarum Seminator."

Richard Masson was committed "quod oneravit et accusavit Johannem Tanner gen. crimine Abbettaconis Invitaconis et Instigaconis ad Murdrandum et Mahemiandum Timotheum Child ubi revera idem Johannes nunquam Abbettavit Invitavit et Instigavit."

A petty constable was fined 13s. 4d. for neglecting and refusing to whip a woman "convicted for pulling of Hedges."

The Justices had to fix the rates to be allowed for quarters and provisions for soldiers marching through the county. For a commissioned officer of horse the allowance was 2s. each night, "for his dyett and small beer, and hay and straw for his horse." For an officer of dragoons the rate was only 1s. 6d. For an officer of foot, 1s., "and 6d. for his horse, if any." For each light horseman and horse, 1s., and for each dragoon, 9d. For each foot soldier, 4d.

There were also long and elaborate orders concerning the locks and weirs on the Thames, and fixing the "Rates of Water Carriages upon the said river," under the Act 6 Wm. III. cap. 16.

Great care was taken of the highways in Bucks, and many persons were presented at the Sessions for neglecting their repair.

The effects of the Assassination Plot, unnoticed in the records of Devon, are clearly reflected in those of Bucks.

At Easter, 1696, an order was made to pay to each of the bailiffs of Hundreds forty shillings for special business, "forasmuch as in the present juncture of Affairs, to obviate the malevolent influence of wicked and Trayterous Conspirators upon the good Subjects of his most sacred Majesty, it was thought fit to tender an Association to the Gentlemen and Inhabitants of this County." And twenty shillings more were paid to the bailiff of Aylesbury, "for his good service to the Country in searching for Armes suspected to have been lodged or gotten into the Custody of disaffected persons for the disturbance of the Government."

The form of the "Association" is entered at the Midsummer Sessions :—

"Whereas there has been a horrid and detestable con-
" spiracy formed and carried on by Papists and other wicked
" and traitorous persons for Assassinating his Majesty's
" Royal Person, in order to encourage an Invasion from
" France to subvert our Religion, Laws, and Liberty ;—
" We, whose names are hereunto subscribed, do heartily,
" sincerely, and solemnly profess, testify, and declare, that
" his present Majesty King William is rightful and lawful
" King of these Realms ; And we do mutually promise and
" engage to stand by and assist each other to the utmost of
" our power in the support and defence of his Majesty's
" most sacred Person and Government against the Late
" King James and all his Adherents. And in case his Majesty
" come to any violent or untimely death (which God forbid),
" we do hereby further freely and unanimously oblige our-
" selves to unite, associate, and stand by each other in
" revenging the same upon his Enemies and their Adherents,

"and in supporting and defending the Succession of the "Crown according to an Act made in the first year of the "Reign of King William and Queen Mary, entitled an Act "for declaring the Rights and Liberties of the Subject, and "settling the Succession of the Crown."

We do not find that the peace of the county was broken on this occasion, though some "cohortes militum" were "quartiatæ apud Le King and Queen's Head, et apud Le Sarazen's Head apud Aylesbury," and one or two prisoners were indicted "quia dixit, utteravit, et loquutus fuit ficta scandalosa malitiosa contemptuosa et mendacia verba, Ad damnum prejudicium scandalum defamaconem et contemptum duorum Justiciorum Willelmi Busby, Ar., et Francisci Ligo, Ar."

The presentment of "Popish Recusants" of course received a new impulse. The same names often came up again and again, and the Court appears to have been satisfied with proclaiming them, without inflicting a fine on each occasion.

The conclusion of the Treaty of Ryswick was signalized, as might have been expected, by a most joyful demonstration.

At the Epiphany Sessions of 1697-8 the following loyal address was "most cheerfully" signed by the Bench and the Grand Jury. It is evidently prophetic of Macaulay's History:—

"Great Sir,

"At our first public meeting after your Majesty's happy "return from infinite dangers to which your sacred person "so oft hath been exposed for our sakes as well as for the "common good of Christendom, we lay at your Royal feet "our hearts full of joy for your safety and the blessing of "an honourable peace, which we hope your Majesty may "long enjoy with us, and never more hazard your Royal

"Person abroad. When we call to mind how by your wise "conduct we have been rescued from Popery and Arbitrary "power, and protected in our just rights and liberties, These "Resentments (*sic*) cannot but melt the most ungrateful "of your people to a willing obedience, and render your "Majesty no less a Conqueror at home than you have "appeared abroad. So that in all future ages *Chronicles* "*will worthily characterize you* to be the true Defender of "the Faith, the Deliverer of oppressed Nations, and the "Redeemer and Asserter of the Common Liberties of "Europe.

"We only beg leave to add our hearty prayers that "Heaven would long continue to us such a Monarch, and "your people always pay your Majesty the tribute of "Loyalty so justly due to the best of Princes, which in our "several stations we do assure your Majesty we shall "always promote to the utmost of our Power."

At the Easter Sessions a general order was made to apprehend Henry Lloyd of Dorney, who was informed against by Joseph Street, as having uttered treasonable words against the person of his most sacred Majesty, and being a person disaffected to the Government, and of wicked and dangerous principles, and who was said to "privily lurk and hide himself in divers obscure places of this county not easily to be discovered."

It may be noticed that *David* Lloyd is mentioned by Macaulay as one of the ablest and most active of the emissaries who carried communications between the exiled King and the Jacobites in England.

At the same Sessions the Justices proceeded to take stringent measures for the effectual prosecution and punishment of all persons guilty of excessive drinking, blasphemy, profane swearing and cursing, lewdness, profanation of the

Lord's Day, and other dissolute, immoral, or disorderly practices. This was in accordance with a special proclamation issued by the King "out of a deep sense of the great goodness and mercy of Almighty God in putting an end to a long, bloody, and expensive war by the conclusion of an honourable peace." Special care was to be taken to apprehend the authors and publishers of books or pamphlets containing impious doctrines "tending to the subversion of the Christian religion."

An Act of 1696 empowered the Justices to fix the price of salt, which they accordingly did by ordering that "Newcastle salt, Wayne salt, and other salt unrefined, made within this realm," should be sold for not more than 4*s.* 4*d.* a bushel, and Bay salt, and other foreign salt, for not more than 7*s.* 6*d.*, "computing fifty-six pounds weight to the bushel." The penalty for disobeying this order was 5*l.* But it was found necessary at the next Sessions to increase the rates to 6*s.* and 8*s.* respectively.

The Window Tax appears in 1697 under the title of an "Act for granting to his Majesty several rates or duties upon houses for making good the deficiency of the Clipped Money." The Justices had a dispensing power similar to that which they exercised under the Stuarts with regard to the hearth-tax. They had to examine the parties complaining concerning the number of windows or lights in their dwelling-houses, and to "increase, *defaulk*, or enlarge the assessments." This caused a considerable increase in the business of Sessions, and compelled the Justices to adjourn them from time to time, not only for their own convenience and for that of the parties, but also to suit the engagements of his Majesty's Inspectors, who had a right to be present.

In 1700 the laws of supply and demand were found to

be too strong for the Justices. The court considered that the wages of artificers and labourers, as settled at the Sessions, had not for many years been altered, notwithstanding that by the consent of masters and servants the same had been generally increased both in the Vale and the Chiltern, "whereby both masters and servants have been and are subjected to indictments for their disobedience and contempts of the orders of this Court." It was therefore ordered that the rates of wages should be reconsidered at the next Sessions. Nevertheless, no alteration was made during either this or the following reign.

It may be worth recording that the registers of the parish of Amersham, quoted in a previous part of this paper, are complete from the year 1561. There are a few leaves containing the accounts of the Churchwardens as early as the reign of Henry VIII. I looked among the baptisms of the time of the Commonwealth for curious Scriptural names of the "Praisegod Barebone" type, but could find nothing more extraordinary than Jonah, Tobyas, Zacchæus, Nathaniel, Jonathan, Ezekiah, Timothy, and Deborah. The certificates of corpses having been buried in woollen, according to the well-known Act of Charles II., begin in August, 1678. There are lists of the names of those who received certificates under the hands and seals of the Minister and Churchwardens "in order to be touched for the disease commonly called the King's Evill." There were five such cases in 1685, eight in 1686, one in 1687, and two in 1688. There are none in the reign of William and Mary, or of Anne, but there is one in the reign of George I.

QUARTER SESSIONS UNDER QUEEN ANNE.

THE contrast between the records of Devon and those of Bucks, which has been remarked in the reign of William and Mary, continues in that of Queen Anne. The Justices of Devon, so far as appears by the Sessions Books, limited themselves strictly to the necessary details of local business, and concerned themselves not at all with questions of Imperial policy. Though the real King of men in this reign, who was turning to flight the armies of the Frenchman, was himself a Devonshire gentleman, no congratulatory addresses on Blenheim or Ramilies seem to have been adopted by the Justices of his native county. It is possible that they had come to think it wrong to bring such subjects forward at Quarter Sessions. But it is more likely that they were still under the influence of Sir Edward Seymour, who was no friend to Marlborough and Godolphin. A few new acts, the execution of which was left to the Justices, are reflected in the records of their proceedings. Otherwise, the entries merely comprise the old routine of familiar subjects, which have been so often mentioned in this series of papers.

One of these subjects appears to have been considered peculiarly pressing at this time, as it had been more than a century before, in the reign of Elizabeth. Both in Devon and in Bucks we find constant orders about vagrants, who were declared to be "a great and increasing chargeto the county."

In 1704 it was recited that the rates for the conveyance of vagrants to another county, or to the House of Correction, had been "lymitted to a penny halfepenny per mile for each horse, and a penny halfepenny per mile for each Guardsman, and sixpence per diem for each vagrant's maintenance." It was ordered that in future "one penny per mile forth and one penny per mile backe be allowed for each Guardsman, and Three halfe pence per mile forth as well as backe for each horse."

In 1707 it was further ordered "that the Constables and Tythingmen be allowed Two shillings and sixpence for each conveyance."

In 1708 it appeared to the Court that, in pursuance of a recent Act of Parliament for conveying vagrants, &c., great numbers of wandering persons were brought from the county of Dorset and other counties into the town of Axminster, "to be there received by the proper officers of that place and by them conveyed unto the next town in the next county, and other remote places." It also appeared that, "by means of the great numbers of such vagrants, and their frequent and sudden coming," the officers and parishioners of Axminster were frequently "disturbed and hindered in the *managery* of their affairs, trades, and professions." In order to prevent these evils, the Justices, "upon mature deliberation," made a regular contract with John Crosse of Axminster, clothier, for providing subsistence and conveyance for such vagrants, at the cost of forty pounds a year, "for his Labour, care, paines, expences, and disbursements."

There are other entries relating to this subject, and

reflecting on "the indiscrete *manegery*, ignorance, and neglect of the Constables and Tithingmen."

"Maimed soldiers" continued to be occasionally relieved, as, for instance, James Palmer, of St. Giles's, who "received greate damage in his body by a bruse of a Greate Gun in her present Majestie's service."

There is a curious order respecting game in the records of 1704. The Court had been given to understand that "diverse mean and disorderly persons, laying aside their lawfull trades and employments, do betake themselves to the taking and killing of hares, pheasants and partridges, and other game appropriated to the Lords of Mannors and other Gentlemen, with Dogs, nets, guns, harepipes, and other Engines, and also the killing and destroying of ffish with Netts, spears, and other instruments, without the consent of the owners of the soile, such persons not being any way qualified as the statute in such cases directs." The Court required and authorized the Constables and Tithingmen to search the houses, out-houses, &c., of such disorderly persons as they might suspect of keeping "doggs, netts, or other Engins," and, having found any such articles in the possession of any person not qualified to kill game, they were directed to forthwith "breake such guns, hang such dogs, burne such netts, and destroy such Engines." But *none of her Majestie's Protestant subjects* were to be "by virtue hereof disturbed in keeping arms for their own preservation."

It was probably about this time that Sir Roger de Coverley "gained universal applause by explaining a passage in the Game Act."

Drovers of cattle and *badgers*, or small dealers in corn, had been required to take out licences by a statute of

Elizabeth. Either this Act had fallen into desuetude, or the Clerks of the Peace had for many years neglected to enter in their books the names of the licensees. In the reign of Anne, the subject reappears, and the cases are entered very minutely, and in considerable numbers. Perhaps one specimen should be given.

"Richard Tulling, of Coombmartyn, in this County of
" Devon, yeoman, being of ye age of Thirty years and up-
" wards, *and a married man*, and having lived in ye said
" parish of Coombmartyn for the space of Three years last
" past and upwards, and being otherwise Qualified as y^e
" Statute in such cases directs, is hereby Lycensed and
" allowed for ye space of One Yeare now next ensueing and
" no longer, to be a Common Drover of Cattle, *Badger*,
" *Lader*, *Kidder*, Carrier, and Byer of corne, graine, butter,
" and cheese, in open markett and out of marketts, as an
" Act of Parliament made in the ffifth yeare of the Raigne
" of Queene Elizabeth directs, intituled an Act touching
" Badgers of Corne and Drovers of Cattle to be Lycenced ;
" so that ye said Richard Tulling doe duly observe and
" keep ye Condicon of the Recognizance which he togeather
" with his Two Sureties have entred into at this present
" Sessions pursuant to the said statute, and doe nothing
" contrary to the statutes prohibiting forestalling, regrateing,
" and Ingrosseing."

The amount of the recognizance was generally 40*l*. for the principal, and 20*l*. for each surety.

A petition from the waggoners *on the Western Wades* passing through the county of Devon " to and from London, and to and from Exeter and other places of Trade," brings before us a long-extinct Act, forbidding any person to use more than six horses " to any travelling waggon, wain, cart, or carriage." The Justices in Quarter Sessions had a dispensing power to permit waggoners to use more than six horses to draw their waggons up certain hills mentioned in the order of Court, and we accordingly find an accurate definition of certain hills on the London road upon which waggoners might "use and drive Seven Horses at Length for drawing their Severall and respective Waggons and Carriages."

The word *wade*, properly a ford, is used here to signify a road, and not merely the crossing of water. It is, I believe, extinct as a noun, though it survives as a verb. Mr. R. J. King has pointed out to me that it is identical with the Saxon *wath*. It must come from the same root as the Latin *vadum*.

In 1709 the Court allowed Mr. John Clopp and Mr. Bickerstave Williams, constables of Honiton, the sum of 12*l*. 7*s*. 9*d*., which they had "necessarily laid out and expended" for conveying "the Armes, Clothes, and Accoutraments of the Lord Tyrawly and Col. Churchill's Regiments" from Honiton to Exeter, over and above the sum of 4*l*. 1*s*. 9*d*. which they had received from the officers of the said regiments, "according to a late Act of Parliament in that case lately provided." And in 1711 the Court made a similar payment for conveying "the Baggages of an Extraordinary Weight and the Sick Soldiers belonging to the Regiment of Collonell Winsor."

It would appear that sign-posts were invented in the reign of William III. At any rate, the Act 8 and 9 Wm. III. c. 16 empowered the Justices to order the surveyors of the highways to erect or fix, in the most convenient place "where two or more cross highways meet," a stone or post, with an inscription thereon in large letters, " containing the name of the next market town to which each of the said joining highways leads." An order of our Court at the Michaelmas Sessions of 1713 directed this Act to be duly put in execution throughout the county, as the Grand Inquest had presented "that the said clause was of great use and benefit to her Majestie's subjects in such places where the same hath been duly observed; but that the due execucon thereof hath in many places of this county been neglected and wholly omitted, to the great inconvenience and damage of her Majestie's liege people."

The Justices continued to have authority to fix the price of salt. In 1713 the Grand Inquest presented that "wee doe conceive that the maker or first seller may take at Barnstaple, Biddeford, and other ye North parts of this County for English Salt made in Chester and ye other parts adjoining, not above one shilling ye Bushell single Winchester measure, each bushell containing 56 pounds." At Plymouth, Dartmouth, &c., not above 1s. 4d. At Topsham and parts adjacent not above 1s. 6d. "And for all salt made and refined at Limington and ye parts adjacent," if imported into any port on the south side of the county, not above 1s. If imported into the north side, not above 1s. 6d. "And for all forreigne Salt," *the first seller* thereof should not take above 1s. 6d. These prices were in all cases "over and above the duty imposed by the said Act." They were recommended to the Justices, and no doubt approved by them. The duty was 1s. a bushel, so that the price of salt in Devonshire was from 2s. to 2s. 6d. The difference of prices caused by the difficulties of carriage in former times is well exemplified by the fact that salt in Bucks cost from 6s. to 8s. a bushel.[1]

[1] See "Quarter Sessions under William and Mary."

Before leaving the records of the Quarter Sessions of Devon, it may be well to quote the last rates of wages settled in the reign of Queen Anne.

A "bayliffe of husbandry, hyne, or miller," was to receive not more than 5*l.* a year.

A "common man-servant in husbandry," if between sixteen and twenty years of age, not more than 3*l.* Above twenty years, not more than 4*l.*

A woman servant, if under fourteen, no wages, but meat, drink, and clothes. From fourteen to eighteen, not more than 40*s.* Above eighteen, not more than 50*s.*

"Husbandry labourers" from Allhallow-tide (Nov. 1) until Candlemas (Feb. 2) were to receive not more than 5*d.* a day with meat and drink, or 11*d.* without. From Candlemas to Allhallow-tide, 6*d.*, or 12*d.* At mowing of corn or grass they might take 8*d.*, or 1*s.* 4*d.*

"Women labourers at hay" were to have not more than 3*d.*, or 6*d.* In corn harvest, 4*d.*, or 8*d.* "At reaping," 6*d.*, or 12*d.*"

"Master carpenters," masons, &c., not more than 8*d.*, or 1*s.* 4*d.*"

Other carpenters, masons, &c., not more than 6*d.*, or 12*d.* Apprentices for the first four years, not more than 3*d.* or 7*d.*

A pair of sawyers, not above 1*s.* 4*d.*, or 2*s.* 8*d.*

All spinsters not above 12*d.* *by the week*, with meat and drink, or 2*s.* 6*d.* without meat and drink.

If we compare these rates with those appointed in the reign of Elizabeth,[2] one hundred and nineteen years before, we may well be astonished at the slowness of the increase, except in the case of indoor servants. A bailiff's wages

[2] See "Quarter Sessions under Queen Elizabeth."

had only advanced from 3*l.* 6*s.* 8*d.* to 5*l.* Those of a farm man-servant had been just doubled. Those of a female servant had been rather more than doubled. Those of a woman employed in making hay had not been increased at all. The wages of ordinary farm labourers had only risen from 7*d.* to 11*d.* a day in winter, and from 8*d.* to 1*s.* in summer.³ Those of foremen in the building trades had only been raised from 1*s.* to 1*s.* 4*d.* a day, and those of journeymen from 11*d.* to 1*s.* And this was in an age when the disparity between the rich and poor was so great that the official income of the Duke and Duchess of Marlborough, from the various places that they held, amounted, according to Lord Stanhope, to the prodigious sum of 64,325*l.*

Turning now to the records of Bucks, we find the Easter Sessions of 1702 held in the name of Queen Anne, William having died on the 8th of March. But little was done until the Midsummer sessions, when a large number of Justices and others attended and took the various oaths required by the Acts concerning supremacy and allegiance, " to prevent dangers which may happen by Popish recusants," and especially by the Act "for the further security of his Majesty's Person, and the succession of the Crowne in a Protestant Line, and for extinguishing the hopes of the pretended Prince of Wales and all other pretenders and their open and secret abettors." The Court was adjourned to Chipping Wycombe, Chesham, Newport Pagnell, and Buckingham, to enable aged and infirm people to attend and take the prescribed oaths.

³ In Bucks the appointed rate of wages for farm labourers in the reign of Anne was no greater than that fixed in Devonshire in the reign of Elizabeth.

Most commissions, such as those of Lord-Lieutenant and *Custos Rotulorum*, were then terminable at the demise of the Crown. Marlborough and Godolphin naturally abstained from reappointing the extreme Whigs, especially those who were disliked by the new sovereign.

The removal of Thomas Lord Wharton from the office of *Custos Rotulorum* for the county of Bucks gave rise to a dispute between Thomas Smith, the Clerk of the Peace who had been appointed by him, and Francis Neale, who claimed the place by a grant from the new Custos, William Viscount Newhaven. Mr. Smith obtained a mandamus from the Court of Queen's Bench commanding the Justices to restore him, or to show cause to the contrary. But Mr. Neale succeeded in retaining his post. The Clerk of the Peace was at this time only the deputy of the *Custos Rotulorum*. Viscount Newhaven was, I suspect, the same nobleman who, as Lord Cheyney, fought a duel with Wharton in consequence of a quarrel for precedence at the Quarter Sessions of Bucks in 1699, and has for that reason been honoured by a place in Macaulay's History.

At Epiphany, 1704, the Earl of Bridgewater, as *Custos Rotulorum* of Bucks, reported that he had received directions from the Privy Council, recommending to his lordship and the Justices the vigorous execution of an Act for raising recruits for her Majesty's Land forces and Marines, "the same being att this tyme of greate importance to her Majestie's service." The constables were ordered to bring before the Justices all such able-bodied men as they should find in their parishes "as have not any lawful calleing or Imployment, or visible means for their Livelyhood, *and that have noe vote in electing of any member or members* to serve in Parliament." They were, of course, "entertained as soldiers in her Majesty's service," that is, enlisted compulsorily. The names of the persons so "listed," and the regiments to which they were sent, were reported to Sessions. Many debtors were at the same time discharged from prison on condition of serving in the fleet or army.

The description given of the recruits would hardly be of much use in case of their desertion. Richard Grove was a "middle-sized man." John Hopkins was a "tall black mann, aged thirty." Richard Kempster was "a thick, short, Brown-haired mann, aged eighteen yeares." John Wood was "a well-sized browne man, aged about twenty yeares," and so on. "John Samms, a Thin-bodyed man," reminds one of Falstaff's recruit Shadow, who "presented no mark to the enemy; the foeman might with as great aim level at the edge of a pen-knife."

In 1705 the Lord-Lieutenant received a letter on the same subject, "being a service absolutely necessary for carrying on the Warr."

A comment is supplied by the application of Mr. Noah Pitcher, "a skillfull chyrurgeon," showing that one Gerard Wilding, a vagrant who had been taken up for her Majesty's service, had, to disable himself from that service, "in a malicious and barbarous manner, cutt and divided the greate Tendon of his Legg," and that Mr. Pitcher, "in order to have made him serviceable," had "made severall operacons, and applyed severall medicaments, and constantly attended him for a considerable tyme." Mr. Pitcher only claimed 3*l.* 13*s.*, but the court cut him down to 3*l.*

The battle of Ramilies was fought on May 23, 1706, and within a few days afterwards almost every city and fortress of Flanders was in the hands of Marlborough. Even the cool-headed conqueror wrote to his wife of that marvellous

Quarter Sessions under Queen Anne.

campaign that "it really looked more like a dream than truth." The capture of Barcelona by Peterborough in the previous autumn was also an exploit of which England might well be proud.

At the Midsummer Sessions, the following address " to the Queen's most excellent Majestie " was made and signed by the Justices, gentry, and freeholders of the county of Bucks :—

"Most Dread Soveraigne,

"Tis the peculiar Prerogative of your Majesty's most "Glorious Reign that your Majesty's dutiful and happy "Subjects have no occasion to use their privilege of peti-"tioning to the Throne for Redress of Grievances, but are "only employed in addressing their great and Victorious "Queen in the style of joy and congratulation.

"With Infinite Pleasure we embrace the present oppor-"tunity of joining in the Universal Acclamations of your "Majesty's Loyal people for the late wonderful Success of "your Majesty's forces and those of your Allies, under the "unparalleled Conduct and bravery of his Grace the Duke "of Marlborough, and of your Majesty's other renowned "Generals the Earl of Peterborough and the Earl of Gal-"loway (Galway) ; and with great satisfaction we admire "your Majesty's wisdom in the choice of your present "Ministers and Generals, under whom the exorbitant "Power of France has been so visibly reduced, and the "ancient Honour of England so gloriously advanced.

" And that your Majesty's Reign may long continue over " us, and your arms for ever flourish, the undaunted courage "of your Troops still prevail, *and the Trepidity of your* "*Enemies increase,* shall ever be the prayers of

"Your Majesty's most Loyal, Dutiful,
"and Obedient Subjects."

It may be doubted whether Marlborough would have felt altogether satisfied at finding his name associated with that of the Earl of Peterborough. But it is certain that neither of them would have been well pleased at being joined in the same sentence with the Earl of Galway, whom Macaulay calls a pedant and a sluggard, "a man who was in war what Molière's doctors were in medicine, who thought it much more honourable to fail according to rule than to succeed by innovation." But Galway, though a Frenchman by birth, was looked upon by the Whigs as a staunch member of their party.

In the next year the county of Bucks was equally pleased at the completion of the Union with Scotland. Here is the address voted on that occasion :—

"May it please your Majesty,

"As no people were ever more prosperous under the "happy influence of a glorious reign, so it is our duty to "take all opportunities to manifest our sincere Affections "and hearty Zeal to the Great Source from whence (under "God) all our Blessings flow. And amongst all the unex-"pected Successes that have attended your Majesty's "prudent Conduct and unwearied Endeavours, nothing can "make us appear more formidable abroad and secure at "home than the long wished for Union of your Two Neigh-"bouring Kingdoms, a work of such difficulty that, though "so often attempted by your Royal Predecessors, it seemed "reserved only to add fresh Glories to your Majesty's most "auspicious Government.

"May the same Spirit of Union that has always inspired "your Majesty's Councils prevent all Differences and "Animosities amongst your United Subjects. May your "Majesty enjoy a long and prosperous Reign over us, and

Quarter Sessions under Queen Anne. 279

"at last receive the Reward of your unexampled Care and
"Concern for the welfare of all your Liege People and
"their posterity."

At Midsummer, 1706, the Justices had received orders
from the Privy Council to make a strict inquiry respecting
all "Papists and reputed Papists, their qualities, estates, and
places of abode," and committees were appointed for each
hundred to carry out this business. It is possible that the
Ministers thought it well to make a display of Protestant
zeal while they were carrying on negotiations for the Union
with the Presbyterians of Scotland.

In looking through so many volumes of County Records
I have of course seen many thousands and tens of thousands
of proper names, belonging to men of all ranks and degrees,
to noblemen, justices, jurymen, witnesses, sureties, inn-
keepers, hawkers, paupers, vagrants, criminals, and others.
And in no single instance, down to the end of the reign of
Anne, have I noticed any person bearing more than one
Christian name. The first instance occurs in 1717, when
Sir Coplestone Warwick Bampfield appears among the
Justices who attended the Midsummer Sessions at Exeter.
The first instances which I have met with in any other
place are those of Henry Frederick, Earl of Arundel, born
in 1608, and Sir Henry Frederick Thynne, who was created
a baronet in 1641. Both these must have been named
after the eldest son of James the First, who was, of course,
born in Scotland. No other child of James bore two
Christian names, nor did any child of Charles the First,
except Henrietta Maria, named after her mother, who was
a Frenchwoman. No King of England bore two Christian
names before William the Third, who was a Dutchman.

It seems probable that the practice of giving children two Christian names was utterly unknown in England before the accession of the Stuarts, that it was very rarely adopted down to the time of the Revolution, and that it never became common until after the Hanoverian family was seated on the throne.

We have now seen what information is to be gleaned from the records of Quarter Sessions, at least from those of the counties of Devon and Bucks, during a space of one hundred and twenty-two years, extending from the thirty-fourth year of Elizabeth to the last year of Anne.

In the administration of justice, we have passed from the multitudinous hangings, brandings, and floggings, which characterized the earlier reign, to the more settled and temperate system which began to be established in the latter. In finance, we have passed from the privy seals of Elizabeth, and the benevolences of James the First, to the National Debt and the scientific taxation of Godolphin and Montague. In religious matters, we have passed from persecution to toleration. If these gleanings are worth anything at all, they ought to serve as contributions to a more accurate knowledge of the condition of the people, and of the government under which they lived, at least in the rural districts. Such knowledge was perhaps too much neglected by the older historians, and was not allowed its fair weight until supported by all the eloquence of Lord Macaulay. The earlier writers had their attention not unnaturally concentrated on the movements of armies, the debates of politicians, the struggles of diplomatists, and the intrigues of Courts. Lord Stanhope, though one of the latest writers who have undertaken to portray the age of

Anne, was yet an historian of the older type. He was dazzled by the military and literary glories of the reign, and could not doubt that, in that Augustan Age of England, the people must have been extremely happy. He compares the days of Queen Anne with the days of Queen Victoria, and declares himself fully convinced "that the people of Queen Anne enjoyed much the larger measure of happiness."

Of the details from which he has drawn this induction he does not favour us with any clear view. He tells us casually that in Queen Anne's time "there was no trace of serfdom or compulsory service, but there lingered the feeling of protection due by the lord of the soil to his retainers in sickness or old age. Labour was then no mere contract of work done for value received. . . . The handicraftsman and the labourer had no difficulty in obtaining employment without dispute as to the hours of work or the rate of wages. Most grievous is the change in that respect which has since ensued!"

The change is simply that the labourer is permitted to make a bargain with his employer for the value of his labour. The labourer of the reign of Anne was compelled "to take a master" at a prescribed rate of wages, and was liable to be flogged and imprisoned if he was out of work, or even if he accepted a higher rate from a willing master.

"As between landlord and tenant," says Lord Stanhope, "a more cordial spirit, a more intimate relation, appears to have prevailed. There was wholly absent that main cause of alienation—whenever at present alienation does occur—the excessive preserving of game." And then he gives us a fancy picture of a shooting party in the time of Queen Anne, which appears very much like a shooting party in the time of Queen Victoria on the estate of a reasonable and good-natured squire; a race, we may hope, which is not yet quite extinct. Nor were all landlords of the former epoch quite perfect, if we may believe Pope's character of Sir John Cutler. Even the good Sir Roger, as we are informed, had destroyed with his gun "many thousands of pheasants, partridges, and woodcocks," though some doubt of the accuracy of this sporting intelligence may be caused by the further information that he had killed "several kinds of deer in the chase," "tired many a salmon with a line consisting of a single hair," and hunted one fox for fifteen hours through half a dozen counties!

The excessive preservation of game has done harm enough, no doubt, in our days, but scarcely so much harm as to deserve to be balanced as a cause of general unhappiness against the ferocity of party spirit in religion and politics, and the constant dread of civil war, which prevailed in the reign of Queen Anne.

Again, we are told that there was at the former period "much less of wealth but much less also of abject poverty. The contrasts were not so sharp, nor stood as it were so closely face to face with each other." Lord Stanhope gives us in another place an account of the emoluments of the Marlboroughs. But he does not mention the wages of the labourers who were toiling for five shillings and sixpence a week in Devonshire, or for three shillings and sixpence in Buckinghamshire, while the price of wheat in bad years rose to fifty-four shillings a quarter. Nor does he mention the multitudes of vagrants of which the Justices so often complained.

There is one part of Lord Stanhope's contrast between the age of Queen Anne and the age of Queen Victoria that certainly appears at first sight to have a great deal of truth in it. I mean the complaint summed up by Mr. Tennyson some forty years ago in the line—

"Every gate is thronged with suitors, all the markets overflow."

Lord Stanhope says,—
"As regards the liberal professions and the employments
"in the Civil Service, it may be deemed, from the absence,
"at least, of any indications to the contrary, that under
"Queen Anne there was more of equality between the
"supply and the demand. The number of men of good
"character and good education who desired to enter any
"career was not disproportioned to the number of openings
"which that career presented. It followed that any person
"endowed with fair aptitude and common application, and
"engaging in any recognized walk of life, was in due time
"certain, or nearly certain, of a livelihood. Riches and dis-
"tinction were of course, as in every state of society, the
"portion of the few, but there was competence for the
"many. How greatly the times have changed! . . .

"It is certainly a great practical hardship, such as we do
"not trace under Queen Anne or under the first Georges,
"that a young man entering life with a good character and
"careful education should see every profession overcrowded,
"every avenue of advancement hemmed in, that he should
"be unable in so many cases to earn his bread, and be cast
"back for subsistence on his family."

There can be no doubt that the number of young gentlemen of good character and fair education has much increased in England since the age of Queen Anne. But the number of opportunities for a successful career, if not at the Bar or in the Civil Service, at least in India, in the Colonies, or in business, has also increased enormously, nor would it be easy to prove that it has not increased in proportion. At any rate, it is quite certain that the difficulty of providing fit occupation for the younger sons of good families was felt in the reign of Queen Anne, as it was felt long before, and has been felt long since. One of the most interesting sketches in the *Spectator* is that of Will Wimble, the younger brother of a baronet of ancient family. He was "bred to no business, and born to no estate," and spent his life in looking after the game on his elder brother's property. His position was very much like that of a young man who has failed in a competitive examination in the reign of Queen Victoria, and who has been "given up to his own inventions." And, lest we should look upon him as an exceptional object of compassion, we are informed that "Will Wimble's is the case of many a younger brother of a great family, who had rather see their children starve like gentlemen than thrive in a trade or profession that is beneath their quality."

No doubt, as Lord Macaulay observes, there was no Joseph Hume in the reign of Anne. Ministers had the power of conferring pensions and sinecure places on their friends, and on the sons of their friends, and exercised it without much regard to their characters or education. But the cessation, or diminution, of this practice is surely not to be much regretted by the public.

The truth seems to be that the age of good Queen Anne was a pleasant time for a general like Marlborough, whose victories were rewarded with titles, and honours, and estates, and palaces, and grants of hundreds of thousands of pounds. It was a pleasant time for a gentleman "of respectable abilities" like James Stanhope, whose civil and military services obtained for him the earldom which has been so worthily borne in our days by his descendant. It was a pleasant time for a poet like Pope, whose genius won for him fame, and friends, and fortune, such as had never before fallen to the lot of an English poet. It was a pleasant time for a writer like Addison, whose polished prose and less perfect verse made him a Secretary of State. It was a pleasant time for at least some of the merchants and speculators, of whom Budgell wrote, " I have observed greater estates got about 'Change than at Whitehall or St. James's," although they must have been haunted by a fear of their investments being all wiped out by the return of James III.

It was, perhaps, not so pleasant a time for the working classes, who were compelled to labour for whatever wages the Justices thought fit to appoint. It was not so pleasant for the Roman Catholics, who were deprived of their horses and arms, and were liable to fine and imprisonment if they refused to take an oath of allegiance to one whom they firmly believed to be an heretical usurper. It was not so pleasant even for the Protestant Dissenters, who found all honours and public employments refused to them. It was not so pleasant for the poor fellows who were taken by force from their wives and families to be shot on the banks of the Danube, or to return home as " maimed soldiers " and beg the Court of Quarter Sessions " of their great charity " to grant them pensions of thirty or forty shillings a year. It was not so pleasant for the prisoners, who were left to perish in the gaols from starvation or fever. It was not so pleasant for the paupers, whose number amounted to nearly one-fifth of the population. It was not so pleasant for the vagrants, who wandered about the country in swarms, in constant terror of being caught, stripped naked, and flogged, women as well as men, "until their backs were bloody," and *præconis ad fastidium*—until the constable was disgusted with his work.

It is surely sufficient praise when we say that the reign of Anne was an age of many great and illustrious men, of many splendid victories, and of many eminent achievements in science, and literature, and statesmanship; that it made the people who lived under her rule happier than their fathers had been, and that it laid the foundation for much of the prosperity and happiness which have been enjoyed by their descendants.

Besides giving us some idea of the condition of the people, the records of Quarter Sessions ought to throw some light on the conduct and the opinions of that ancient and peculiar body, the Justices of the Peace. Their opinions on some subjects may be gleaned from the sentences they passed and the orders they made, especially in the matters of "Popish recusants" and Protestant Nonconformists. Still more may be learned from the addresses of a political or quasi-political character which they sometimes adopted. Unfortunately we have no specimens of the speeches by which these addresses were supported or opposed, and which might, perhaps, have been sometimes more instructive than the addresses themselves. We know that Sir Roger de Coverley was said to have died from the effects of a cold he caught at the Sessions of his county, as he was very warmly promoting an address of his own penning, in which he succeeded according to his wishes. "But this particular comes from a Whig Justice of Peace, who was always Sir Roger's enemy and antagonist."

Of the private habits and mode of life of the Justices of bygone times we learn little or nothing from these records.

On those points we are left to seek information from diaries and letters, and still more from works of fiction, which often preserve facts which history has disdained to record. The lighter literature of England contains plenty of sketches of Justices, from which we may easily gain a notion of what manner of men they were who transacted the business of Quarter Sessions at different periods. Many such may be found relating to the space of one hundred and twenty years with which we have been dealing. Among these there are three immortal portraits which stand out conspicuous, each painted by the hand of a master, though of very unequal merit. And, curiously enough, these portraits belong respectively to the beginning, middle, and end of the space of time to which I refer. One belongs to the age of Elizabeth, one to that of the Commonwealth, and one to that of Anne.

The first portrait is by the most illustrious master, though it is not one of his greatest works. But, as Mrs. Browning has said, a face carved on a cherry-stone may reveal in its lines the mallet-hand. Among all the fools of various sorts and degrees that we find immortalized in the plays of Shakespeare, the greatest fool, except perhaps the constable Dogberry, is Robert Shallow, Esquire, one of the Justices of the Peace "of the coram and custalorum" for the county of Gloucester. There are few characters drawn with more evident enjoyment on the part of the artist. In Master Shallow we see a combination of almost everything that can render a man ridiculous and contemptible. He is an old man, yet ever boasting of the dissipations of his youth, "and every third word a lie, duer paid to the hearer than the Turk's tribute." He is full of self-importance, yet capable of the meanest actions ; a tyrant to his inferiors, and cringing to his superiors; somewhat given to liquor, regardless of justice, a mere tool in the hands of his own servants, and an easy prey to the wily Sir John Falstaff. We know how that witty knight remarks upon Master Shallow's character: " It is a wonderful thing to see the semblable coherence of his men's spirits and his. They, by observing him, do bear themselves like foolish justices; he by conversing with them, is turned into a justice-like serving man;—their spirits are so married in conjunction with the participation of society, that they flock together in consent, like so many wild geese. If I had a suit to Master Shallow, I would humour his men with the imputation of being near their master; if to his men, I would curry with Master Shallow, that no man could better command his servants. It is certain that either wise bearing or ignorant carriage is caught, as men take diseases one of another, therefore let men take heed of their company."

There is no character in Shakespeare that more decidedly bears evidence of having been intended as a personal attack than that of Master Shallow. It fortunately happens that we know the reason of this. It seems tolerably certain that the poet was in his youth caught poaching in the park of Sir Thomas Lucy, and that he had with that worshipful knight an interview, of which he retained the most unpleasant recollections. Indeed his first attempt at poetry is said to have been a satirical ballad on Sir Thomas Lucy. There can be no doubt that Justice Shallow is a caricature of the same personage. He is identified by his coat-armour, which Master Slender describes as bearing a dozen white *luces*. But it may be feared that the poet, being by no means exempt from the frailties of more ordinary mortals, was eager to avenge his grievance against Sir Thomas upon the whole class to which the knight belonged. His brother justice, Master Silence, is as great a fool as Shallow, though he does not talk quite so much nonsense, except when he is in liquor. His cousin Slender is merely a reflection of the same character. Even the humbler peace-officers, Dogberry, Verges, and the like, were equally objectionable in the eyes of " the immortal Williams."

Shallow is represented as living in the reign of Henry IV. But that goes for nothing. It may be taken as certain that Shakespeare intended to satirize the justices of his own time, and it is likely enough that some of them were no wiser than Shallow, and more like serving-men than justices.

We know, however, that there were others of a very different type. The class from which sprang men like Walter Raleigh must have contained many individuals not destitute of brains or of culture. It is probable that Warwickshire and Gloucestershire, the counties with which Shakespeare was best acquainted, were at that time less enlightened than Devonshire. At any rate, we know exactly who the justices of Devon were at the end of the reign of Elizabeth. They were only fifty-four in number, and, as there were some hundreds of families in the county entitled to bear coat-armour, it seems likely that some care was taken in their selection. Most of them, we may suppose, knew a little Latin, as all law proceedings were then written in that language. We may also suppose that they knew a little law, as justices' clerks were not yet a regular institution, and it was an ordinary part of a gentleman's education to read law for two or three years at one of the Inns of Court. Several of them played a not undistinguished part among the men of that remarkable generation. Some of them, as Periam, and Prideaux, and Glanvyle, were lawyers whose names are still

U

remembered. Others, as Sir William Pole, author of the *Description of Devonshire*, and Richard Carew, author of the *Survey of Cornwall*, were men of considerable literary ability. Others, as Drake, and Gilbert, and Cary, were among the foremost of the men who reared up a very small kingdom into a very great empire. Others, if not heroes themselves, were at any rate the sons, or brothers, or fathers of heroes, and it is reasonable to suppose that they were not very far below the average of their relatives.

On the whole, Shakespeare's sketch must be pronounced a caricature, though with sufficient likeness to render the features easy to be recognized.

Some sixty years afterwards, the Presbyterian Justice of the Commonwealth was drawn in a much more elaborate manner, though by a far inferior hand. If Shakespeare was prompted by personal hatred, Butler was actuated by political and theological hatred as well. It may be considered settled that Sir Samuel Luke sat for the portrait of Hudibras. The idea of describing the adventures of a knight and squire, or master and man, was probably taken from Cervantes. Don Quixote has in that respect served as the model of many writers, down to the time of Mr. Pickwick and Charles O'Malley. But some of the touches in the character seem to have been borrowed from Shallow, with the addition of pedantry and intolerance, which we do not find in the earlier worthy. Of course accuracy is not to be looked for in a burlesque poem. It is a caricature, and an extravagant caricature. Yet the work of Butler must always retain some historical and literary importance, though no generation except the subjects of Charles II. would be likely to value it more highly than the *Paradise Lost*. Dr. Johnson seems to have been persuaded that Butler's descriptions of "the sour solemnity, the sullen superstition, the gloomy moroseness, and the stubborn scruples," which he alliteratively attributes to the ancient Puritans, were accurately true. " Our grandfathers knew the picture from the life ; we judge of the life by contemplating the picture."

There was no doubt as much truth in the picture as may reasonably be required in a caricature. But the justices, even of that period and that party, comprised many accomplished and liberal-minded gentlemen, as we know from many sources, and especially from the lives of Eliot and Hampden.

But if Shakespeare and Butler set themselves to ridicule the country justices of their time with the utmost ferocity, no such charge can be brought against the gentle artist who undertook the portrait of the Justice of the reign of Queen Anne. He had executed pictures of Cato and Marlborough, not without a fair measure of success, but he found his most congenial subject in the good Sir Roger de Coverley. The Worcestershire baronet is undoubtedly Addison's masterpiece, and one of the best known and best loved characters in the whole range of English literature. Flattered he may be in some respects, but his little absurdities and failings are by no means concealed, though a cunning hand has introduced them in such a way as to heighten the effect of his greater qualities. We have all laughed at the eccentricity, and admired the kind-heartedness, of the worthy baronet. We have watched him at church, where he suffers nobody to sleep but himself, and, after a short nap, jumps up and looks about him, and wakes up anybody who appears to be nodding. We have envied the power which he exercised in making his chaplain pronounce every Sunday a sermon of one of the best English Divines, instead of inflicting upon his congregation one of his own compositions. We have entered into his feelings of pride, when, at the age of twenty-two, he served the office of sheriff, and rode at the head of a whole county, with music before him, a feather in his hat, and his horse well bitted. We see him "filling the chair at a Quarter Sessions with great abilities." We accompany him to the Assizes, and see him make his way through a crowd of red-coated country gentlemen, in order to favour the Judge with a remark on the state of the weather. We share the surprise and anxiety of the Spectator when his friend gets up in the midst of a trial to make a speech, " with a look of much business and great intrepidity." A general whisper runs among the country people that Sir Roger is up. The speech proves to be very little to the purpose, and, in Mr. Spectator's opinion, " was not so much designed by the knight himself to inform the Court, as to give him a figure in my eye, and keep up his credit in the country." In this respect it succeeds perfectly, so that the county gentlemen compliment him, and the ordinary people gaze upon him at a distance, "not a little admiring his courage, that was not afraid to speak to the Judge."

Many little touches complete the picture of the time—the laced hats of the squires, the exaggerated head-dresses of their wives, the elaborate etiquette of a country neighbourhood, and the extraordinary fuss about place and precedency. But all this is merely the background to the portrait of the good baronet, with his overflowing kindness to every one he meets in town or county—to the watermen, the hackney coachmen, the vergers,—as well as to his own tenants and servants, and the poor of his own parish, though the dear old man is a little puzzled about the Coverley witch, and advises her as a Justice of the Peace to avoid all communications with the devil, and never to hurt any of her neighbour's cattle.

The moral of the story is pointed out in the letter of Captain Sentry, "that a man of a warm and well disposed heart, with a very small capacity, is highly superior in human society to him who, with the greatest talents, is cold and languid in his affections." And so Sir Roger leaves behind him a reputation which would be worth the pains of the wisest man's whole life to arrive at.

Attempts have been made to identify Sir Roger de Coverley with Sir John Pakington, who was undoubtedly a Worcestershire baronet, and Knight of the Shire in the reign of Anne. But there, it seems, the resemblance ends. Sir John is said to have been a fierce partisan, and by no means an amiable character. It is certain that he did not spend forty years in pining after an impracticable widow, for he was twice married, and had several children.

It is more probable that Sir Roger is not modelled from any individual. Still less is he a fair representative of his class. There must have been plenty of Justice Shallows and Squire Westerns in his time, and since. He must be considered as an ideal country gentleman, intended as an example for the uncivilized squires of his day, showing them how much goodness and usefulness were compatible with a very moderate share of brains and acquirements. The character of "the fine old English gentleman" was, no doubt, a popular one long before his time. We find a sketch of him in Chaucer, which is not very unlike the Sir Walter Vivian of five centuries afterwards :—

> An householder, and that a great, was he,
> Sir Julian he was in his countrie.

> His table dormant in his hall alway
> Stood ready covered all the long day.
> At Sessions was he lord and sire,
> Full oft-times was he knight of the shire,
> A Sheriff had he been, and à countor,
> Was nowhere such à worthy vavasor.

But it was Addison who gave him immortality, and the fame that extends wherever the English language is spoken. The name of De Coverley is, indeed, too Norman to be accepted as the typical name of an Englishman. That post was assumed about the same time by Mr. John Bull. But Arbuthnot's John Bull was a clothier. Later generations have turned him into a country squire. Many of the best qualities which characterize the John Bull of *Punch* and the other light literature of our own day, many of the virtues and failings which we love to associate with the idea of an English gentleman, are those of the model justice of the reign of Queen Anne, the good Sir Roger de Coverley.

THE TRIAL OF TWO QUAKERS IN THE TIME OF OLIVER CROMWELL.

IT is well known that the Puritans, for some mysterious reason, entertained a particular objection to the Quakers. Not even under Charles the Second were the " Friends " so harshly treated as they were under the Commonwealth. According to the historian of the Society, the messengers of the testimony "were entertained with Scorn and Derision, with Beatings, Buffetings, Stonings, Pinchings, Kickings, Dirtings, Pumpings, and all manner of abuses from the Rude and ungoverned Rabble. And from the Magistrates, who should have been their Defenders, they met with Spoiling of Goods, Stockings, Whippings, Imprisonments, Banishments, and even Death itself."

The extreme penalty was, it would seem, seldom inflicted in England, except indirectly, for an indefinite imprisonment in one of the foul and pestilential dungeons of the period was in many cases equivalent to a sentence of death. But in New England, where the Puritans were triumphant and absolute, the unfortunate Friends were treated with still greater barbarity. They were not unfrequently hanged, and many of them met a worse fate, receiving hundreds of lashes, being kept chained tightly by the neck and heels, and being sold as slaves in the West Indian plantations. It is curious that some of our instructors should insist on confounding the Quakers with the Puritans. A writer in a well-known newspaper, describing the funeral of Mrs. John Bright, remarked on the "utter absence of ceremonial parade, and of any sort of ecclesiastical attire, which distinguishes this sober, steadfast, God-fearing community of *old-fashioned English Puritans.*"

The Quakers of the time of Cromwell would scarcely have been recognized as brethren by the Puritans of that epoch. It is true that the Protector himself was inclined to religious toleration, except in the cases of Popery and Prelacy. But the subordinate magistrates took every opportunity of persecuting the Friends, and sometimes perverted for their oppression the laws which had been passed for very different objects. It seems to have been usual to tender them the oath of abjuration which had been provided as a test for the Roman Catholics. The Quakers, it was well known, were quite as ready to renounce the Pope and all his works as the Presbyterians could be. But they were determined not to swear in any cause, and therefore the offer of an oath was a certain way of bringing them into collision with the law. In the case referred to in the following pages not only was the oath of abjuration employed in this way, but, with ludicrous ingenuity, the culprits were committed for provoking to fight a duel—the provokers being Quakers, and the party provoked being a clergyman, so that both sides might fairly have been supposed incapable of fighting.

The case, no doubt, is only one of many hundreds that happened nearly at the same time. It is only remarkable as having been one of the first of its class, and as having been unusually well preserved. We have the records of important State trials, such as those of Strafford and Laud, but it is rare to find any full record of the ordinary administration of justice in the case of more obscure offenders. In searching among the records of the county of Devon for an example of that administration in the time of the Protector, I met with some sheets of depositions taken with greater care and at greater length than usual. They proved to be the depositions taken in the case of Thomas Salthouse and Miles Halhead, two of the earliest " public Friends," otherwise " messengers " or missionaries, who followed George Fox in bringing the testimony into the West of England. Both of them seem to have been important members of their Society, and founders of meetings in Devonshire. Extraordinary efforts were made to procure their liberation. I have met with a curious pamphlet printed in 1656 " for Giles Calvert at the Black spread Eagle, near the West end of Paul's," and entitled " The Wounds of an Enemie in the House of a Friend, being a Relation of the Hard Measure sustained by Miles Halhead and Thomas Salthouse for the Testimony of Jesus; particularly in a long, and sore, and close imprisonment, first at Plymouth, and then at Exeter, in the county of Devon, though they have neither offended the Law of God or of the Nation." It is for the most part, as might be expected, a rather tedious and rambling production, in part composed of a curious *cento* of texts, but not without an occasional strain of eloquence in pleading for religious liberty, and appealing from the magistrates to the people.

" Was persecution of tender consciences unjust in the
" Bishops, and is it righteous now in them who suffered by
" the Bishops for the tenderness of their consciences, and
" shed so much blood for a secure provision therein, and
" put it to this issue of the sword, *either they and theirs not*

"*to be or not to be without it*, to outstrip the Bishops, yea,
" the latter ages, in a cruel and barbarous persecution of
" their brethren because of the tenderness of their con-
"sciences ? Was the infringement of Liberty, the endea-
" vouring to subvert the fundamental Laws of the Nation,
" and the violation of Right, unrighteous in the King, and
" Strafford, and Canterbury, and that generation, and
" judged tyrannical, and traitorous, and Justice executed
" upon them for so doing, and the King's Family rooted up,
" and thousands of Families destroyed, and the three
" Nations made fields of blood, and hazarded in many years'
" fierce and cruel Wars to bring it to pass? And is it just
" now in inferior Ministers, who are in Commission and
" sworn to execute the Law, to preserve Liberty, and to
" defend Right, as saith also the Instrument of Government,
" to exceed them all in violation of Law, and the destruction
" of Right and Liberty, as if so be the Cause and the Jus-
" tice of the War were to destroy one Generation for ano-
" ther to exercise the same and far greater violences and
" oppressions upon those who were instrumental in the
" destruction of the other ?"

But the chief importance of this tract is that it contains copies of some legal documents which, added to the depositions already mentioned, enable us to form a pretty clear idea of the procedure of the period.

We may now leave the witnesses to tell their own story, only premising that the accused, on their first apprehension, addressed a letter to the Mayor of Plymouth, which is preserved in the pamphlet. It is very Biblical, but slightly incoherent. The following sentence is a specimen of it :—

" Now, Friend, to thee for Justice doe we call, that the
" truth may be freed from scandals and false reports, and

The Trial of Two Quakers.

"the oppressed set free, which is pure religion; that we
"may have that favour at thy hands, which the Law doth
"afford, to bring our Accusers to us, that have anything to
"lay to our charge worthy of Bonds, that things may be
"tryed by the light, and actions weighed in the balance of
"Equity; that truth may spring up out of the Earth, and
"righteousnesse may run down as a mighty stream, and
"peace and Justice may kisse each other; for know
"assuredly, although we are counted deceivers, yet are we
"true, and nothing doe we desire from thee, as thou art a
"Magistrate, but to have the truth cleared by the light, and
"truth set at liberty."

The first witness whom we call is Mr. Peter Popham.

"The Examinacon of Peter Popham of Plymouth had
"and taken before the Right Worshipful John Paige,
"marchant, Maior of the Borrough of Plymouth aforesaid
"and Richard Spurwell, marchant, two Justices of the
"Peace within the said Borrogh the 22*th* day of May, 1655.

"The said deponent sayth *on Oath*, That on Sabbath
"day last being the 20th of this moneth of May in the
"afternoone hee this deponent goeing towards Stonehouse
"to heare one Mr. Titchen that is the present Minister
"there to preach, in his way thither he overtooke one Mr.
"George Brookes and Ralph Ansley—and this deponent
"askinge them where they were goeinge they said to heare
"some Quakers neere a place called the Old Mills that
"were at a howse, as this deponent hath heard, belonging to
"one John Harris within the Burrough of Plymouth afore-
"said. Whereupon this deponent went with them the said
"George Brookes and Ralph Ansley unto the said Harris
"his howse, and from there into a garden belonging to the
"same howse, where were about 70 or 80 persons, amonge

"whome this deponent saw three Strangers who went by
" the name of Quakers, which are the same Three persons
" now present at the time of this deponent's examination,
" owning themselves by the names of Thomas Salthouse,
" Myles Hallhead, and Nicholas Ganniclffe, as they are
" written in two papers now shewed unto this deponent.
" And this deponent further sayth, That he heard the said
" Salthowse (that was then speakinge to the people) say,
" That they should follow noe more their old Ministers, for
" they are those that will bringe them to destruccon, and
" they are Baal's priests, and there is that within a man
" that must carry him to heaven, and there is noe neede of
" other teachinge. And this deponent further sayth, That
" the said Salthowse havinge ended his discourse without
" any prayer, that afterward hee heard the said George
" Brookes open a place of Scripture which was 2 Cor. vi. 1.[1]
" In openinge of which said Scripture the said George
" Brookes spake somethinge of the holy Trinitie. And
" after the said Brookes had done speakinge the said
" Thomas Salthowse spake to the said Brookes, and said
" these words, Thou Lyest in sayinge there were Three
" persons in the Trinitie, I deny itt, there is no such
" Thinge. But thou art a deluding Spiritt come to draw
" away the hearts of the people from God. And hee the
" said Salthowse then and there spake to the people, that
" they should not hearken to him, meaninge the said
" Brookes, for that hee was a theefe and was come with a
" Lye in his mouth, and had stollen what he had from
" others, and had it in his hand, pointinge to the Bible
" which was then in the said Mr. Brookes his hand open.

[1] "We then, as workers together with Him, beseech you also that ye receive not the grace of God in vain."

The Trial of Two Quakers.

"And this deponent further sayth, That the said Myles
"Halehead did speake the same words as aforesaid,
"And said severall times that itt was a Lye that the said
"Brookes had brought.

"JOHN PAIGE, *Maior*.
"RI: SPURWELL."

Then follows —

"The examinacon of George Brookes, Chaplain in the
"*Nightingall* ffrigott in the State's Service, had and taken
"as aforesaid.

"*On Oath.* The said deponent sayth, That on Sabboth
"day last hee hearinge that there were some men that went
"by the name of Quakers, and intended to exercise at a
"howse leadinge to Stonehowse within the Burrough of
"Plymouth which as this deponent is informed is one John
"Harris his howse. And this deponent cominge into the
"said howse went into a garden belonginge to the same
"howse, where were a great concourse of people, about 70
"or 80 persons, and after a little time this deponent had
"beene there, one Thomas Salthouse, one of the people
"called Quakers, beganne to speake to the people there
"assembled, without either seekinge of God in prayer or
"takinge any portion of Scripture to speak from itt, did
"runne on in such a way as was not at all to the edifyinge
"of the people (in this deponent's Judgment) but to dis-
"traction. Which stirred up this deponent (after the said
"Salthowse had ended speakinge) to speake somethinge
"by way of exhortacon to the edificacon of the people then
"present to and for the glory of God. And then and there
"this deponent made choice of a portion of Scripture,
"which was 2 Cor. vi. 1, from which this deponent exhort-
"inge the people to Virtue and Love and used this Simile,
"That as the Father, Son, and Spiritt, were Three in

"Trinitie bur one in Unitie, soe although there were severall sectts of Religions yet wee should bee all one in Unitie and Love. And afterward this deponent proposed to all the people that they should seeke to God for a blessinge by prayer, and if any there present had a larger portion or measure of the true light and spiritt of God than this deponent had, that then hee should pray, if not, this deponent would. Whereupon the said Salthowse with Myles Halhead and Nicholas Gannicliffe (as this deponent now perceives their names soe to bee) being the same Three persons which hee this deponent now seeth att the time of his examinacon, and att the time aforesaid were in the said Garden, they fell upon this deponent with unsutable and inhumane speeches, sayinge Thou Lyest, there is noe such thinge in Scripture as the Trinitie, and therefore thou Lyest and art a theefe, and thou hast stollen that which thou hast from others, and brought itt in thy hand, pointinge att the Bible then open in this deponent's hand, and thou, meaninge the deponent, hast a deludinge spiritt, and thou art come to deceave the people, and to draw away the hearts of the people from God, and therefore admonished the people that they should not hearken or beleeve what this deponent had said.

"JOHN PAIGE, *Maior.*
"RI: SPURWELL."

Nicholas Gannicliffe appears to have been discharged. The other two prisoners seem to have been remanded until the next day, when they were examined by the Mayor and three of his brethren. We are apt to forget that the rule of not questioning a prisoner, by which English jurisprudence is distinguished from that of most foreign States, is one of very modern adoption.

"The Examinacon of Thomas Salthowse of Druglebecke, "in the County of Lancaster, husbandman, aged Thirtie years "or Thereabout, taken before the Right Worshipful John "Paige, Maior of the Burrough of Plymouth in the County "of Devon, and Richard Spurwell, Robert Gubbs and Wil- "liam Birch, fower Justices of the Peace within the same "Burrough, the 23th day of May, 1655.

"The said examinate being demanded the Cause of his "cominge to this towne sayth itt was to visitt some friends, "and beinge asked what those friends were and if hee had "any friends or relacons in Plymouth, sayth hee knew "Nicholas Cole and Arthur Cotton and some other per- "sons, and beinge demaunded where and how longe since "hee became acquainted with the said Cole and Cotton "sayth, That about the end of March last this examt beinge "under restraint att Exon togeather with one Myles Halhead, "the said Cotton and Cole came thither to this examt and "the said Halhead, and that after they had been under "restraint 16 daies they were sent with a guard by "Col. Coplestone to Taunton, and from thence were sent "from tithinge to tithinge to Bristow by Col. Buffett of "Taunton, but the messenger that went with this examt "and the said Halhead from Taunton, beinge (as this "examt conceiveth) drunke and fallinge on the ground "about a myle from Taunton, and itt growinge towards "night, this deponent with the said Halhead and the mes- "senger returned to Taunton to the said Col. Buffett, and "two daies afterward this examt and the said Halhead by "leave from the said Col. Buffett departed and went to "Bristow. And this examt further sayth that he came "hither to this Towne of Plymouth on ffriday last to Arthur "Cotton, and afterward that eveninge went to Stonehowse,

"at the howse of one Lippingcott. And being demaunded
"where this Examt was the last Lord's day, sayth that hee
"was the last *first day* in a garden of one John Harris
"within the Burrough of Plymouth, where there were a
"Companie of people mett together, and this examt spake
"somethinge to them both in the howse and in the garden.
"And this deponent being further demaunded whether he
"did not in his discourse to the people say these words
"followinge, (vizt) That they should follow noe more their
"old Ministers, for they are those that will bringe them to
"destruccon, and they are Baal's preists, and there is that
"within a man that must carry him to heaven, and there
"is noe neede of other teachinge, denyeth the same. And
"beinge further demaunded whether hee did not speake
"these followinge words to one George Brookes (who had
"alsoe then spoken to the people, in which discourse of the
"said Brookes hee menconed the holy Trinitie and the
"Three persons in the Trinitie) Thou lyest in sayinge there
"were Three persons in the Trinitie; I deny itt, there is
"noe such thinge, but thou art a deludinge spiritt come to
"draw away the hearts of the people from God, and that
"they should not hearken to him the said Brookes for that
"he was a Theefe and was come with a Lye in his mouth,
"and had stollen what hee had from others and had itt in
"his hand, pointinge att the Bible which was in the said
"Brookes his hand open, denyeth the same. And beinge
"further demaunded by what authority hee spake to the
"people in that publique way, sayth hee was imediately
"called of God to goe out and declare the truth as hee is
"moved. And beinge demaunded if hee bee not one of
"those that are called Quakers sayth hee is one of them,
"and somtimes he has had shakings on him. And this

"examt beinge demaunded att what place he intendeth
"to goe from this towne, sayth, to Bristow. And beinge
"demaunded when hee did make use of his callinge as a
"husbandman or any other lawfull callinge to procure a
"Lyvelyhood, sayth, itt was about Three months since.
"And beinge demaunded where hee hath had money for
"his subsistance since that time, sayth, That if hee come
"to any Towne or citty he hath money to pay for what hee
"calls for, and if hee goe into any friend's howse hee can
"eat bread or drinke water with them. And this deponent
"beinge asked whether Nicholas Ganniclifle and Myles
"Halhead bee of the same Judgment and opinion with
"this examinate, sayth they are, and doe goe under the
"name of Quakers.

"The oath of Abjuration conteyned in his highnesse the
"Lord Protector's proclamacon was tendred to the said
"Thomas Salthowse, and hee refused to take itt, sayinge
"the Lord Jesus forbids him to sweare."

"JOHN PAIGE, *maior*.
"RI: SPURWELL."

After this Miles Halhead was similarly examined.

"The examinacon of Myles Halhead of Kendall in the
"county of Westmerland had and taken as aforesaid.

"The said Examt sayth. That hee is a marryed man,
"and left his wife and Three children att Kendall aforesaid
"about Three moneths since. And being demaunded why
"hee left his family sayth hee was drawne to London and
"from thence towards this towne to see his freinds, and att
"Exon this examt and Thomas Salthouse were taken upp
"for goinge the country without a passe, and after 16 daies
"(beinge there under restraint) were sent to Taunton to
"goe towards Bristow where this examt went. And beinge

x

" demaunded why he came hither to this towne of Plymouth
" and when, sayth on ffriday last hee came thither to see
" his freinds, beinge mooved thereunto. And beinge asked
" what freinds, sayth Arthur Cotton and Nicholas Coles.
" And beinge demaunded how longe hee hath been acquainted
" with them, sayth that hee came acquainted with them att
" Exon when hee this examt was under restraint there.
" And beinge demaunded whether hee were not in a garden
" within the Burrough of Plymouth on the last Lord's day,
" sayth hee was. And beinge further demaunded whether
" hee then spake these words followinge to the people there
" assembled, vizt. They should follow noe more their old
" ministers, for they are those that will bringe them to
" destruccon, &c. (as in Salthowse's examinacon) denyeth
" the same. And beinge asked if he bee not of the com-
" pany of those people that are called Quakers sayth hee is.
" And beinge demaunded why hee left his callinge and doth
" not apply himselfe to itt, sayth hee was drawne to itt and
" to goe and see freinds. And beinge demaunded when hee
" did employe himselfe about his callinge as a husbandman,
" sayth not since hee left his family, which was about Three
" moneths last past. And beinge further demaunded how
" and by what meanes hee is supplyed with moneys for his
" lyvelyhood in regard hee doth not worke, sayth hee hath
" enough of his owne to maintaine himself. And beinge
" demaunded by what authoritie hee goes upp and downe
" the Country, and gathers people togeather to withdraw
" them from their publique attendance on the preachinge
" of the Gosple and other religious duties performed by
" the ministers of Jesus Christ, sayth hee knoweth the
" nation gyves men free Libertie to meete togeather. And
" beinge demaunded where hee intendeth to goe from this

The Trial of Two Quakers.

"towne, sayth towards Bristow. And this examt beinge
"further demaunded if hee doe acknowledge the Trinitie
"of persons in the unitie of essence, and whether the
"Father bee God, the Son God, and the Spirit God, sayth
"hee owneth the Father, Sonne, and Spiritt, but refuseth
"to gyve an answeare and will not say they are God. And
"this examt being tendred the oath of abiuration enjoyned
"by the Lord Protector by a late proclamation of 26th of
"April last, denyeth to sweare at all, and will not take the
"said oath of Abjuration.
  "JOHN PAIGE, *maior.*
  "RI: SPURWELL."

After this the Mayor must have remanded them again, and we find that they took the opportunity of addressing to his Worship another letter, pointing out the iniquity of swearing. It may be thought, perhaps, that the way in which they called God to witness was as decided an oath as kissing a book would have been. In fact, a Quaker named Thomas Courtis was actually fined by the Court of Quarter Sessions soon after this time for profane swearing, because he said "God is my witness," and " I speak in the presence of God." The epistle begins thus, the word " friend " being no longer used :

"John Page, Mayor of Plymouth,
  "Forasmuch as it hath pleased thee to cast us into
"Prison, and hast examined us, and hast found no breach
"of any Law, by which thou canst lawfully punish us ; but
"under a pretence hast tendred us an Oath to swear against
"the Supremacy and Purgatory. We doe, *in the presence of*
"*the Lord God of Heaven and Earth*, deny the Pope and all
"things therein mentioned, with as much detestation as
"thou thyself, or any in the world can or doth, our con-

"sciences also bearing us witnesse, *in the presence of our*
"*God*, who is able to deliver us, although we are cast into
"a Prison ; nay, if we be cast into a Den of Lyons, and a
"fiery Furnace, with the three Children, as you may read
"in Daniel, that would not fall down to worship the Image,
"neither will we disobey the Command of Jesus Christ,
"who saith, Swear not at all ; and the Apostle James saith,
"'Above all things, my brethren, swear not, neither by
"Heaven nor by Earth, nor by any other Oath, but let
"your yea be yea, and your nay nay, lest ye fall into con-
"demnation.'"

Shadrach, Meshach, and Abednego were quoted by George Fox as examples, having worn their hats when they were cast into the burning fiery furnace.

Their worships of Plymouth saw plainly that it was a case for the Sessions. It was clear that the prisoners were Quakers, but it was not equally clear on what charge they could be committed. They had refused the oath of abjuration, but that was, I believe, a matter of summary jurisdiction rather than for committal. The ordinary offence committed by Quakers was penetrating into a "steeple-house," insisting on addressing the congregation, and "disturbing the Minister." But in this case the minister had disturbed the Quakers. It was hardly safe to commit them on that charge only. Under these circumstances the mayor, or his legal adviser, bethought him of an ordinance made by the Lord Protector in the previous year, "for preventing of Duells." So, after a few days' deliberation, the Quakers were sent to the common gaol at Exeter under the following *mittimus :—*

"*Devon.*
"John Page, Merchant, Maior of the Burrough of Ply-

The Trial of Two Quakers. 309

"mouth in the County aforesaid, and one of his High-
"nesse's Justices of the Peace within the said Burrough.
"To the keeper of his Highnesse's Gaol at Exon Castle,
"or to his lawfull deputy in that behalfe, greeting. I send
"you herewithall by the bearer hereof the bodies of Thomas
"Salthouse late of Drugglibeck in the County of Lan-
"caster, husbandman, and Miles Halhead late of Kendal
"in the County of Westmorland, lately apprehended here
"as disturbers of the public peace, and for divers other
"high misdemeanours against a late Proclamation pro-
"hibiting the disturbing of Ministers and other Christians
"in their assemblies and meetings, and against an Ordi-
"nance of his said Highness the Lord Protector and his
"Counsel lately made against Duells, Challenges, and all
"provocations thereunto, who have refused to give suf-
"ficient security for their personall appearance at the next
"general Sessions of the Peace to be held for the County
"of Devon, and in the meantime to be of good behaviour
"*against* his Highnesse the Lord Protector and all his
"liege people. These are therefore in his said Highness
"his name to will and command you that, when the bodies
"of the said Thomas Salthouse and Miles Halhead shall
"be unto you brought, you them safely detain, and keep
"them until by due course of law they shall be thence de-
"livered. Hereof fail not at your perill.
  "Given under my hand and seal of Plymouth aforesaid,
"the 28th day of May, in the year of our Lord God 1655."
                      "JOHN PAGE, *Mayor.*"
  John Desborough was at this time the Major-General in
command of the Western District, and to him the prisoners
and their friends determined to appeal. An answer,
specifically denying every charge mentioned in the warrant,

was drawn up and placed in his hands, with the following letter, which at any rate effectually disposes of the accusation of refusing to give security. Arthur Cotton was a man of good position and education, and a leading member of the Society of Friends in Devonshire until the reign of James the Second. He was a correspondent of William Penn. The readiness of the Quakers to suffer for one another was most remarkable from the very commencement of the Society. A petition was presented to Parliament in 1659 by one hundred and sixty-four of them, offering to suffer imprisonment in lieu of an equal number of Friends whose lives were endangered by their long confinement in filthy gaols and houses of correction.

Letter to General Disbrow (*sic*) :—

"We whose names are hereunto subscribed doe testifie,
"That the severall particulars in this Answer made by our
"friends are true (to wit) That they did not at all disturb
"the publick Peace. Nor were they at any other Meeting
"(but that which was appointed by us) to disturb any
"Ministers or other Christians in their Assemblies or
"Meetings. Nor are they guilty of any Challenges, Duells,
"and Provocations thereunto in the least Measure, whilst
"they were among us. And as for their refusall to give
"security, two of us, whose names are Robert Cary
"and Arthur Cotton, had given security to the Mayor, by
"entring into Recognisance for their appearance at the
"next Sessions, the day before their sending to Prison, but
"that the Town Clerk made it void the next day, pretend-
"ing that it could not be according to Law."

This letter was signed by eleven Friends. It was no doubt forwarded to the mayor by Desborough with a request or his remarks, and we have a humble letter from his

The Trial of Two Quakers. 311

worship in reply, dated June 1, 1655. He sends the General copies of the examinations of the Quakers, and assures him that

"Their carriage here was not becoming men, much lesse
"Christians, and besides their contempt of authority, and
"all the while they were in Prison, they never sought God
"by prayer at any time, nor desired a blessing on any Crea-
"ture they received, or gave thanks for them. . . . They
"wander up and down in all parts, to vent their wicked
"Opinions, and discover their irregular Practises in the
"breach of Peace, and disturbance of all good People.
"Indeed, Sir, they hold many sad Opinions, destructive to
"the true Religion, and power of Godlinesse. I have hereby
"according to my Duty given your Honour an account of
"what passed here in reference to these men; I could say
"much more in reference to their Examination, and discourse
"with them, but I fear I have already trespassed upon your
"Honour's patience in the perusal of these lines, and humbly
"desiring your excuse for giving you this trouble, and doe
"most thankfully acknowledge your Honour's continued
"favours to this place, and for which we stand very much
"obliged, desiring your Honour still to retain such an
"opinion of us, as those that desire to doe nothing un-
"becoming Christians, and persons that desire the welfare
"and peace of this Common-wealth and Government, and
"shall ever labour to appear
"Your Honour's very Humble Servant,
"JOHN PAGE, *Mayor*,
"for myself and Brethren."

Such was the way in which one of Cromwell's major-generals was addressed by the Mayor of Plymouth. It may be doubted whether any of the Tudors were approached with greater servility.

Desborough gave the Quakers an opportunity of answering this letter, which they did with considerable sharpness, informing the Mayor that he had manifested himself to the children of light, by his flattering Major General " Disbrow " *in feigned humility*, and by his railing accusations against them, to be of the generation and spirit of Tertullus, who accused and informed the Governor against the Apostle Paul as a pestilent fellow, &c. The Mayor had said they were offenders, " as I conceive." They reply, " Thou hast laid open thine ignorance in imprisoning us because *thou conceivest* we are offenders, which indeed is nothing but *thy conceiving*. . . . Because *thou conceivest* we are offenders, doe we suffer; but thou makest *thy conceiving* a Law to imprison us by." And so, having given the Mayor the lie through two or three pages, they observe that they never render railing for railing, but in the spirit of love and meekness exhort him and his brethren to repent and fear to offend the Lord, and the least of them who believe in His name.

The author of the pamphlet uses still stronger language in "improving the occasion," and points out twelve distinct lies in the letter of his Worship, whose future destination he precisely defines, for " all lyars shall have their part in the lake that burneth with fire and brimstone, which is the second death."

The Mayor thought it necessary to fortify his position by sending up some additional evidence to Sessions. Two more depositions were annexed to the others.

"PLYMOUTH B.

" The Examinacon of Jacobb Jennens of Plymouth, mer-"chant, had and taken as aforesaid the 5th of June, 1655.

" The said Examt sayth, that hee beinge in a Garden of "one John Harris neere the old mills within the Borrough

The Trial of Two Quakers.

"of Plymouth on Sabbath day the 20th day of May last heard
" Thomas Salthouse and Mylles Halhead that went by the
"name of Quakers speake these words to the people then
" present ; That they should follow the Light of their owne
" minds and Consciences within them, and bee not deluded
" nor deceived by these teachers and Preachers (as you call
"them) but follow the Light of your owne minds, for that
" will condeme you or save you. And the said examt sayth
" that all the tyme the said Saltehouse and Hallhead spake
" they had their hatts on their heads, and they did not pray
" beefore or after they spake to ye people. And this depo-
" nent farther saith that after they had done speakinge, one
" Mr. Brookes that is Chapplayne of the *Nightingall* ffryggett
" spake somethinge to the people from that place of Scrip-
"ture the 2 Cor. vi. 1, speakinge of the Holy Trinitye.
" After hee had ended, the said Thomas Salthouse said
" to the said Brookes, Thou Lyest. And the said Brookes
"replyed, Wherin ? And the said Saltehouse replyed, Thou
" hast said there are three persons in the Trinity, I tell thee
" thou Lyest, for there is noe such word as three persons in
" Trinity in the Scripture. And the said Brookes said, I will
"make it appeare. And this deponent sayth That the said
" Haleheade sayed to the (said) Brookes, Thou art a theife
" for thou hast stollen that which thou hast brought in thy
" hand, meaninge the Byble that was in the said Brookes
" hand, as this deponent beeleiveth, for hee had a byble then in
" his hand, out of which he noted severall places of Scripture.
" JOHN PAIGE, *maior*.
" RI : SPURWELL."

We may suspect that what the Quakers meant was that the Chaplain had stolen his sermon, which is a more common offence than stealing a Bible.

"PLYMOUTH B.

"The examinacon of Ralph Ansley of Plymouth, in the "County of Devon, Barker, had and taken before the Right "Wor¹¹ John Paige, merchant, Maior of the burrough afore-"said, and one of the Justices of the Peace within the "burrough aforesaid the 7th day of July, 1655.
"*On Oath.*

"The said deponent sayth, That hee goinge towards "Stonehouse with one Mr. George Brookes and Mr. Peter "Popham uppon Saboth day the twentieth of May laste and "they hearinge there weare some Quakers att the house of "one John Harris neere the old mills within the burrough "of Plymouth, this deponent together with the said Brookes "and Popham went into the said house to heare the said "Quakers. And this deponent saw in a Garden belonginge "to the said house about 70 persones, amonge whome weare "three strangers which went by the name of Quakers. And, "as this deponent hath been informed, their names were "Thomas Salthouse, Myles Halehead, and Nicholas Ganni-"cliffe, whome this deponent heard to speake to the people "these words; That they should follow noe more their old "*Ministers*, for they are those that will bringe them to "destruccon, for they are Baall's preists, and there is that "within a man that must carry him to heaven, and there is "no neede of other teachinge. And this deponent further "sayth, That the said Salthouse havinge ended his discourse "without any prayer, that wee heard the said Mr. Brookes "who is chaplinge aboard the *Nightingall* ffryggote open a "place of Scripture (to the people) which was the 2 Cor. vi. 1, "in the openinge of which said Scripture the said Brookes "did speake somethinge of the holy Trinitie. And after "the said Brookes had done speakinge the said Thomas Salt-

"house did speake to the said Brookes, saying, Thou Lyest
"in sayinge there were Three Persons in the Trinitie; I deny
"itt, there is noe such thinge, but thou art a deludinge spiritt
"come to drawe away the hearts of the people from God.
"And the said Salthouse did alsoe speake to the people
"they should not hearken to him, meaninge the said Brookes,
"for that hee was a theefe and was come with a Lie in his
"mouth, and had stollen what hee had from others, and had
"it in his hand, pointinge to the Bible that ye said Brookes
"had then in his hand open. And the said deponent further
"saith, That he heard the said Myles Halehead speake the
"same words as aforsaid, and said severall tymes it was a
"Lye that the said Brookes had brought.

"JOHN PAIGE, *maior*.
"RI: SPURWELL.".

The Sessions began at Exeter on July 10. The first name on the list of Justices present is John Disbrow, from which we may infer that the Major-General took the chair on the occasion. Salthouse and Halhead were indicted for provoking George Brookes, though it is evident that the only duel likely to ensue was an oratorical one. Since the establishment of the Commonwealth indictments had been framed in English instead of Latin. As it is our object to give a complete example of the legal procedure of the period, we subjoin a copy of the "Indictement exhibited against, and read to them at the Sessions."

"The Jurors for His Highnesse the Lord Protector of the
"Commonwealth of England, Scotland, and Ireland, and
"the Dominions thereunto belonging, upon their oaths doe
"present, That whereas, by an Ordinance of His Highnesse
"the Lord Protector, and his Counsell, bearing date the
"29th day of June, in the year of our Lord one thousand

"six hundred fifty-foure, for preventing of Duells, and all
"occasions of challenges and quarrells, and using any dis-
"gracefull provoking words or gestures tending to that effect,
"it was ordered, That no persons whatsoever should from
"and after the publishing of the said Ordinance, use any
"provoking words or gestures, whereby Quarrells or Chal-
"lenges may arise, as by the said Ordinance may more at
"large appear. Neverthelesse Thomas Salthouse, late of
"Drugglybeck, in the County of Lancaster, Husbandman,
"and Miles Halhead of Kendall in the County of Westmor-
"land, Husbandman, not fearing nor regarding the said
"Ordinance and the penalty therein contained, after the
"publishing of the said Ordinance, to wit, the twentieth day
"of May in the year of our Lord, one thousand six hundred
"fifty and five, at Plymouth in the County aforesaid, in the
"presence and hearing of divers honest persons of the
"Common-wealth of England there then being, did use
"divers disgracefull provoking words, and gestures, to
"George Brooks, Clerk in the *Nightingale* Friggot, he being
"then opening and declaring unto the said persons a certain
"place of Scripture wherein the said George said something
"of the Holy Trinity, to wit, *Thou*, the said George Brooks
"meaning, *lyest in saying there were Three persons in the
"Trinity, we doe deny, there is noe such thing, but thou art
"a deluding spirit come to draw away the hearts of the people
"from God.* And further they the said Thomas Salthouse
"and Miles Halhead did further speak to the people then
"present, that they should not hearken to the said George
"Brooks for that he was a Theif, and was come with a Lye
"in his mouth, and had stollen what he had from others, and
"had it in his hand, poynting to the Bible which was then
"in the said George Brooks his hand open. And further

The Trial of Two Quakers.

"did say it was a lye which the said George Brooks had "brought, and other harmes to the said George Brooks then "and there did, contrary to the form of the said ordinance, "against the peace publick."

For the manner of their trial we are again indebted to the pamphlet. The indictment having been read to them, they were asked whether they were guilty or not guilty.

"*Answer.* We are not Guilty in what is there charged "upon us.

"*Court.* By whom will you be tryed?

"*Answer.* By you whom the Lord God of power hath "set in Authority, to judge righteously between man and "man, and to put a difference between the precious and the "vile, and set the oppressed free, from whom we do expect "justice and equity.

"*Court.* Will ye be tryed by God and the Country?

"*Answer.* We are willing to be tryed by this Bench, and "desire that our accusers may be brought in, and that we "may have liberty to speak for ourselves, and make our "defence against the false accusations laid to our charge.

"*Court.* Will ye be judges of your own case? Jaylor, "take them away.

"This was done immediately."

There are copious comments on these proceedings, both by the defendants and the author of the pamphlet. With their usual obstinacy, the Quakers refused to adopt the form of words "to be tried by God and the country," and this was construed as contempt of court.

About an hour afterwards they were again called in, and required to take the Oath of Abjuration. As before, they refused to take it, and then proceeded to make a declaration which most people would consider as much an oath as the other.

"*Answer.* In the presence of the eternall God, and before
"all this people, we doe deny, with as much detestation as
"any of you doth, the Pope, and his Supremacy, and the
"Purgatory, and all therein mentioned, and declare freely
"against it. And we doe not deny to swear because of any
"guilt that is upon us, but in obedience to the command of
"Christ, who saith, Swear not all. And we will not come
"under the condemnation of an Oath for the liberty of the
"outward man."

After this they were sent back to prison.

The next day they were brought up again and asked,—

"Will ye confesse that ye wronged G. Brookes, in calling
"of him Thief, and be sorry for it, and make him satisfaction?

"*Answer.* One of us did not speak one word to him, and
"therefore I deny to make him satisfaction, or to be sorry for
"it, and what was spoken was no such thing; therefore we
"will not lye for our liberty, nor confesse that we are sorry
"for that which we never spoke.

"*Court.* You are fined five pound a piece, and must goe
"to the House of Correction till payment, and find sureties
"for your good behaviour; and for refusing to take the Oath,
"we shall take course to send to the North to seize on your
"Estates, according to the Proclamation."

Their names appear in the Calendar as having used provoking words against George Brooks, clerk, and "refusing to be tryed by the Countrey."

Such was the end of their trial, or rather of the proceedings which served instead of a trial. They were kept in the Bridewell more than a twelvemonth, and were still there

The Trial of Two Quakers.

when the pamphlet was written. They wrote long descriptions of their "uncivil and barbarous usage," and complained that the friends who came to see them, "who were in scorn called Quakers," were also detained and imprisoned. Their friends at Plymouth made strenuous efforts for their liberation, and drew up a memorial with certificates appended, which, if genuine, give us a favourable idea of the naval discipline of the Commonwealth, and certainly dispose of Master Brookes' character. " Loe, hear what a filthy worker of iniquity this Priest is, for denying of whose spirit before the people these long and cruel sufferings are inflicted on the innocent!"

"The Testimonies of the Captaines of the *Nightingall*
" Friggot, and of the *Nantwich*, and of the *Constant Warwick*,
" concerning the deboyst, filthy, and drunken conversation
" of George Brooks, Priest, or Clerk, with the reasons where-
" fore he was put on shore, or turned out of the said Friggot.

"'I having been formerly desired to relate upon what
" account that Mr. George Brooks, Chaplin of the Friggot,
" and under my command, was put on shore ; Because he
" was a busy body, and disturbed the whole Ship's Company.
" Secondly, being on shore, it was his common practice to
" abuse the creature in such sort that he was drunken, voyd
" of good reason, that he would abuse any one that came in
" his company by ill language, besides the abuse of himselfe
" and the good creature, daily complaints coming unto me
" both aboard and on shore. Therefore knowing him to be a
" *deboyst* fellow, and not fit for that imployment, therefore I
" put him on shore, and I dare own it, who shall ever call
" me to question. Witnesse my hand,

"' ROBERT VESSAY.

"' Mr. Brookes being formerly with me in the *Nightingale*,

"I found him to be very idle, and continually drunk, which once made me to *put a quarter can about his necke*, whereunto I subscribe.

"'JOHN JEFFERY,
"'Captain of the *Nantwich*.

"The person above mentioned I have seen drunk at shore, in testimony whereof I have set my hand.

"'RICHARD POTTER,
"'Captaine of the *Constant Warwick* Frigot.'"

My purpose of giving an example of the legal proceedings of the period is accomplished. After the "messengers" regained their liberty, one at least of them seems to have remained in the West. The name of Thomas Salthouse occurs in the records of the Friends in Devonshire as late as the year 1681.

THE JUSTICES OF THE PEACE FOR THE COUNTY OF DEVON IN THE YEAR 1592.

A LECTURE DELIVERED BEFORE THE EXETER LITERARY SOCIETY.

IN the reign of Queen Elizabeth of famous memory, as the men who lived under the Stuarts delighted to call her, this country, I need hardly say, was inhabited by a very remarkable generation. They were the men to whom was allotted by Providence the task of rearing up a very small kingdom into a very great empire. Among them were the men who, with few resources besides their own skill and courage, confronted and beat down the vast overbearing power of Spain; who, in ships that we should call "cockle-shells," sailed round the world, and explored the Arctic Regions with very much the same results that have been attained in our time by brave men supplied with all the engines and contrivances that the science of the nineteenth century has been able to invent; who laid the foundations of the British Colonies in America and of the British Empire in India. Nor were the men of less active occupations unworthy companions of the founders of the greatness of England. If the men of action of that generation were Drake and Raleigh, Sidney and Essex, Davis and Frobisher; the statesmen were Burleigh, and Walsingham, and Bacon; the poets were Shakespeare and

Y

Spenser; the scholars were the translators of the Bible; and the Sovereign was Elizabeth.

Other generations of Englishmen may have been as brave and enterprising, but probably no generation has been so wise, and cautious, and far-seeing, so skilled in knowledge of the world and of the workings of the mind of man. They had been trained in a school very different from any known to the easy-going Englishmen of the last two centuries. They, and their fathers, had lived in the age of the great religious revolution. They had seen the nation and its rulers pass backwards and forwards, from Romanism to Protestantism, from Protestantism to Romanism, from Romanism to Protestantism again. They had seen at one time Protestants burnt at Smithfield, at another time Romanists hanged and quartered. They had lived in times of plots, treasons, disputed successions to the Throne, insurrections amounting to civil war. Above all, they had to guard their country against the imminent danger of foreign invasion, against the peril of an alien government and an alien church being imposed upon it by a most cruel and persecuting enemy. These things, which might have crushed the spirits of a more servile race, only served to brace the courage and sharpen the faculties of the high-minded Englishmen of the sixteenth century.

I have always looked upon those times, which reached their culminating point in the battle with the Spanish Armada, as the greatest age in the history of England, and indeed one of the greatest epochs in the history of the world. It is not merely because the men of Devonshire happened to stand in the front of the battle on that occasion, but because it was on that point that the question of the religion and liberties of our country mainly hinged,—and not only of our country, but also the religion and liberties of the better part of Europe and America,—that this period must always be to us one of surpassing interest.

The deeds of the statesmen and warriors of those times, the works of the great authors, are probably sufficiently familiar to us. What is not, perhaps, so familiar is the daily life of the people, especially of the people who lived in the country. We must all see that history, as it has generally been written, is for the most part a record of courts, and camps, and councils, a gallery containing the portraits of Sovereigns, and Commanders, and Ministers, but which does little to make us understand the ordinary life of the millions of private persons who tilled the fields and produced the food on which the great men lived, who built the houses in which they dwelt, who served in the armies which they commanded, who paid the taxes of which they disposed, who bore their share in the administration of Local Government, and who carried on in their respective stations all the varied business that fills up the time of civilized nations.

It is chiefly from other sources, from original records, diaries, letters, and so forth, that we are enabled to fill up the blanks of the grander histories, and to understand something of the different degrees and classes of former generations.

It is of one of these classes that I have undertaken to speak this evening, a class that has often been abused, and often ridiculed, but which has yet managed to retain for itself a fair share of respect, and, we may hope, has done the State some service. I mean, as I need hardly tell you, the ancient class of Justices of the Peace, or, as they are more commonly termed, county magistrates; a class which has existed in this country for many centuries, and which does not seem likely to die out with the present generation.

What manner of men, then, were the Justices of the Peace in the reign of Queen Elizabeth? That is the question which I mean to try to answer. Some of you may perhaps be aware that I have been occupied, by permission of the Lord Lieutenant, in examining the records of this county, which have been seen, I believe, by few eyes besides my own since they were stowed away by the Clerks of the Peace in long past generations, and which have furnished materials for certain papers which have appeared elsewhere. These records commence in the year 1592, four years after the great battle with the Armada. Nor is it difficult to account for this. The imminent danger of foreign invasion, which had cast a gloomy shadow over the country for so many years, had at last been dissipated. The government had at last some leisure to attend to domestic affairs, to the internal organization of the kingdom, and to the administration of justice. The form of the commission of Justices of the Peace was re-modelled in 1590 by Sir John Wray, Chief Justice of England. At the commencement of the Devonshire records, we find a letter from the Lords of the Council to four Commissioners, the Earl of Bath, Lord Lieutenant of the county, Sir William Courtenay, Sir John Gilbert, and Sir Francis Drake. I venture to quote it at length, as it shows the endeavours of the Government of Elizabeth to reform the Commission of the Peace, and to purge it of those who were called " popish recusants."

" After our hearty commendations. The Queen's Majesty

Justices of the Peace for the County of Devon. 325

" being lately informed that sundry persons in many of the
" counties of her realm, being placed to be Justices of the
" Peace, yet have not taken such oaths as by the laws and
" statutes of the realm they ought to have taken before they
" might exercise such office, hath therefore thought very
" necessary to have speedy remedy hereof. And for that
" purpose considering it is uncertain who they are that have
" not taken the said oath, her Majesty's pleasure is (with-
" out intent to prejudice such as have their oath) that by
" virtue of these our letters before the 20th day of Novem-
" ber next, or within 15 days after the receipt of these our
" letters, you shall procure a Sessions of the Peace to be
" holden at such open and accustomed place within that
" county as is used, and by notice and warning from you to
" be given to require and cause that all the Justices of the
" Peace dwelling in that county be personally present at the
" same Sessions, after the usual manner of keeping Sessions
" for the Peace, to the accomplishment of her Majesty's plea-
" sure and service. At which time and place you occupying
" the place of *Custos Rotulorum*, and you the Sheriff, with
" such other of the said Justices as shall be appointed by
" her Majesty's writ of *Dedimus Potestatem* that shall be
" directed unto you and them for that purpose, shall require
" all and every of the Justices of the Peace there present
" openly and publicly to take the oath accustomed for the
" Justices of the Peace, and the oath also of her Majesty's
" supremacy, as is prescribed by the Statutes, and therein
" you and as many of the other Commissioners appointed
" by the said writ of *Dedimus Potestatem* as shall be then
" and there present, shall make due return of the said writ
" under your hands, thereby certifying unto the Chancery
" how many of the said Justices shall in the said Sessions

"have taken their said oaths, so as the same may come to
"me the Lord Keeper of the Great Seal of England with-
"out any unnecessary delay, to be recorded in the Chan-
"cery. And if any of the said Justices that shall be there
"at the said Sessions shall refuse or forbear to take the
"said oaths, you shall also cause the same to be in like
"sort certified to me the Lord Keeper. And therewith
"you shall declare to me every such person so refusing or
"forbearing, that her Majesty's pleasure is that he shall
"from that time forbear to exercise the office of a Justice
"of Peace, until he shall conform himself so to do and be
"newly placed in commission and sworn accordingly.
"And if any Justice dwelling in that county and being
"warned to come unto the said particular Sessions, shall
"not come thither, you shall by your letters declare unto
"him that her Majesty will have him forbear from the
"exercise of that office until he shall have taken those
"oaths, either in the Chancery before me the Lord Keeper,
"or upon reasonable excuse of such his absence to be
"allowed to have a writ of *Dedimus Potestatem* to certain
"persons to give him the said oaths in some open Sessions,'
"and shall cause the same duly to be returned and recorded
"in the Chancery. Which said oaths if the Justices so
"dwelling in that county and absent from the said Sessions
"shall not take before me the Lord Keeper or the said
"special commissioners, and cause to be duly returned and
"recorded in the Chancery as aforesaid within 20 days
"after the next Sessions of Justice, they so thereof failing
"shall be removed out of the Commission of the Peace.
"And because many are commonly in Commission that
"are not residently dwelling in the county where they are
"named commissioners, you shall by your letters signify

Justices of the Peace for the County of Devon. 327

"unto them that so shall reside out of that county and be
"absent from the so prefixed Sessions of that County, that
"they shall forbear to execute the office of a Justice of
"the Peace in that County until they shall certify you
"credibly that they have by virtue of our letters sent at
"this time to the county where they shall reside taken
"those oaths in the said other county where they are Jus-
"tices and have their dwellings, or before me, the Lord
"Keeper in manner aforesaid.

"Furthermore her Majesty is informed that divers
"persons do occupy the offices of Justice of the Peace who
"do not repair to their church or chapel accustomed, or
"upon reasonable lett thereof to some other place where
"Common Prayer is used and accustomed for Divine
"Service, or whose wives living with their husbands, or
"sons and heirs living in their houses or within that county
"where their fathers do dwell, are known to refuse to come
"to the church, contrary to the Statutes in that behalf
"made. A matter not agreeable with the vocation of any
"that ought to inquire of such offenders and to reform the
"same. For which purpose also her Majesty willeth you
"to certify her pleasure to all persons being Justices in that
"county, that if any of them do forbear to resort commonly
"to the church, or that their wives remaining and living in
"house with them, or their sons and heirs being above the
"age of 16 years and living in their fathers' houses or
"dwelling in the country where their fathers do dwell, do
"not usually come to the church to Divine Service as by
"the Laws and Statutes they are bound to do, the fathers
"understanding or knowing of their sons' recusancy, that
"the persons being themselves recusants or husbands or
"fathers of such recusants shall forbear to exercise the

"offices of Justice of the Peace and shall be left out of the
" Commission of Peace during the time of such recusancy
" of themselves, their wives, or sons and heirs. And to the
" intent that this her Majesty's determination may take
" effect without delay, we will that you shall forthwith give
" notice to every such Justice within that county of this
" her Majesty's last determination for their forbearing from
" exercise of their offices upon the causes next here above
" alleged, so as they may be withdrawn out of the commis-
" sion for that county. So, nothing doubting of your good
" care in the accomplishment hereof according to her
" Majesty's pleasure and expectation, we bid you heartily
" farewell.

" From Hampton Court, the 20th of October, 1592.
" Your very loving friends,
" JO. PUCKERINGE, C.S.   " T. BUCKHURST.
" W. BURGLEIGHE. (sic.)   " RO. CECYLL.
" C. HAWARDE. (sic.)   " J. WOLLEY.
" J. HUNSDON.   " J. FORTESCUE.

"*Postscript.*—We require you all that are named in the
" writ of *Dedimus Potestatem* that yourselves will first
" openly in Sessions take the oath, one of you administer-
" ing to the other, saving that the Lords of Parliament are
" excepted by the Act from taking the oath of supre-
" macy."

With this letter were sent copies of the writ of *Dedimus Potestatem*, of the oath of a justice, and of the oath of supremacy. The oath of a justice is identical with that taken in the reign of Queen Victoria.

The four Commissioners executed their office, and returned the following letter:—

"Our humble duties to your good Lordships remem-

"bered. These may be to advertise you that, according to
"the tenor of your Lordships' letters to us directed, bearing
"date the 20th of October last, for the administration of
"the oaths to the Justices of the Peace in this county of
"Devon, annexed to her Majesty's writ of *Dedimus Potes-*
"*tatem*, in like sort to us addressed for the same cause, we
"(in open Sessions held at the Castle of Exeter the
"24th day of this present November) have thoroughly
"accomplished our duties in that behalf, and made return
"of the said writ of *Dedimus Potestatem* unto the Chancery,
"as to you our very good Lord the Lord Keeper shall by
"the same return more at large appear. The which we
"humbly leave to your honourable considerations, and our-
"selves to your accustomed favours, praying God long to
"preserve your Lordships in all honour.
"From Exeter the 25th day of November, 1592.
"Your Lordships' humble to command,—
"W. BATHON. "JOHN GILBERTE.
"W. COURTNEY. (*sic.*) "FRA. DRAKE."

The return referred to is in Latin, and contains fifty-five names, a complete list of the Justices of the County of Devon. One of these, as we shall find, died about this time, making the actual number fifty-four. I have never seen it stated that the number was limited, but I think there is some reason to believe that it was. Twenty years afterwards, when James I. was levying a benevolence, another list was entered in the Sessions Books, and that list contains exactly fifty-four names. The number at present is unlimited, and I believe is not far from four hundred.

Thirty-four Justices appeared and took the oaths in open court. Two were sworn before the Lord Keeper at

Hampton Court. Five, being Justices for Cornwall also, were sworn at Bodmin. Nine, most of whom seem to have been lawyers, were absent from the county. Two were prevented from coming by age and infirmity. One was not living in the county. One, being Sheriff, could not act as a Justice, and the administration of the oath to him was therefore deferred. And one of those named in the Commission had recently died.

I propose now to run rapidly over the names of these fifty-five Justices, and I shall be obliged for any information that may be given me respecting those of whom I know nothing.

WILLIAM BOURCHIER, EARL OF BATH, was for many years Lord Lieutenant of Devon. He lived at Tawstock Court, near Barnstaple. He seems to have been the only peer in the county at this time, as the Earl of Bedford was seldom resident, and the titles of the great houses of Courtenay and Seymour had been forfeited, or were in abeyance. He married, at Bedford House, Exeter, in 1582, Elizabeth Russell, daughter of the Earl of Bedford. The Countess is one of the characters in Kingsley's *Westward Ho!* The Earl, being Lord-Lieutenant, must have had a great deal to do with organizing the defences of the county during the period preceding the approach of the Armada. If the letters and other documents that must have been in his hands at that time could be discovered, it is probable that they would form a most important addition to the history of Devon, if not of England. I am informed, however, that nothing of the kind has been preserved by his descendants. There are many letters of his in the Calendars of State Papers for the reigns of Elizabeth and James I. I may mention

Justices of the Peace for the County of Devon. 331

that the editor of those calendars, never having heard of Tawstock, enters all these letters as dated from *Tavistock*. The Earl died in 1623, and was succeeded by his son Edward, at whose death in 1636 the title became extinct. His estates at Tawstock and elsewhere passed to his daughter Anne, who married first the Earl of Middlesex, and secondly Sir Chichester Wrey, ancestor of Sir Bourchier Wrey, who now represents the ancient family of Bourchier.

The next Justice on the list is the Bishop of Exeter. It is recorded that at one time during the reign of Elizabeth, the Bishop tried to exercise jurisdiction within the city, but was resisted successfully by the Mayor and other authorities. The county Justices were more polite. The name of the Bishop appears frequently in the list of those present at Quarter Sessions, and, as it appears first, I infer that he was placed in the chair. The Bishop at this time was JOHN WOLTON, a native of Lincolnshire. He seems to have been a distinguished preacher on the Protestant side, and was forced to fly to Germany during the reign of Mary. He was Bishop of Exeter from 1578 to 1593. He was buried on the south side of the choir of the Cathedral, in a tomb adorned with an epitaph abounding in puns and rhymes about " ingenium genium," " busta perusta," " Ultonus tonus," and so forth. He wrote a work entitled *The Christian Manual, or Of the Life and Manners of True Christians*, which has been published by the Parker Society.

EDWARD, DOMINUS SEYMOUR, as he is here called, was no doubt Sir Edward Seymour, head of the great family that dwelt at Berry Pomeroy Castle. He was eldest son of the first Duke of Somerset, whose sister was married to Henry VIII., and who was Protector of the Realm in the time of his nephew Edward VI. On the fall of the Duke, his honours were forfeited, but his son may perhaps have been sometimes called Lord Seymour, as having borne that title by courtesy in the lifetime of his father, which would account for his being entered as *Dominus*. He was generally known as Sir Edward Seymour, and sat in Parliament for the County of Devon. He was Sheriff in 1583, and commanded a regiment of militia in 1588. The present Duke of Somerset is a direct descendant of his, as also was the famous Sir Edward Seymour, leader of the Tory Party in the Parliaments of Charles II.

SIR WILLIAM COURTENAY of Powderham Castle was, I need hardly say, an ancestor of the present Earl of Devon, and the representative at that time of one of the noblest names of Europe. He ought to have been Earl of Devon himself, as heir male of the Earl who died at Padua in 1566. But he appears never to have claimed the title, nor did his descendants until the reign of William IV., when their right to it was established, after it had remained dormant for two hundred and sixty-five years. He was Colonel of a regiment of militia, High Sheriff in 1581, and in 1585 was employed as what was called "one of the undertakers for the better planting of Ireland." He obtained the estate in that kingdom still enjoyed by his descendants. He married Elizabeth, daughter of the Earl of Rutland. There is extant a funeral sermon preached on the Lady Elizabeth Courtenay at Chudleigh in 1605, but this may have been his mother, who was also named Elizabeth. He married secondly the widow of Sir Francis Drake, and thirdly a Mistress

Justices of the Peace for the County of Devon. 333

Bruerton of Taunton. He died in 1630. His son married a daughter of Sir Edward Seymour, the first Baronet.

SIR JOHN GILBERT, of Greenway near Dartmouth, and of Compton Castle near Torbay, was one of a most illustrious brotherhood. His younger brothers were the distinguished sailors Humphry and Adrian Gilbert, and his half-brother bore a still more famous name, Walter Raleigh. Sir John, as the eldest brother, did not lead so adventurous a life as the others, but he had a very considerable share in providing for the home defences of the country. He was knighted in 1570, and was Sheriff in 1572. In 1588 he seems to have been entrusted with the care of a large number of Spanish prisoners, and, if we may believe Sir George Cary's letters preserved in the State Paper Office, I am afraid he did not take much trouble to prevent their being starved to death, though he made 160 of them work in levelling the grounds about his own house. There was plenty of sherry on board some of the Spanish vessels, and George Cary wrote; "Though I have spoken and written to Sir John Gilbert, to understand of his proceedings and of what is becum of all the wynes I left in his custody, yeat I can receave no directe answer from him; but this I know by others, that all the best wynes are gone!" I fear the great men of the West in the times of Queen Bess had a certain taste for Spanish plunder. Cecil said of one of them, "On my faith I do think him wronged in this, albeit in other things he may have done *as a Devonshire man!*" *i.e.* a buccaneer. Sir John Gilbert is said to have been *Custos Rotulorum* of Devon, but I do not find this mentioned in the county records. He seems to have died shortly after this time, and both he and his wife, a daughter of Sir Richard

Chudleigh, were honoured by a stately monument in Exeter Cathedral. He left no child, and was succeeded by his brother Sir Humphry, from whom is descended Col. Walter Raleigh Gilbert, of the Priory, Bodmin.

SIR FRANCIS DRAKE is the next on the list, but if I were to enter upon his biography, I should have to devote a whole lecture to it. It appears to me that the "old warrior," a s Devonshire folk called him, really did more than any other man, or any other three men, to found the present British Empire. He was literally

"Curibus parvis et paupere tecto
Missus in imperium magnum."

His parentage is scarcely known. According to one story, the paternal mansion in which he was born was a boat turned bottom upwards. He was apprenticed to the captain of a small vessel, which he inherited from his master. The vessel was taken by the Spaniards, and Drake lost everything he possessed. He made a personal quarrel of it, and declared perpetual war against the King of Spain. How "the name of Francis Drake rang through the world, and startled Philip in the depths of the Escurial," has been told by many historians. We all know how, in his own words, he "singed the King of Spain's beard," by burning thousands of tons of shipping under the guns of his forts; how he avenged his early loss by the capture of hundredweights of gold, and tons of silver; how, in the crowning fight with the Armada,—

"When that vast fleet of Spain
Lay torn and scatter'd on the English main,"

he fulfilled the intention he had previously expressed, of "so handling the matter with the Duke of Sidonia, as that he shall wish himself back at St. Mary's Port among his orange-trees." What education he received I do not know, but the quaint felicity of his sayings and letters seems to me almost as remarkable as his actions. Take for example, the few words in which he summed up the history of the Armada, ending with, "As for the Prince of Parma, I take him to be like a bear robbed of her whelps!" I know nothing more romantic than the story of how he climbed up a high tree on a mountain above Panama, and, first of all Englishmen, beheld the vast expanse of the Pacific Ocean stretch before him illimitably, and how he prayed to Almighty God "to give him life and leave once to sail an English ship in those unknown seas." We know that that prayer was heard. Of all Englishmen, he was

"The first that ever burst into that silent sea,"

and the first of all men who succeeded in sailing round the globe. He was knighted by Queen Elizabeth in 1581. In the intervals between his voyages he purchased Buckland Abbey, married a daughter of Sir George Sydenham, served the office of Mayor of Plymouth, acted as a Justice for Devon, and accomplished the great work of bringing a stream of water into the town of Plymouth. But it was not fated that his bones should rest in his native county. The great sailor died in 1596 on his own element. According to the ancient ballad,—

"The waves became his winding-sheet, the waters were his tomb;
But for his fame the ocean sea was not sufficient room."

EDWARD SEYMOUR, son of Sir Edward, was Sheriff in 1606, and was created a Baronet in 1611, the first who attained that rank in Devonshire, and one of the first in England. He married a daughter of Sir Arthur Champernowne. He died in 1613. There is extant a funeral sermon on him, entitled "The Barronett's Burial," by Barnaby Potter, B.D., who was afterwards Bishop of Carlisle.

HUGH FORTESCUE, of Filleigh and Wear Gifford, an ancestor of Earl Fortescue. He was admitted student of the Inner Temple in 1562. He married Elizabeth, sister of Sir Arthur Chichester, Lord Deputy of Ireland.

WILLIAM ABBOTT, of Hartland, was son of William Abbot, serjeant of the cellar to Henry VIII., who obtained a grant of the Abbey and lands of Hartland, at the time of the dissolution of the monasteries. This William Abbot was sheriff in 1607, and died in 1609. He left no son, and one of his co-heiresses married Andrew Luttrell.

TRISTRAM GORGES, of Budokshed, in the parish of St. Budeaux. His daughter married her cousin Sir Ferdinando Gorges, who became commandant of the fortress of Plymouth in 1595, and held that post for thirty-three years. Sir Ferdinando was a Justice for Devon, and his name occurs very frequently in the records of subsequent Sessions. He appears in the history of England as having behaved very discreditably in connexion with the trial of Essex. But in a pamphlet written by Mr. Tuttle, of Boston, Massachusetts, who shows a most minute acquaintance with the Devonshire families, Sir Ferdinando Gorges is elevated to a place among the heroes, Raleigh, Drake, and Gilbert. Mr. Tuttle declares that he was the real "founder of English empire in America," that he directed the course of colonization from his post at Ply-

Justices of the Peace for the County of Devon. 337

mouth, and that, without his action, "it is doubtful whether England would ever have come to the possession of an acre of American territory."

GEORGE WYOTT appears to have lived at Braunton.

RICHARD SPARRY had a "house in St. Peter's Churchyard," Exeter, as we find by a subsequent entry.

RICHARD BAMPFIELD was head of the ancient house of Poltimore. He was Sheriff in 1576. He married Elizabeth, daughter of Sir John Sydenham. (All the ladies in this reign appear to have been called Elizabeth.) He died in 1594. His son Amias was created a baronet.

THOMAS WYSE, of Sydenham and of Mount Wise, close to Plymouth, sat in the House of Commons, and was created a Knight of the Bath at the coronation of James I. He was Sheriff in 1612, and died in 1629. His representative in the female line is J. H. Tremayne, Esq., of Sydenham and Heligan, M.P. for Cornwall. The younger branch is represented by John Ayshford Wise, Esq., late M.P. for Stafford.

EDWARD AMEREDITH, of Crediton and Slapton, son of Griffith Amcredith, who was Sheriff of Exeter. I am sorry that this pretty name is only kept alive by a charity which he and his father founded for providing shrouds for poor prisoners hanged at Exeter, "and not leaving sufficient to buy a shroud!"

EDMUND PARKER, of North Molton, an ancestor of Lord Morley, was Sheriff in 1600.

ROBERT DRAKE was of Wiscombe Park, in the parish of South Leigh. He was brother of Sir Bernard Drake of Ash, a famous soldier and sailor, who occupies a place among *Prince's Worthies*, and who, according to the old story, (which deserves to be true,) objected to the great Sir

Z

Francis assuming the arms of that ancient family. John Churchill, Duke of Marlborough, was born at Ash, his mother being a daughter of that house, now represented by Sir William Drake of Oatlands, Surrey, and Thomas Tyrwhitt Drake, Esq., of Shardeloes, Bucks.

HUGH ACKLAND (*sic*), of Ackland in Landkey, was the head of the well-known family now represented by Sir Thomas Dyke Acland, Bart. He married in 1585 Margaret, daughter of Thomas Monk of Potheridge, and great-aunt of General Monk.

JOHN ACKLAND, of Columb John, brother of the preceding, is one of the *Worthies of Devon*. He inherited his mother's estates in Middlesex. He was long in Parliament, and was knighted at the accession of James I. He was Sheriff in 1609. He bought the estate of Columb John, and built the house and chapel. He also built the hall of Exeter College, Oxford, and founded various charities, of which the City of Exeter administers at present nearly 400*l.* a year. He married first a daughter of George Rolle, Esq., and secondly a daughter of Sir William Portman, but had no children, and his estates were inherited by his nephew Sir Arthur. He died in 1613, and his "very stately monument" may be seen in the church of Broad Clyst.

GEORGE GALE, of Crediton, is recorded to have been very active in hunting down "Popish recusants." It has been suggested that his zeal was not quite disinterested, as he held a good deal of church property.

ANTONY MOUNCKE (*sic*), of Potheridge in the parish of Merton, brother-in-law of Hugh Ackland, and grandfather of George Monk, Duke of Albemarle.

THOMAS HEALE (*sic*), of Wisdom, afterwards of Flete, was Sheriff in 1601. The name of this family, once the most prosperous and widely-extended in Devonshire, is now kept alive only by Hele's School in Exeter and other charities founded by Eliseus Hele. It is recorded that, when one of them was Sheriff, he summoned a Grand Jury consisting of 23 gentlemen of his own name. The Judge hearing the name of "Hele of Wisdom" called among the rest, observed that he thought they must all be "of wisdom" to have attained such prosperity.

WILLIAM WALROND of Bradfield, where the family has been seated since the reign of King John. He was Sheriff in 1596. His present representative is Sir J. W. Walrond, Bart.

WILLIAM KIRKEHAM, of Blagdon and Pinhoe, afterwards knighted, was Sheriff in 1586. There is a fine chantry in the parish church at Paignton, erected by this family. According to the Sessions books of the reign of James, Sir William and Lady Kirkham appear to have been frequently in trouble for not attending Church, and for not taking the oath of allegiance. Summonses were issued against them, and Sir William did at last take the oath, but I do not find that Lady Kirkham ever did. She appears to have belonged to an old Roman Catholic family in Hampshire, which has been occasionally mentioned in our time. Would you be surprised to hear that her maiden name was Tichborne?

EDWARD WHIDDON, of Chagford, son of Sir John Whyddon, Justice of the King's Bench, who is one of Prince's *Worthies*.

ROBERT DILLON, of Chimwell, in Bratton Fleming. Like Hugh Fortescue, he married a sister of Sir Arthur Chichester.

HUMPHREY SPECCOTT, of Speccott in Merton, Sheriff in 1585.

GEORGE CARY, of Clovelly, Sheriff in 1587. He is introduced by Mr. Kingsley into his *Westward Ho*, and his son is Amyas Leigh's chief companion.

WILLIAM CRYMES was afterwards knighted, and was Sheriff in 1610. His predecessor was the original grantee of Buckland Monachorum at the Reformation.

ROGER GIFFARD, of Tiverton Castle, was son of Sir Roger Giffard of Brightleigh. He died in 1603, aged seventy, and was buried at Tiverton, and commemorated by a very long Latin epitaph. Prince assures us that he was a very eminent person, but he does not know why, except that he married successively three rich widows, "which greatly increased his estate."

ARTHUR HARRIES (*sic*), of Cherston, was half-brother of Sir Thomas Harris, Serjeant-at-law, whose name occurs afterwards.

THOMAS REYNELL, of Ogwell, built West Ogwell House in 1589, and was knighted at the coronation of James I. This family was long one of the most distinguished in the West of England. Three brothers of Sir Thomas were also knighted.

WILLIAM STRODE, of Newnham, also of a famous family. He was Sheriff in 1593, and knighted in 1597. He died in 1637, aged seventy-six. He was father of Richard Strode, M.P. for Plympton, and also of William Strode, the celebrated parliamentary leader, M.P. for Beeralston in 1640, and one of the five members whom Charles I. attempted to seize.

WILLIAM POLE, of Colcombe and Shute, a distinguished lawyer and antiquary, treasurer of the Inner Temple, and author of the *Description of Devonshire* and several other works. He married a daughter of Sir William Peryam, Chief Baron, of whom I have to speak presently. He was

Justices of the Peace for the County of Devon. 341

Sheriff at the time of the accession of James I., and was knighted in 1606. He is one of Prince's *Worthies.*

The next two, being attached to the Court of Elizabeth, were sworn in at Hampton Court before the Lord Keeper Puckering.

SIR THOMAS DENYS (*sic*), of Bicton and Holcombe Burnell, was knighted in Holland by the Earl of Leicester in 1586, and was Sheriff in 1594. He married a daughter of the Marquis of Winchester, and left two daughters, one of whom married Sir Henry Rolle of Stevenstone, and made the Rolle family the largest land-owners in the county of Devon. His grandfather Sir Thomas Dennis, one of Prince's *Worthies*, was a Privy Councillor of Henry VIII. and acquired enormous estates at the dissolution of the monasteries. He lived in the reigns of eight Sovereigns of England, and was eight times Sheriff of Devon. He is said to have also been *Custos Rotulorum.*

GEORGE CARY, of Cockington, was the head of one branch of that famous family, who were connected with the great Queen herself. One of them married a sister of Anne Boleyn, and his son was created Baron Hunsdon and a Privy Councillor by his Royal cousin. George Cary commanded a regiment of the Devonshire militia at the time of the Armada. He sat in Parliament for the county. He was afterwards employed in Ireland, was knighted in 1597, and appointed Treasurer of Ireland in 1598, and Lord Deputy in 1603. He lived till 1617, and acquired large estates in addition to his patrimony. He is of course one of Prince's *Worthies*, and many details respecting his life and family have been published by Mr. Dymond, to whom I am indebted for much information respecting him and several other justices. The Cary family lost Cocking-

Justices of the Peace for the County of Devon. 343

The next nine justices were those returned as absent from the county.

SIR WILLIAM PERYAM, one of the justices of the Common Pleas, and raised to be Chief Baron about this time. His father was Mayor of Exeter, and he himself bought the estate of Little Fulford, now Shobrooke, near Crediton. His third wife was sister of Lord Bacon. He died in 1604, aged seventy. I need hardly add that his life has been written by Prince. His representative is Sir Alexander Bateman Periam Acland Hood.

EDWARD DREWE, Serjeant-at-law, is also one of the *Worthies*. He was Recorder of Exeter and of London, and acquired the large estates of Killerton in Broad Clyst (now Sir T. D. Acland's) and the Grange in Broadhembury, where his descendants still reside. He died in 1622, and was honoured by a sumptuous monument in the church of Broad Clyst.

THOMAS HARRIS, Serjeant-at-law, another of the *Worthies*, was knighted at the coronation of James I. He died in 1610, and was buried at Cornworthy. He was half-brother of Arthur Harris, who was mentioned before.

JOHN GLANVYLE, of Killworthy, also a Serjeant-at-law, and one of the *Worthies*, was made a Justice of the Common Pleas in 1598, and knighted. He died at Tavistock in 1600, and was buried in the parish church, where his stately monument may still be seen. His descendants are seated at Catchfrench in Cornwall.

JOHN HELE, of Wemberry, near Plymouth, recorder of Exeter in 1593, made Serjeant-at-law in 1594, and knighted at the coronation of James I. He too is one of the *Worthies*.

EDMUND PRIDEAUX, also one of the *Worthies*, and a

distinguished lawyer, founded the family of Prideaux of Netherton. He was a younger son of Roger Prideaux of Soldon, Sheriff in 1578. He was created a Baronet in 1622, and died in 1628. The baronetcy became extinct at the death of Sir Edmund Prideaux in 1875.

HUGH POLLARD, of King's Nympton, afterwards knighted, was son of Sir Lewis Pollard, one of the Judges of the Common Pleas, who may be found among the *Worthies*. Sir Lewis had eleven daughters and eleven sons, of whom four were knighted. Hugh had the honour of being Sheriff of Devon in 1588, and is therefore the one commemorated by Macaulay in his ballad of "The Armada:"

"With his white hair unbonneted, the stout old sheriff comes;
Behind him march the halberdiers ; before him sound the drums ;
His yeomen round the market cross make clear an ample space ;
For there behoves him to set up the standard of Her Grace."

His daughter married an ancestor of Sir Stafford Northcote, and became the mother of Sir John Northcote, the first baronet, member for Ashburton in the Long Parliament, and member for Devon in 1660.

THOMAS RIDGEWAY, of Torwood, Sheriff in 1590 and 1599, and knighted in the latter year, was sometime M.P. for the county. He was Commander-general and treasurer of the wars in Ireland under James I., created a Baronet in 1612, and afterwards Earl of Londonderry. He acquired Tor Abbey in 1598. He died in 1620, and his monument may be seen in Tor Church. I need hardly say that his biography is to be found in Prince.

THOMAS PRIDEAUX, probably of Orcharton in the parish of Modbury, the head of the family from a younger branch of which Edmund Prideaux was descended.

Justices of the Peace for the County of Devon. 345

The next two Justices were prevented by age and infirmity from coming to the Sessions.

SIR JOHN ST. LEGER, of Annery, near Bideford, a name familiar to the readers of *Westward Ho*. He was Sheriff in 1560. One of his daughters married the great Sir Richard Grenvile, and another married Tristram Arscot, who bought Annery.

THOMAS SOUTHCOTT, probably of Mohun's Ottery, Sheriff in 1557 and 1569.

Of ROBERT CROSSE the Commissioners reported that he was not living in the county, and had no lands in it to their knowledge. I do not pretend to know more about him than they did. But, if one were to make a guess, I should say that the officials in London may perhaps have translated the ancient British name Cruwys, still borne by one of the oldest families in Devonshire, into the modern English Crosse.

SIR ROBERT DENYS was reported to have recently departed this life. He was father of Sir Thomas, whom I have already mentioned. He was Sheriff in 1556 and 1567. He built the mansion and made the park of Bicton, where had formerly been the prison of the county, and which is now the seat of Lady Rolle.

RICHARD CHAMPERNOWNE, whose swearing in was postponed on account of his being Sheriff for the year 1592, was no doubt of the ancient family of Champernowne of Modbury, now of Dartington. He was knighted in 1599, and was, I believe, the elder brother of Sir Arthur Champernowne, who was knighted by Essex in the Irish war, and who occupies a place among the *Worthies of Devon*, like so many others whom I have had occasion to mention.

You may perhaps have noticed the absence from this list of the greatest man, perhaps, of that age, who was undoubtedly a Devonshire man, and at one time M.P. for the county. Sir Walter Raleigh was not a Justice for Devon, because he was Lord Warden of the Stannaries, and therefore held an independent jurisdiction over a great part of Devon, as well as over Cornwall.

I have now run through the list of the fifty-five Justices, I fear at too great length, though I have omitted a great mass of information which has come to my knowledge. I was thinking at one time of hitching them into a ballad after the manner of Macaulay, or rather of Homer;—

> "Bourchier, whose stately mansion
>   O'erlooks the brimming Taw;
> Seymour, whose haughty father
>   Rose above king and law;
> Sir Francis Drake of Buckland,
>   Who smote the Spaniard down;
> And Courtenay, whose ancient kin
>   Grasp'd the Byzantine crown!"

Probably most of you do not care much for archæological and genealogical studies, nor, to say the truth, do I, except as they illustrate general history. But I maintain that it is not without importance to our knowledge of history that we should understand what manner of men were the Justices of the Peace in the reign of Elizabeth. And I venture to say that my story has proved that the Justices of Devon at least at that period were a very distinguished body of men. There were only fifty-five of them, and they must have been selected from a considerable number of country gentlemen. In Cornwall at the same time there were only thirty. How many esquires

Justices of the Peace for the County of Devon. 347

there were entitled to bear coat-armour, I do not know, but there were certainly several hundreds. We know of many families flourishing at the present day who were certainly flourishing at that time, such as the Northcotes, Fulfords, Chichesters, Quickes, and so on, who are yet not included in this list. The representatives of some of them may have been minors. The representatives of others may have been serving their country at sea, or in the Irish wars, as was the case with the head of the great house of Chichester. But, even after these deductions, I think we must suppose that many of them were not appointed because they were not considered fit for the office. I do not mean that the Government of Elizabeth appointed justices by competitive examination, but I do believe that a good deal of care was taken in their selection. For one thing, it was not safe for a justice to act unless he had a certain knowledge of Latin. All law proceedings were in Latin, and a justice who was unacquainted with that tongue would constantly have to sign papers that he did not understand. Again, it was not safe for a justice to act unless he had a certain knowledge of law. Justices' clerks were not a regular institution. Those that did exist were often not attorneys, and those that were attorneys were often of a very different class from the solicitors of our day. We find that it was at that time almost a regular part of a country gentleman's education to read law for two or three years at the Inns of Court in London. Even Master Robert Shallow was of Clement's Inn. In our list we find several professional lawyers, of whom one was Chief Baron, one was a Judge, and four were Serjeants-at-law. The Court of Quarter Sessions exercised the power of life and death, and I believe it was the custom for at least one serjeant-at-law to be present at the trials of prisoners. Some of the more eminent justices were "of the *quorum*," and certain matters could not be transacted without the presence of one or more of them.

But, if the Commission of the Peace was in itself a distinction, many of those in my list attained far higher honours. Only one, the Earl of Bath, held an hereditary title, and he was Lord Lieutenant. That office was not hereditary, and it comprised the command of several thousand men, on whom, there being no standing army, the safety of the country depended to a great extent in very dangerous times. Of the rest, one was a Bishop, and one rose from the rank of a country squire to an Earldom. Two of them wrote County Histories which are still of high account. As there was only one Peer in the county, and the order of Baronets did not then exist, the rank of a Knight conveyed an importance very different to that which we attach to it, and that rank was attained by at least twenty-three out of the fifty-five. Baronets were not created until nearly twenty years afterwards, yet three of our list lived to attain that honour. It must be remembered that the list consists mainly of landed proprietors, or of eldest sons of landed proprietors, without that stimulus to seek fortune and honour which is supplied in the case of those who are otherwise circumstanced. I am inclined to think that no similar body could give a better account of themselves than that furnished by the Justices of the Peace of the County of Devon in the year 1592.

THE JURISDICTION OF THE LORD WARDEN OF THE STANNARIES IN THE TIME OF SIR WALTER RALEIGH.

(READ AT ASHBURTON, JULY, 1876.)

[*Reprinted from the Transactions of the Devonshire Association for the Advancement of Science, Literature, and Art.* 1876.]

IN the reign of Queen Elizabeth a conflict of jurisdiction arose between the deputy-lieutenants and justices of Devon on one side, and the officers of the Stannaries on the other. Among the county records is a copy of a letter from the Queen, " Given under our signet at Nonesuch, the 27th day of June, in the 31st year of our reign," mentioning that the " privileges, liberties, and immunities " of the tinners and duchy tenants of Devon and Cornwall had been of late infringed " by some that had intermeddled with the government of the tinners," and had " by foreign authority charged and rated them for divers payments without consent of their warden." The letter proceeds to confirm in the fullest manner the ancient customs and privileges of the Stannaries, and commands " that no sheriff, commissioner, or other officer whatsoever, do from henceforth muster, rate, or charge any of our tinners, or duchy tenants, or otherwise offer any grief, molestation, or disturbance to the jurisdiction of the Duchy or Stannaries ; neither do convent, precept, or compel any bailiff or officer of the Stannaries, or any of the tinners or duchy tenants, to answer for any abuses arising or growing within the said Stannaries, determinable there."

I should quote this letter at length, but I find that it has been already printed in Westcote's *View of Devonshire*, p. 87.

I have found among the county records some other matters bearing upon this conflict of jurisdiction, which I propose to bring before the Association. The first is a letter from Sir Walter Raleigh, who then held the office of Lord Warden of the Stannaries :—

" *To my very loving friends the Justices of Peace of the County of Devon.*

" After my very hearty commendations. Complaint hath
" been made unto me by Peter Burges, Richard Lanxford,
" William Stockman, and Anthony Sleeman, tinners within
" the County of Devon and Constables of Hundreds and
" several parishes there, that they have been summoned to
" appear before Mr. Serjeant Glanvyle, and refusing to con-
" tribute towards the reparation of a private bridge (induced
" thereunto for the maintenance of the charter and customs
" of the *Stannaries*), were compelled to enter into recog-
" nizance for their appearance at the last Sessions holden in
" Devon, and do yet stand bound for answering their refusal
" therein at your next Sessions, contrary to their said
" Charter and her Majesty's late letters. Forasmuch as the
" said bridge was in former time accustomed to be repaired
" by the borough of *Okehampton* at the charges of the
" inhabitants, and for that tinners are not usually constrained
" to yield to any taxations and impositions for repairing of
" bridges out of their own hundreds and parishes, being
" continually charged with expense bestowed upon the ruins

"of their own, and not holpen with any contribution from
"other hundreds, I have thought good to signify unto you
"that in mine opinion they ought to be forborne in any of
"these courses, and do therefore pray you to discharge
"them of their recognizances for further answering this cause,
"and to desist from demanding any rate or tax which is
"over-burdensome to poor men is regard of their daily
"travel and disbursements employed about the mines. If
"you do persist in the contrary, I shall be urged to have the
"cause heard before the Lords of Her Majesty's Privy
"Council, and then, if it shall appear that they ought to
"contribute, I will by my authority cause them to yield to
"any reasonable charge that shall be thought indifferent.
"And so I commit you to God. From Durham House.
"The 15th of February, 1592. Your loving friend,
"W. RALEIGH.
"I will myself give order that the tinners shall contribute
"unto the bridge if upon examination I find cause to urge
"them thereunto, but not by any foreign authority."

The postscript seems to me rather characteristic of some of the less admirable qualities ascribed to the great Sir Walter by his biographer, Mr. St. John: "insatiable in the pursuit of power, and not over-scrupulous in the use of it." I suspect there was a sharp correspondence between him and the Justices of Devon, which might be of considerable interest, if we could recover the whole of it.

In the records of 1595, three years afterwards, I find the following epistle :—

"*A Letter written by the Justices unto Sir Walter Raleigh.*

"Sir,—We have received your letter, by the which we
"perceive that you are informed that some of us have gone

"about to intermeddle in your jurisdiction of the Stannaries.
"We find by due examination that you are misinformed by
"some inadvised and indiscreet persons, who, we think,
"rather desire to set some discord between you and us than
"to uphold your liberties, which we noway go about to in-
"fringe. We have bound Robert Lake and George Martyn
"to their good behaviour till the next sessions, for divers
"misdemeanours committed by them, noway concerning you
"or your office. And where you write that Voysy and
"Wright have delivered slanderous and scoffing speeches
"touching your late occasion at sea, we have examined the
"said parties and as many others as could best inform us,
"and find no such matter; for if we had, you should assure
"yourself we would have dealt in it *according to the quality of*
"*the offence.* These with our very hearty commendations."

We may be quite sure that the privileges and immunities of the Stannaries led to many frauds and abuses, as such things usually do. The last order of Sessions entered during the reign of Elizabeth relates to the subject. I may mention that I have modernized the spelling in this and the preceding documents. The term foreigners was habitually employed to signify all who were not "tynners."

"*Order for contribution to the Queen's service by foreigners and tinners.*

"Upon a general complaint made unto this Court that
"divers of the principal inhabitants of sundry parishes within
"this county have of late time very fraudulently interested
"themselves in some tinwork, under colour thereof to be
"protected and discharged against the general and necessary
"charges for the service of her Majesty, wherewith they have
"in former times been indifferently rated and taxed, together

The Jurisdiction of the Lord Warden, etc. 353

"with the rest of the inhabitants of the said parishes. It is
" therefore thought fit by this Court, and so ordered, that
" such as are newly crept in to be tinners, at any time
" within six years last past, of purpose to exempt themselves
" from any charge of her Majesty's service, or have at any
" time contributed with the foreigners within six years last
" past, and which have not been ancient tinners, or to whom
" any tinwork is not descended or acquired by marriage, shall
" from henceforth pay to all services of her Majesty with
" foreigners, as before their so making themselves tinners
" they have and were accustomed to do and pay, so as the
" foreigners of the said parishes, or the greater number of
" them, shall or have not wilfully refused to contribute in
" equal charge with such as are accounted tinners within the
" said parishes; and also that as well the parishioners of
" Lamerton, as others now in this Court in question for the
" same, shall pay all such charges as formerly have been
" imposed upon them. And this order is conceived to agree
" with the pleasure of the Lord Warden in this behalf
" formerly signified unto this court, and not with any intent
" to make wilful breach of the privileges rightfully belong-
" ing to the court of Stannary or to the authority of the
" Lord Warden in that behalf."

The last sentence shows the fear that the justices entertained of the illustrious Sir Walter. His power, I need not
say, soon came to an end under the new sovereign. In 1604
he was superseded by the Earl of Pembroke in the office of
Lord Warden of the Stannaries.

ton during the Civil War, but in 1662 they acquired Tor Abbey, where they are still seated.

The next five were also Justices for Cornwall, and took the oaths there before Sir Francis Godolphin, Sir William Bevill, and George Kekewiche, Esquire.

PETER EDGCOMBE, ancestor of the Earl of Mount Edgcumbe, was son of Sir Richard, who built the well-known mansion of the family, and is one of Prince's *Worthies*. He was M.P. for Cornwall, and Sheriff of Devon in 1565. He died in 1607.

RICHARD CAREW, of Antony, where the family is still flourishing, was the author of the *Survey of Cornwall*. His mother was an Edgcombe, and he was born in 1555. He was one of the *Quorum* in Cornwall in 1581, Sheriff in 1586, and Deputy Lieutenant and Colonel of a regiment in 1599. He was one of that early Society of Antiquaries formed by Sir Robert Cotton, Sir J. Dodderidge, Camden, Stow, and others. He died in 1620, and was honoured by a splendid monument in the church of East Antony.

ANTHONY ROUS, of Edmerston and Halton, was of the family previously seated at Modbury. He was one of the executors of Sir Francis Drake. He was twice Sheriff of Cornwall, M.P. for East Looe in the reign of Elizabeth, and for Cornwall in the reign of James I. The family is now settled in Glamorganshire.

CHRISTOPHER HARRIS, of Radford in Devon, and Trecarrell in Cornwall, M.P. for Plymouth, was knighted in 1607, and died in 1624. He was also one of the executors of Sir Francis Drake.

JOHN WREY, of Wrey in Devon, and Trebigh in Cornwall, was Sheriff of the latter county in 1586. He was an ancestor of Sir B. P. Wrey.

THE CASTLE OF EXETER.

A PAPER READ BEFORE THE MEMBERS OF THE BRITISH ASSOCIATION ON THEIR VISIT TO EXETER, AUGUST 18, 1877.

GREATLY to my surprise, I was informed, a day or two ago, that I had been told off to show the Castle to the members of the British Association. Had the task been one requiring any technical knowledge of architecture, I should certainly have been compelled to decline it. Unfortunately, the state of the Castle is such that there are very few architectural features remaining, and its interest must be considered historical, rather than architectural. The distinctive interest that I venture to claim for the Castle of Exeter is this, that it is one of the very few spots in this country which have undoubtedly been inhabited by man from pre-historic times continuously down to the present day. There can, I imagine, be little doubt that this spot was a British camp or fortified town before the Romans ever set foot in Britain. It is a place peculiarly well adapted for defence in the ages before artillery was invented. The site of the City of Exeter, as you may observe, is an elevated platform of a rude oblong form, approaching indeed to the form of a triangle. The base is formed by the valley of the Exe. On the north side, speaking roughly, it is bounded by the deep glen now occupied by the London and South Western Railway. On the

The Castle of Exeter. 355

south is a smaller glen, which may be seen from the Magdalen Road and Holloway. On the east it is connected with the country beyond by a narrow neck of land, along which runs St. Sidwell's Street. Its form is in fact somewhat like that of the domestic fire-shovel, the edge being towards the river, and the handle being St. Sidwell's Street. The northern corner of this platform is occupied by a knoll, rising pretty steeply to the height of about 200 feet above the sea level, and formed by an upheaval of trap rock of a reddish colour, which gave rise to its Norman name of Rougemont, well known to all readers of Shakespeare, and, though this had been alluded to before, I feel that I must again quote it.

> "Richmond! When I was last in Exeter,
> The Mayor in courtesy shewed me the Castle,
> And called it *Rougemont;* at which name I started,
> Because a bard of Ireland told me once
> I should not live long after I saw Richmond!"

This knoll, as I said before, is so conveniently adapted for defence, that it was held and fortified by the Britons at a very early period. They dug out a ditch round it, and excavated the earth and rock on the crown, and with the materials they threw up the high bank which formed the original camp or Castle of Exeter, and which, through all changes, remains for the most part to this day. The ditch from the north-east to the north-west has been filled up so as to make the public gardens of Northernhay. The outer scarp on this side descends to the railway. The bank and wall have been removed to make room for the Assize Courts. On the south and south-east, and especially in the grounds belonging to Mrs. Gard, the ditch remains, and is considered a very fine example of an ancient British earth-work.

This original hill-camp, then, was taken by the Romans, and the rude fortifications were no doubt improved by them, as they made it an important station. On the platform to the south, as we may fancy, were clustered the rude huts of the British town of Caer-Wisc, the Castle of the Exe. The Romans laid out a new town on their usual cruciform plan, and, still taking the name from the Exe, called it Isca Damnoniorum. The cross may still be traced where North and South Streets meet the High Street, though the latter is probably not identical with the street which carried the Ikenild way through Exeter. Of the Roman city the Castle was, of course, the Citadel.

After the Romans left England, the name became Exanceaster, but it was still the Castle of the Exe. It was the residence of the West Saxon Kings, and was often attacked by the Danes. It was taken and retaken in the time of Alfred. In the reign of Athelstan, the place having been demolished by the Danes, the city and Castle were for the first time surrounded by walls of stone. But, as far as the Castle is concerned, these walls were built exactly on the lines of the ancient earthworks. It is thought that some pieces of Athelstan's work remain to this day. It was in great part destroyed by the Danes under Sweyne, in the year 1003, but it must have been restored before the Conquest, as it stood a siege of 18 days from the Conqueror in 1067. After its capture, William, according to his usual policy, caused a strong castle to be built to overawe the city, for which its situation was admirably adapted. You may observe that it is quite as strongly fortified towards the city as it is towards the country. The office of Castel-

The Castle of Exeter. 357

lan was hereditary in the family De Brioniis, Barons of Okehampton and Viscounts of Devon, and kinsmen of the Conqueror. From this time, I believe, the Castle has always been connected with the county.

The earliest masonry of which we can feel sure is the Gate-house, which was fortunately spared when the new entrance was made. It used to be called Athelstan's Tower, but I believe there is no doubt that it is early Norman—that is, of the latter part of the 11th century. The windows have curious triangular heads, not arches. The arched gateways are very plain, but show some traces of Norman carving. It may be noticed that there is no appearance of a keep, and it is probable there never was one. The whole place was so strong that no keep was required —or perhaps we may say that the whole Castle was a keep. All the ancient buildings which must have existed within the court have been removed. We know there was a chapel in comparatively modern times, and there were, of course, barracks, stables, and their appurtenances. The walls are in general of rubble, but part of the N.E. front is good ashlar, perhaps of the time of Richard II. There is a fine bastion of late Norman work.

The Castle was besieged and taken by Stephen in the war with the Empress Maud. It was annexed to the Earldom of Cornwall by Henry III., and the connexion has continued ever since. For many centuries it was the most important post in the West of England. It was besieged by Perkin Warbeck in 1497, and by the Cornish insurgents at the time of the Reformation. In the reign of Elizabeth we find that the County Assizes and Sessions were held in it, as they have continued to be, with some intervals, ever since. I have been occupied of late in turning out the old records of Sessions, which are kept in the Castle, and find them complete from the year 1592. In the reign of James I., I find orders for building a Sessions-house and Grand Jury rooms at the expense of the county. During the Civil War, the Castle was of course devoted to more warlike purposes. The Sessions were then held in the garden of the Gaol, which stood near the entrance of the Castle. The fortress was held by the Earl of Stamford for the Parliament, and taken by Prince Maurice in 1643. It yielded to Fairfax in 1646, and was garrisoned again by the Parliament. I find that in 1655 a sum of 688*l.* 6*s.* 6*d.* had been disbursed by John Coplestone, Sheriff, "for erecting houses, places, and seats of judicature within the Castle of Exon, by order of His Highness the Lord Protector." So it was again used for civil purposes. But during the Dutch War of Charles II., the Castle was again fortified, and the Courts used as a magazine. The drawbridge was repaired in the reign of James II., which shows that it still existed. The castle was garrisoned by William of Orange when he came to Exeter in 1688, perhaps as a place of retreat in case of failure. It has never, I believe, been since used as a military post. Queen Anne agreed to lease it for ninety-nine years, at a nominal rent, to trustees for the county of Devon, and the agreement was carried out by George I. The fee-simple was granted by Act of Parliament in 1773, subject to the rent of 10*l.* and reserving to the Crown the right of resuming the Castle in time of war. The existing Courts, of which we are not proud, were built in 1775. But we ought to remember, in justice to the Justices of a hundred years ago, that they were limited to an expenditure of 4000*l.*

The Castle of Exeter. 359

What we are proud of, as I said before, is the continuity of life which has, for so many centuries, clustered round the Castle of Exeter. In the darkness of pre-historic ages, before Sarum and Uriconium were thought of, the Castle of Exeter stands out as an important settlement of the Britons. Now, when Sarum and Uriconium have become mere deserted mounds, the Castle of Exeter still remains—still retaining the importance which has never departed from it from the time of Cassivelaunus—still the meeting-place of a great district at times of Sessions, of Assizes, of elections, and other public gatherings—and still on such occasions presenting one of the most animated scenes in the whole county of Devon.

INDEX.

ABBOTT, William, 336.
Aberdena, Moses, 214.
Acland, Sir H., 191; Hugh, 338; Sir John (1592), 338; (1646), 148.
Addison, 291.
Address to William III., 263.
Address to Queen Anne, 277, 278.
Albemarle, the first Duke of, 171; the second Duke of, 199, 226, 228.
Alehouses, 71, 74, 115, 138, 150, 190.
Ameredith, Edward, 337.
Amersham, Parish Register, 256, 266.
Anne, Queen, 267; state of England in her reign, 281.
Annesley, Dr., Dean of Exeter, 226.
Ansley, Ralph, 299, 314.
Armada, 98, 322.
Assassination Plot, 262.
Assizes, 30, 236.
Association of County of Bucks, 262.
Athelstan, 356.
Austen, John, 131.

Babbington, Mr. 133.
Babington, Bishop, 19; Thomas, 74.
Bacon, Lord, 35, 38, 47.
Badgers, 26, 270.
Bagg, Sir James, 107, 109.
Bampfield, Sir Coplestone, 185, 191, 279; Thomas, Speaker, 169; Richard, 337.
Baronets, creation of, 56.
Bath, William, Earl of, 2, 3, 10, 57, 78, 324, 330; John, Earl of, 218, 226, 242, 254.
Bedford, Earl of, 4, 50, 128.

Benevolence of 1614, 42; of 1622, 52, 65.
Billeting soldiers, 107, 261.
Black Assize, the, 29.
Bloody Assize, the, 236, &c.
Bohemia, 57.
Bradninch, 245.
Bridgewater, Earl of, 275.
Brioniis, De, 357.
Brookes, George, naval chaplain, 299, &c.
Brugis, Richard, 247.
Buckhurst, Lord Treasurer, 2, 7, 24.
Bucks, county of, 222, 246, 255, 274.

Calendar of prisoners in 1598, 33.
Carew of Antony, 99, 290, 342; of Haccombe, 77; Sir Thomas, 211, 213, 218.
Cary, Sir George, of Cockington, 3, 8, 9, 11, 21, 23, 341; George, of Clovelly, 340; Sir Henry, 130; William, 51.
Cavaliers, 137, 141.
Champernowne, Sir Richard, 345.
Charles I., 100.
Charles II., 172, 201.
Chevalier, M. 100.
Chichester, Amias, 67.
Christian names, 166, 266, 279.
Chudleigh, Sir George, 107, 134.
Church ales, 73, 99.
Churchill, Lord, 235.
Civil War, 127.
Claimant, a, 87.
Clapp, Maudlin, 140.
Clarendon, Earl of, 219.

Index.   361

Clerk of the Peace, 68, 145, 253, &c.
Cliffe, Jacob, letter from, 230.
Coffin, John, 77; Richard, 227; letters to him, 228, &c.
Coke, Sir Edward, 44.
Commission of the Peace (1592), 2, 324; (1647), 144; (1651), 151; (1653), 152; (1659), 153.
Commonwealth, the, 150.
Conventicles, 177, 222.
Cornwall, 8.
Corruption, 82, 244.
Corporations, disloyalty of, 184, 186, 188.
Cottage, licence to build a, 27, 164.
Cotton, Arthur, a Quaker, 303, &c.
Council, letters from the, 2, 7, 10, 19, 21, 42, 48, 52, 67, 73, 78, 95, 97, 116, 186, 217.
Council, of Elizabeth, 2, 7, 328; of James I., 44, 54; of Charles II., 187, 217.
County rates, 207.
Courtenay, Sir William, 2, 8, 77, 78, 89, 205, 255, 324, 332.
Coventry, Sir W., 205.
Coverley, Sir Roger de, 291.
Crediton, 94, 137.
Cromwell, Oliver, 147, 148, 160, 296; Richard, 161, 165.
Crosse, Robert, 345.
Cruwys of Cruwys Morchard, 77.
Crymes, William, 340.
Cucking, 84.
Cullompton, 20, 116.

Dearth (1608), 91; (1630), 101.
Debtors, 210.
Dennis, Sir Thomas, 341; Sir Robert, 345.
Desborough, Major-General, 153, 167, 309, &c.
D'Ewes, Sir Simonds, 44, 139.
Dialect, Devonshire, 112.
Dillon, Robert, 339.
Dodridge, Sir John, judge, 50.
Dohna, Baron, the Bohemian ambassador, 57.
Drake, Sir Bernard, 337; Sir Francis (1592), 2, 19, 324, 334; (1660) 170; Robert, 337.

Drewe, Edward, 3, 343.
Duchy of Cornwall, 5.
Dunning, Richard, on Devonshire labourers, 14.

Edgcombe, Peter, 342.
Eliot, Sir John, 108.
Elizabeth, Queen, 2, 4, 22, 349.
English, Peter, 135.
Essex, Earl of, 87, 135.
Evans, Richard, 148, 241.
Execution of prisoners in 1598, 30; in 1685, 238.
Exeter, 117, 130, 136, &c.; Castle of, 29, 128, 142, 166, 195; account of, 354.

Fairfax, 136, 144, 147; letter of, 141.
Fee farm rents, 216.
Feversham, Lord, 235.
Fines, 179, 180.
Fires, 19, 90.
Fish, salting, 24, 26.
Fisheries, 220.
Fitzwilliams, Henry, 199, 207.
Flear, Mrs., 76.
Fortescue, 9, 336; Sir Peter, 185; Sir John, 222.
Fox, George, 308.
Frederick, King of Bohemia, 57.
Fulford, Sir Francis, 51, 130.
Fuller, 3.
Fursdon, 76.

Gale, George, 338.
Galleys, 31.
Galway, Earl of, 277.
Game laws, 89, 162, 269.
Gannicliffe, Nicholas, a Quaker, 300.
Gidley, Captain, 128.
Gifford, Roger, 340.
Gilbert, Humphrey, 205; Sir John, 2, 8, 324, 333.
Gill, Nicholas, 84.
Gipsies, 220.
Glanvyle, Serjeant, afterwards Judge, 3, 343.
Godolphin, Sir Francis, 342.
Gorges, Sir Ferdinando, 4, 77, 336; Tristram, 336.

Gray, Lord, 236.
Green Cloth, Board of, 9, 41.

Halhead, Miles, a Quaker, 297, &c.
Hampden, Richard, 259.
Hancock, Mr., 25.
Harris, Arthur, 340; Christopher, 342; John, 299, &c.; Serjeant, 3, 343.
Hawkins, Sir Richard, 62.
Hearth-money, 201, 224.
Hele, Elize, 217, 339; John, 343; Thomas, 338.
Holsworthy, 18.
Hudibras, 85, 290.
Hughenden, 122.
Hunsdon, Baron, 9.
Hutchinson, Dr., 75.

Inchiquin, Lord, 150.
Indictments, 157, 176, 186, 242, 248, 260.
Irish, 204.

James I., 32, 35, 66, 71.
James II., 225, 234, 246.
Jeffrey, John, Captain of the "Nantwich," 320.
Jeffreys, Judge, 223, 227, 239.
Jennings, Abraham, 62; Jacob, 312.
Justices of Assize, 68, 81, 82, 115.
Justices of the Peace, 1, 67, 286.
Justices of Devon, letters from, 8, 10, 45, 91, 93, 116, 169, 328, 351.
Justices of Devon in 1592, 321, &c.
Justices who subscribed to the benevolence of 1622, 65.

Kas Isa, a Chaldean minister, 214.
Kekewich, George, 342.
Kingsley, Charles, 330.
Kirkham, Sir William, 77, 339.
Knollys, Sir W., 37.

Lamplugh, Bishop of Exeter, 241.
Larke, Sampson, 181.
Leach, Simon, 54.
Lee or Leigh, of Northam, 98.
Lenthall, William, Speaker, 152, 153, 169.

Libels, 241.
Licences, 26, 89, 270.
Lucy, Sir Thomas, 288.
Luttrell, Colonel, 232.
Lydford, 151.
Lyme, 141, 219, 228.

Macaulay, on hearth-money, 202.
Machim, William, 87.
Maimed soldiers, 18, 141, 151, 173, 253.
Malt, prohibition of, 101.
Mariners, 107, 217, 275.
Markets, 103.
Marlborough, Duke of, 274, 277.
Martyn, Sir Nicholas, 134; William, 253.
Maurice, Prince, 128, 130.
Maynard, Sir John, 215.
Monk, Anthony, 338; Sir Thomas, 167; George, Duke of Albemarle, 168, 171.
Monmouth, Duke of, 225, 232, 236.
Monopolies, 23.
Morrice, Sir William, 170, 187, 205, 219.
Mulberry-trees, 95.

Newhaven, Viscount, 275.
Nonconformists, 173, 196, 234, 251, 258.
Northcote, Sir Arthur, 185, 191, 236; John, 120; Sir John, 134, 170, 171; John, Clerk of the Peace for Devon, 213.
Northmore, Thomas, letters from, 227, &c.

Oath of Clergy, 198.
Oath of Justices, 2, 325, &c.
Offences, 83, 111, 154, 155, 156, 159, 178.
Orders, public, of Sessions, 16, 138, 143, 182, 188, 192, 197, 212, 352.

Paige, John, Mayor of Plymouth, 299, &c.
Pakington, Sir John, 293.
Parker, Edmund, 337.
Paulet, Lord, 138.

Index. 363

Peamore, 136.
Pembroke, Earl of, 353.
Penruddock, Colonel, 174.
Pepys, Samuel, 177, 206, 211, 218.
Perkins, Major, 143.
Peryam, Sir William, Chief Baron, 3, 343.
Peterborough, Earl of, 277.
Petition to the King, 124; to the Parliament, 122.
Piracy, 64, 88.
Plague, 90, 105, 219.
Plymouth, 107, 297, &c.
Pole, Sir William, 290, 340.
Pollard, Hugh, 3, 344; Sir Hugh, 219.
Poor, Relief of the, 15.
Popham, Peter, 299.
Posse Comitatus, 129, 230.
Potter, Richard, Captain of the "Constant Warwick," 320.
Powderham, 136.
Prague, battle of, 62.
Price of corn in 1608, 92; in 1630, 102.
Price of meat in 1593, 10; in 1622, 40.
Prideaux, Edmund, 145, 239; Sir Edmund, 343; Thomas, 344.
Pringe, Agnes, 85.
Prisoners, 30, 101, 208, 243, 260.
Privy Seals in 1598, 21.
Protestation, the, of 1641, 132.
Purveyance under Elizabeth, 6; under James I., 36; under Charles I., 110.

Quakers, 164, 258; Trial of two, 295.
Quicke of Newton St. Cyres, 153.

Raleigh, Sir Walter, 4, 5, 346, 349; letter from, 350.
Ramilies, battle of, 276.
Rates of carriage, 259; of quarters, 261.
Recusants, 2, 27, 74, 81, 121, 222, 258, 324.
Renell, Hilary, 157.
Revels, 28, 115, 139.
Reynell, Sir Thomas, 340.

Richards, Roger, 84.
Ridgeway, Sir Thomas, 37, 39, 344.
Robertshaw, Benjamin, 257.
Rogues, 17, 104, 247.
Rolle, Sir Henry, 56; Sir John, 185; Sir Samuel, 134.
Rosemond, Thomas, 131.
Rous, Anthony, 342.
Rowe, Nicholas, 145.
Russell, Francis, 257.
Rye House Plot, 192, 223.
Ryswick, Treaty of, 263.

Sainthill, Captain, 135.
St. John, Oliver, 47.
St. Leger, Sir John, 345.
Salt, price of, 265, 272.
Salthouse, Thomas, a Quaker, 297, &c.
Searle, John, 129; Robert, 144.
Sedgemoor, battle of, 226, 236.
Sentences, 30, 84, 112, 154, 160, 178, 180, 199.
Sexton, Gawen, 159.
Seymour, Sir Edward (1592), 8, 37, 331, 335; (1682) 191, 246.
Shallow, 287.
Sheriff, 12.
Ship-money, 118.
Sidmouth, 129.
Sign posts, 271.
"Skolster," a, 85.
Smyth, Sir George, 51.
Soldiers, 107; pressing, 19, 107, 275.
Southcott, Thomas, 355.
Spain, war with, 107, 322.
Sparry, Richard, 337.
Speccott, Humphry, 339.
Spurwell, Richard, 299, &c.
Stannaries, 4, 6, 349.
Strode, William, 12, 89, 340.
"Strubbing," 220.
Style, James, 130.
Sunderland, Lord, 234.
Sutclif, Dean, 60.
Swearing, 153.

Tanfield, Sir Lawrence, 82.
Taunton, 228, 233.
Teignmouth, 259.

Throckmorton, Sir Robert, 222.
Tichborne, 78, 339.
Tiverton, 19, 90, 128.
Toleration Act, 252, 258.
Topclyff, Richard, 76.
Topsham, 129, 225.
Torbay, French fleet in, 254.
Trankmore, John, 221.
Transportation, 174, 219.
Treasurer of the Household, letter from, 36.
Treasurer, County, 114, 199, 208.
Turkish captivity, 62, 211.
Turks, 213, 238.

Union with Scotland, 278.

Vagrants, 16, 104, 247, 268.
Vaughan, Charles, Clerk of the Peace for Devon, 51, 129, 145; Hugh, 213.
Venner, Robert, 76.
Vessay, Robert, Captain of the "Nightingale," 319.
Vynton, Julian, 64.

"Wades," 270.
Wages in Devon in 1594, 12; in 1654, 163; in 1714, 273.

Wages in Bucks in 1688, 249.
Walrond, William, 339.
Walton, Christopher, purveyor, 7, 11 37, 40.
Warwick, Earl of, 129.
Wells, 238.
Westward Ho! 98, 330.
Wharton, Thomas, 256, 259, 275.
Whiddon, Edward, 339.
Whipping, 32, 160, 223, 238.
"Whither-witted," 133.
William III., 206, 246, 251, 263.
Window Tax, 265.
Witchcraft, 220.
Wollocomb, 159, 233.
Wolton, John, Bishop of Exeter, 3, 331.
Woollen trade, 92, 117.
Worth, Robert, 156; William, 157.
Wray, Sir John, Chief Justice in 1590, 324.
Wrey, Sir Bourchier, 242; John, 342.
Wyott, George, 337.
Wyse, Sir Thomas, 337.

Yonge, Walter, Diary of, 54, 60, 75, 76, 89, 112, 119; Sir Walter, 205.

GILBERT AND RIVINGTON, PRINTERS, ST. JOHN'S SQUARE, LONDON.

www.ingramcontent.com/pod-product-compliance
Lightning Source LLC
Chambersburg PA
CBHW020259240426
43673CB00039B/645